Dear JANE

HAPPY CHRISTMAS 2022

Hope ya enjoy the book. Despite its seemingly dull topic
it is actually rather engaging. It's all about rethinking
ownership =) ... gives us plenty to think and talk
about next year td.

Been a pleasure to get to know you over this last
year.
Enjoy. STEVE & fAMily x

The Art of Passing the Buck

The Art of Passing the Buck - Volume I

The Art of Passing the Buck

VOLUME I:

The Secrets of Wills and Trusts Revealed

by Charles Arthur

Publisher:
Charles Arthur Enterprises
12228 Venice Blvd., No. 303
Los Angeles, CA 90066

Second Printing: March 2008

Cover art design by www.arttmann.com

ISBN 978-0-6151-5288-2

Warning

This information was created to help you, the reader, to make better choices for your progeny, loved ones and causes you support. This book does not provide you with the paperwork to create any Will or Trust. We expect you will consult with professionals in estate planning before you make final decisions that affect the lives of the people who depend on you.

Likewise, for you who are Beneficiaries, we present key questions for you to ask about your inheritance. You will find this book can aid you; we are not offering legal advice.

Information has been gathered from many sources to create this book. We do not claim to have all the answers. We present this view to add to your capacity to make informed choices.

Special Note to Lawyers and CPAs.

Although designed specifically to be easy to read and to understand, we fully recognize that some of what we cover will, of necessity, not just be technical and detailed, but may be new, even alien, to you. For these reasons, we have elected to place much meaty material, both legal and historical, in the Appendices or in Volume II. Here you will find the case cites, IRS and legal opinions, and much more. Enjoy, then, the fruits of our research into obscure texts, little-known books and the mists of history.

"Do not put your trust in money, but put your money in Trust."

Oliver Wendell Holmes, Sr. (1809-1894)

Acknowledgments

The pen name "Charles Arthur" represents a group of people contributing to this work either through sharing direct experience with us, by writing articles or taking part in an interview.

The information is not only built on experience, but decades of extensive research. Much of this information has been expressed in various newsletters and documents published by different Trust organizations and a stream of articles, and court cases. Not only do we include interviews, but also we describe experiences. These resources have been summarized and presented by those who deal in the Trust world, thus creating the broad database now available in *The Art of Passing the Buck*.

We thank our Editor, who worked with a team of people while he researched and wrote portions of new text himself since receiving the assignment. He raised and addressed many issues, the inclusion of which improved this book. He labored to excellent effect to make a complex, scary, often forbidding topic so user-friendly that one of our assistants volunteered she enjoyed reading it and learned a lot from it. Since readability and user-friendliness were major objectives in this first-of-its-kind book aimed not just at the legal and financial communities, but at most American families, we are thrilled by her reaction.

The resulting two-volume set will, we firmly hope, open eyes and shake the complacent to their very roots. We aim to give the American people the information, the options and the power once the sole province of the Super-Rich and others who are well-connected.

We give thanks to the fine work of all attorneys who continuously grapple with the difficulties of this subject, and for those who make a special effort to keep others in the legal community informed. References to those who work in the legal community, though, do not imply or infer they contributed to this book in any other way than what they published, and we used as references.

We would be remiss if we did not acknowledge how much we gained through reading the book *The Constitutional Common-Law Trust*[1]. Within those pages we had our first glimmer of many aspects of the **Common-Law Trust**, which until that point was lost in obscurity, vagueness and the confusion caused by complicated legal jargon.

Those who are most directly involved in creating *The Art of Passing the Buck* drew on the wisdom and the courage of the nation's founders, who fought tyranny and sought to preserve privacy. We are especially thankful to the Quakers (See Appendix A) whose great contribution seems to have been lost in history. It is thanks particularly to those who gave what President Lincoln aptly called in his Gettysburg Address, "The last full measure of devotion" that we still have the Right to Contract and thus, can write this set of books.

---

[1] James Mathers, *The Constitutional Common-Law Trust*, Renaissance Publishers, Tulsa, OK (1997)

Foreword

Most people have heard of Trusts, but few understand them. Fewer still know the types of Trusts and their relative advantages and disadvantages.

All of us face transition from this plane to the next. Most of us get involved as either recipients of monies and goods passed on to us or as people who will bequeath assets to others upon our deaths.

This work attempts to present you with the major strategic, technical and emotional issues surrounding one of the most significant events of your life–inheritance. The information applies to both givers and receivers of wealth. For those of you who received a windfall, have oodles of money and do not know what to do with it, this book may just save, not only relationships with your family and friends, but allow you to keep that wealth for the rest of your life.

We will parade before you various Trusts and Trust issues to give you an overview of the value of each Trust type, as well as warn of the traps inherent in this age-old issue of passing wealth.

We even dare to take you into an in-depth discussion of one of the most controversial subjects in the realm of inheritance: the Irrevocable Common-Law Trust. This, when set up properly and managed with care, becomes the "King's Trust." This Trust can perpetuate dynasties. It is the subject of deep intrigue, and has been constantly under siege by those who would like to dismantle it by confusing all issues surrounding it. We will show you why.

Even lawyers and CPAs are generally unfamiliar with the immense power, potential and perfectly legal tax leverage afforded by a properly structured Irrevocable Common-Law Trust, also known as a Private Trust.

As we will show, ignorance of *The Art of Passing the Buck* can be expensive, yet once shown the ropes, you and yours can be savvy when determining which Trust works best for your circumstances. And to those of you caught in the muddle of receiving an inheritance, we know this will clarify many aspects of your own situation. We also hope, if you care to take on mastering the same techniques the Super-Rich have used for centuries, you have enough knowledge to separate the con artists from the knowledgeable.

We believe you should be able to expand your wealth over centuries, just like the Super-Rich—while minimizing the tax bite and maximizing privacy.

Further, we seek to discourage those who are unqualified from meddling in the sophisticated area of estate planning and especially the complex domain of Trusts. Conversely, we encourage those who have the ability to determine the future of their progeny.

Join us, then, on this journey into Trusts and learn *The Art of Passing the Buck*.

Introduction

Simplification

The subject of Trusts is complex and mysterious. An ancient system used to pass wealth has gone through a metamorphosis that only time can produce. Despite this, though, the basics of setting up assets for Beneficiaries remains. Keeping this one thought in mind, the variety of ways to do this becomes simpler, and the complexity drops away.

In reality, the average person with a high school education can understand the basic concept of any Trust. Within this knowledge is the art of wealth building and management–a subject that everyone should know, at least at a working level.

Those matters considered technical, or that seem more suitable for professionals, appear in Volume II where we included court cases and the more intricate details of Trust structuring. Other matters, some controversial, are in the Appendices of this book.

So, even if you feel inadequate to the task of sorting out wealth and inheritance, feel free to charge right in. We wrote this book for you.

"No Classroom Text Available"

We discovered, after over a decade of devoted research, that most people are woefully ignorant when it comes to the subject of inheritance.

The emotional aspects of inheritance are daunting. When combined with a forest of jargon, complex financial issues and the possibility that lawyers and CPAs are themselves usually not taught certain key concepts, the subject rapidly becomes overwhelming. According to CPAs with whom we have spoken, the subject of Trusts is not taught in any complete form, and the IRS volunteers nothing about the subject.

You might be disturbed to learn that it is common that most lawyers and CPAs have not been properly educated in the basics of Trusts. This is because there has been a concentrated effort to narrow the field of legal instruction and to control the courts. The book, *Justice for Sale*, documents a multifaceted, comprehensive, and integrated campaign set in motion by large corporations to create taxpayer-subsidized law firms to . . . shape law school curriculum and to affect the minds and decisions of sitting judges.[2]

This is also reinforced by a statement in *A Trustee's Handbook* (7th ed) by Loring:

> In the late 1960s law schools set about the process of downgrading courses in the law of trusts from required to elective status, so that while almost all the law books have made courses on state regulation mandatory, only a few continue to afford the law of trusts the status it enjoyed at the turn of the century. In most law schools trust law is now an afterthought, buried somewhere in the elective course on estate planning.

> Likewise, in the preface to *Income Taxation of Trusts, Estates, Gran tors and Beneficiaries*, author Jeffrey Pennel states: "Unfortunately, when I first recommended to our curriculum committee that we add a course on this subject, there was simply no classroom text available."

> Because Trust literature is seldom published, it is virtually impossible to go to any single source to get reliable information about bene-

---

[2]   Richard L. Grossman, *Justice for Sale: Shortchanging the Public Interest for Private Gain;* Alliance for Justice, 1993; reviewed in *The Workbook, Vol. 18, No. 3 Fall 1993*

fits of every Trust. Further, available information on Trusts has been complicated to the point that the average person has almost no chance of understanding even the basic principles. The information is out there, though, if you know where to look. The basic principles of Trusts and their management are simple, and proper administration of a Trust is no more difficult, and often easier, than running your basic small business.[3]

Our purpose is to demystify inheritance by explaining, in clear, straightforward terms:

- The basic ideas;

- The nature and history of Trusts;

- What the various kinds of both Statutory and Common-Law Trusts can and cannot do for you and yours;

- What you should know about the Irrevocable Common-Law Trust that offers, among all the Trust types, the best combination of asset protection, for

  o Asset growth

  o Tax minimization

  o Privacy in an ever less private world

  o Flexible Beneficial distribution

Once you have a picture of a sophisticated and complete Trust, you can more easily discover what other Trust type suits your needs, or whether the Trust from which you receive benefits properly handles administration.

---

[3]   Glen Halliday "The Truth about Trusts," *AntiShyster News Magazine*, Volume 7, No. 1, Pg. 39
http://famguardian.org/Published
Authors/Media/Antishyster/V07N1-TheTruthAboutTrus
ts.pdf

Whether or not you use the information contained here, we are certain that reading *The Art of Passing the Buck* will better prepare you and yours to deal with the emotionally charged matter of preparing for your passing. This alone pays big dividends by giving you clarity about your choices and in reduced personal and family stress.

Table of Contents

We dedicate this book to the next generation in the hope that lives can be more fulfilling, the People better educated about inheritance, and the legal profession more fully informed.

Chapter 1

The Core Issue—Results

To see why ignorance is not bliss when it comes to inheritance, please read and carefully consider the following item:

If Only He Cared . . .

In an article in the Los Angeles Times[4], the Trust Grantor, the one who started the Trust, remarried a longtime girlfriend, and died suddenly several weeks later. The new wife inherited the estate. Since the Declaration of Trust restricted her use of neither Trust principal nor income, she was able to do as she chose. She chose to deprive the original Beneficiaries (her dead husband's children) of their rightful inheritance.

When she was finally, expensively, forced into court by the original Beneficiaries and made to produce the Trust documents, they found she had been given *carte blanche* with all funds, named her relatives as new Beneficiaries, and planned to pay the original Beneficiaries a pittance . . . eventually.

---

[4] Liz Pullliam Weston, *Los Angeles Times*, "Two Trustees Would Protect Estate,", Section C3, Money Talk, September 3, 2000

The column writer advises that this could have been avoided if the husband named both his wife and a Cotrustee to the estate. This would restrain her actions as she needed the Cotrustee to cooperate before she could use funds. The bottom line in the article, written to the ex-wife, the mother of the children suing the estate, is expressed clearly in these two sentences,

> One would like to think the dear departed didn't know his wife was not trustworthy, but that rather strains credulity. It's more likely that, for whatever reason, he didn't care enough about making sure your kids got an inheritance to put sufficient checks and balances on her.

And here's another point to ponder: This stems from what might be termed a "bypass" Trust–although the column writer wasn't sure–which is another name for a Revocable Living Trust.[5] When the Grantor of a Revocable Living Trust passes on, the Trust automatically turns into an Irrevocable Trust. Why? Because the Grantor is no longer alive to change his or her mind, and what is written in the Declaration of Trust, from now on referred to as Trust Indenture or Indenture, is cast in stone.

In reviewing some Revocable Living Trusts, we discovered they are weak, lack direction, and in general, the Trust Grantor casually assigns funds after his or her death. We suggest that even a Revocable Living Trust, in which it states the Trust Grantor is the primary focus of the receipt of funds until his or her death, be written from the view of irrevocability. The Trust Grantor needs to consider the results of nonchalant assignments and to ensure the Beneficiaries' needs are more broadly and seriously addressed.

---

[5] A Living Trust is when the Grantor remains as the Trustee and can change the terms of the Trust during his or her lifetime. There will be much more about this in following chapters.

There is also another choice: set up a Testamentary Trust[6] with people selected as Trustees. When you pass on, the assets are then placed into this newly created Irrevocable Trust. It is administered by a Board of Trustees or only one Trustee—preferably not a family member—whose job it is to take care of *all* the Beneficiaries.

---

[6] A Testamentary Trust is created by the Testator through a Will. He or she sets the terms of the Trust to be created and names a Trustee, or a Trustee can be court appointed.

The Art of Passing the Buck - Volume I

Chapter 2

What is a Trust?

B efore we go on much further, though, we need to make sure you understand what a Trust is.

Refer to Figures 1 and 2. A Trust is a collection of assets transferred into financial accounts under the name of a Family Trust. For example, the name of the Trust might be the Smith Family Trust. These assets, now identified as belonging to the Smith Family Trust, are managed for the benefit of Smith family members or other appointed people and groups.

All recipients of goods or funds are identified as Beneficiaries. They receive the benefits of the Trust which may be assets kept or cash flow generated. The relationships of the Beneficiaries to the Trust and how these benefits are given to them control what type of Trust is set up.

The collection of transferred assets, identified as corpus, can be investments, rental property, promissory notes, business ventures, etc., all designed or selected to produce a cash flow for the Beneficiaries.

Some Trusts pay most of funds at the death of the Grantor(s), from now on referred to as Grantor, and some Trusts provide a cash flow to Beneficiaries during the lifetime of the Grantor. The Grantor does not have to die to benefit his or her family. Remember, though, that ALL Trusts become Irrevocable on the death of the Grantor.

How Does a Trust Work?

There are two types of Trust—Revocable and Irrevocable. The Living Trust is the most common Revocable Trust type. This means you can revoke the Trust at any time. A Revocable Trust, though, eventually becomes Irrevocable. This means the person who set up the Trust passed and can no longer change the terms of the Trust, thus making it irrevocable. Please refer to the following two Figures to see how funds flow through these two types of Trusts.

If you would rather not deal with these details, you may turn to Chapter 3 at any time to read about the benefits derived from being born into a Trust environment.

Grantor/Revocable Trust - Figure 1

The person(s), such as the husband and wife, who sets up the Trust has assets to establish the initial corpus. This is how the Trust is funded. He or she transfers title to the Trust. In this diagram—Figure 1, the Family Trust is set up. The name of this Family Trust can be the last name of your great-grandmother, or it can be your name. By creating a contract known as a Trust Indenture (also known as a Declaration of Trust), a Trust is established. The Grantor as the Trustee sets forth the rules and regulations under which he or she agrees to manage funds for the Beneficiaries. In a Revocable Trust, the immediate Beneficiary is usually the Grantor and spouse, after which are what is known as the Contingent Beneficiaries. These are those people who receive funds after the Grantor passes. During the life of the Revocable Trust the Grantor can give gifts to the Contingent Beneficiaries, but most of the inheritance remains under the control of the Grantors—usually the parents.

Acting as the Trustee, the Grantor Trust financial accounts by opening them in the name of the Family Trust.

For funds to pass without going through probate, the Grantor adds the name of the successor Trustee to these bank accounts, so when the Grantor passes on, the successor Trustee becomes the Trustee with signature power on the Trust accounts. If this step is not taken, then the Revocable Trust may need to go through probate to allow the bank to recognize the signature of the successor Trustee.

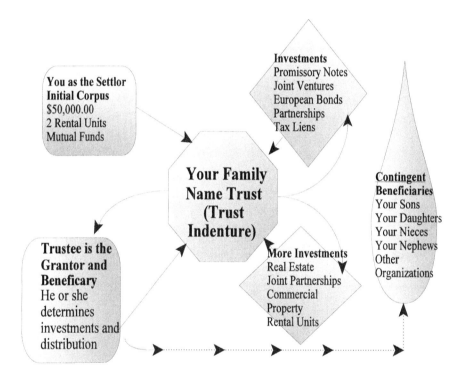

Figure 1 - Revocable/Living Trust

The most common type of Revocable Trust is a Living Trust.

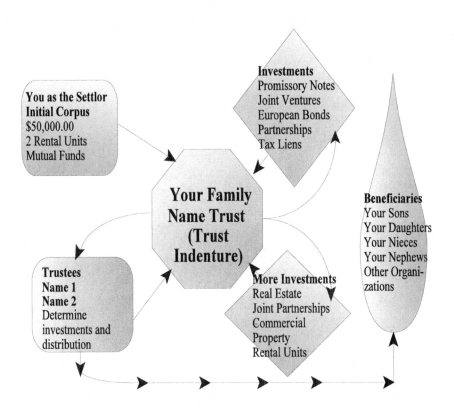

Figure 2 Irrevocable Trust

Irrevocable Trust

The Grantor can establish an Irrevocable Trust at any time during his or her life. Once he or she places funds into the Trust, that person no longer owns them. The funds are the responsibility of the Trustees in the name of the Trust, and the Grantor is neither responsible for them, nor pays taxes on any increase.

The Beneficiaries are now eligible for distribution and pay taxes on what they receive. They do not need to wait until the Grantor passes. They can also take part in the financial decisions of the Trust if the Trustees invite them to do so, and they interact with the Trustees chosen to ensure their welfare.

The role of the Grantor and his or her relationship to the Beneficiaries changes. Without direct financial control over the Trust assets, the Grantor can remain as an advisor to the Board of Trustees, if he or she so chooses. The Grantor can keep control over the distribution throughout his or her lifetime. We will go more into detail about that later in this book.

With funds in the Trust, the Trustees invest and manage any income earned. They can sell the initial corpus and buy different assets, or they can administer the original assets. Because the purpose of the Trust is to increase assets and especially the cash flow, the Trustees receive a percentage of distribution as an incentive. It is likely that an aggressive Board of Trustees (or just one Trustee), will take action to find strong, profitable investments that have a reasonable margin of safety.

The objective is to ensure the welfare of the Beneficiaries, and so profits produced from investments the Trust holds are either reinvested or the Beneficiaries receive some or all the profits.

General Summary of the Trust Basics

The Grantor puts his or her assets into the Trust, and either the Grantor acting as Trustee, or the Trustees then invest the funds. When there is a payout of the investments, the funds go directly into the Trust bank account, where they are distributed to the Beneficiaries. In a Revocable Trust, the Beneficiary(ies) is the Grantor. In an Irrevocable Trust, the Beneficiaries are usually the children and/or close relatives of the Grantor. In both cases, a percentage of the profits can be reinvested.

A Little Beyond Basic

The following section about Divided Title and the U.S. Constitution is for those of you who want to explore the subject of Trust mechanics and definitions more deeply.

For those who feel you are not ready for more details about the mechanics of inheritance, and would like to move onto a more friendly presentation, please go to Chapter 3.

In Chapter 3 we discuss what life might be like if you were a member of a strong Trust Group, which offered both financial security and ample mentoring. The support described mostly applies to an Irrevocable Private Trust where Trustees may personally interact with and be attentive to the Beneficiaries. Here you will discover why those with enough funds are more likely to be successful.

When you feel more comfortable with the ideas of inheritance, we invite you to return to this chapter to read this key additional information.

Divided Title and The U.S. Constitution[7]

The fundamental feature of any Trust is the division of *full title* (complete ownership) of a particular property into *legal title* (technical ownership) and *equitable title* (the beneficial right to possess and use the particular property).

Trustees retain legal title to the property within the Trust and are responsible for administering and enforcing all Trust rules. Beneficiaries receive equitable title to use Trust property they do not own—provided they obey all the Trust's rules.

---

[7] Adask, Alfred, "Divide and Conquer," *AntiShyster News Magazine*, Volume 7, No. 4, pg. 220.

The United States Constitution declares, "no State shall . . . pass any . . . law impairing the obligation of contracts."[8] Therefore, when a Trust is created without fraud by contract, not statutes, it holds a position in law superior to any state law. In other words, by voluntarily and honestly contracting with your Trustee, you establish a lawful Trust. No State can then "impair" or void the obligation you created. Therefore, Trust rules stand superior not only to state constitutional law; they form private law which operates legally outside the U.S. Constitution—as guaranteed by that document itself.

This does not give you any guarantees, though. Your Trust can still be challenged whether or not it is set up correctly.

You might wonder why this is so important? Consider the ownership of residential property. Once put in Trust, several people have a vested interest. Seizure of the property by the government becomes a greater consideration because it is unknown how many of the Beneficiaries will contest the matter, and how much money is behind the Trust veil. This idea of having the property seized by government authorities is not so uncommon. In fact, Eminent-domain abuse is widespread.[9] The issue of divided title comes into play concerning whose property is well guarded and whose is not.

---

[8] U.S. Constitution, Article 1, Section 10.

[9] Jon Daugherty, "Improperty," Report: Eminent-domain abuse widespread," *World Net Daily*, April 22, 2003 www.worldnetdaily.com/news/article

Trusts: What They Are and What they are Not

Many people think that a "Trust" is a group of stocks, bonds and other investments held by a Trustee to produce money for Beneficiaries. This would be the most minimal of definitions.

Others believe the rich use Trust to evade taxes, and people spend years searching for the tax loopholes. Granted, there are enormous tax advantages to a properly formed and managed Irrevocable Trust, but tax breaks are only a small part of the picture.

The legal and IRS definitions limit the scope and purpose of Trusts and so do not adequately or properly describe them. No wonder people have misconceptions!

The Business of a Trust

A good working definition for our purposes here would be: a Trust is a particular type of artificial legal entity structured in such a way and for such a purpose that it can legally take advantage of *passthrough* accounting principles. "Passthrough accounting" means the proceeds (profits, earnings, etc.) pass through it to a secondary recipient (the *Beneficiary*) without producing a tax liability for the Trust. The business is *granted* or settled by a *Trustor, Donor, Grantor* or *Settlor*. Its purpose is to acquire, hold and increase assets for its Beneficiaries. It is administered by a Trustee or a Board of Trustees. Within this business may be many other businesses run by managers who work for it, or it may hold and manage the stock of other businesses to help them all prosper and produce income. Since the Trust is a business, it has its own income flow.

> According to *Black's Law Dictionary* (*First Edition*), a Trust is "an equitable or beneficial right or title to land or other property, held for the Beneficiary by another person, in whom resides the legal title or ownership . . ."

The IRS does not classify a Trust as a business. We use this term because it is in the business of increasing family assets, and should be run accordingly.

Types of Asset Collections

A Trust can be complex and diversified, holding stock in various other entities and operating several businesses. On the other hand, a Trust may be just one business[10], one piece of real estate and/or a collection of priceless household goods. It need not be large and complex. Often, a small Family Trust can grow over several generations into a large, smoothly run group of businesses such as the Grantor could never have envisioned. The fundamental requirements of a Trust are simply that it manages and control assets and that, as a business using passthrough accounting, its structure provides the maximum tax advantages allowable under the law. Again, its entire reason for being is to protect the interests of its Beneficiaries.

Now, let us consider a common legal definition. According to *Black's Law Dictionary First Edition*, a Trust is "an equitable or beneficial right or title to land or other property, held for the beneficiary by another person, in whom resides the legal title or ownership," recognized and enforced by chancery courts." (Chancery courts are courts of equity; see Glossary)

Black's provides a second definition of the word Trust as "an obligation on a person, arising out of a confidence reposed in him, to apply property faithfully and according to such confidence." The Trustee is the one who holds the title to the property due to the "confidence reposed in him" by the Grantor.

So, the most basic activity is the Grantor creates a Trust by granting property into the care of a Trustee, who administers it for the benefit of some third party(ies) known as the Beneficiary(ies). The Trustee can be the Grantor in a Revocable Trust.

---

[10]   There are certain restrictions when a Trust owns a business. This is covered later in this book.

Internal Revenue Code (IRC) Definition

> <u>Ordinary Trusts</u>. In general, the term "Trust" as used in the Internal Revenue Code refers to an arrangement created either by a will or by an inter vivos (see Glossary) declaration whereby Trustees take title to property for the purpose of protecting or conserving it for the Beneficiaries under the ordinary rules applied in chancery or Probate Courts. Usually the Beneficiaries of such a Trust do no more than accept the benefits thereof and are not the voluntary planners or creators of the Trust arrangement. Generally speaking, an arrangement will is treated as a Trust under the Internal Revenue Code if it can be shown the purpose of the arrangement is to vest in Trustees responsibility for the protection and conservation of property for Beneficiaries who cannot share in the discharge of this responsibility and, therefore, are not associates in a joint enterprise for the conduct of business for profit.[11]

Further, a classic court case defines a particular Trust type as, "an agreement by which the property of a syndicate is vested in managers who have absolute control of it and the funds contributed by certificate holders, the latter of whom have merely a right to share in the profits in proportion to their certificate holdings, create a common-law Trust."[12]

We will enlighten the reader on the Common-Law Trust later in this work.

---

[11]   IRC §301.7701-4(a) Trusts

[12]   *Darling v. Buddy,* 1 S.W. 2d 163, 58 A.L.R. 493 (1927).

Chapter 3

Mentors, Money and Trustees

This chapter addresses mostly situations found in a Private Trust where Trustees may have greater motivation and be more involved with Beneficiaries. We describe the ideal here to give you a sense of the possibilities for you and yours.

The Private Trust is not dependent on court-appointed Trustees, and beneficial interest is more flexible. Details are found later in this book and in Volume II.

Further, we include the more common Irrevocable Statutory Trusts throughout this book and compare these two asset-protection modalities.

Windfalls

Sally received a cool half a million dollars when her grandmother died. It was arranged that she would get a cash payout every five years in increments of $100,000.00 and $50,000.00. Sally managed to invest the funds in various projects, but over a 10-year period she eventually lost all of it.

Sally is like many people who receive large sums of money. Most lottery winners have the same fate: 299 out of 300 lose their funds and/or lose their friends, and become quite distraught and unhappy.[13]

Connections

How could this be? Although it seems that everyone dreams of having money, in reality few keep it. Perhaps it is an evil plot to keep us enslaved, or maybe it is simply a matter of education, training, and most important of all, "connections." If Sally had mentors to help her understand money, and especially Trustees with investment experience or connections to income streams unknown to most people, perhaps her half a million dollars would have doubled or tripled. The sad reality is Sally did not have support to help her multiply the assets.

So, what does support look like? The ideal is when a parent is well positioned in his or her profession, or perhaps the entire family owns a particular type of business, and the children grow up under the guidance of, not only the family, but the advisors.

J.P. Morgan is one of those people who grew up with connections. His father, a well-placed financier, associated closely with leaders of other countries. J.P. Morgan's father designed a mentorship program for J.P. to provide schooling in various countries so J.P. would learn several languages and meet the children of those in power. At the age of 13, J.P. acted as ambassador, delivering

---

[13]   People Magazine, *Payday or Mayday?* May 17, 1999, p.128.

important documents to France. These responsibilities and experiences placed him in various leadership roles in his life.[14]

Managing a Large Sum of Money

Managing a large sum of money can be a full time job, and it takes significant experience. Lack of foresight, and simply not knowing how to set up and pass on money are the biggest problems with inheritance issues. The rich are well positioned because they understand the importance of mentors, connections in the world of finance and trade, and seasoned Trustees.

If Sally had only known that a Board of Trustees could have given her incredible advantages .

The Magical Mentor System

There are many things in life we can buy, but have you ever thought of buying a support system, an entire family or a bevy of mentors?

Pirates and Vested Interest

Perhaps you have never thought about buying support. In fact, what is a support system? It consists of several people who have an interest in seeing that you are successful. The best way to create this support is to reward people who assisted you to achieve success. Examples of such interest include both pirates and privateers, with everyone involved receiving a share in the gain.

It is easy to take this same example and apply it to everyday life. If you have a successful business, then the people who support you are given a piece of the action in the form of bonuses and unexpected rewards. This is about shared victory. Victory comes in all sizes and shapes, and is not limited to money. For

---

[14]   Jean Strouse, *Morgan American Financier*, Random House, New York (1999)

example, suppose you received an inheritance that included a large amount of jewelry, far more then you could ever wear? Would you share it with your friends, relatives, and others loyal to you? If the answer is yes, then you already learned how to build the support you need.

Swap Weakness for Strength

But how about buying an entire family? What could an encouraging family do for you that your natural family may not be able to supply? If you come from a dysfunctional family, where brothers, sisters, mother and father do not get along, you may be quite willing to trade it in for a new set of relatives. So, how do you get this family? That will be revealed as we explain the proper structure of a Private Trust also known as the Common-Law Trust with its built-in mentors.

The Advantage of a Long Range View

We come now to the core subject, the magical mentor. Mentors sometimes are difficult to find, especially those willing to help you through life. Mentors usually have a long-range view and want to guide and steer you in the right direction. Mentors are often focused on a particular area. For example, if you have a passion to race cars, your mentor would probably be a race car driver or one who could engineer one of the fastest cars in the world. In fact, without a mentor, you would probably never rise to any great competitive status. Of all the people in your life whom you need to help move you forward, the magical mentor is probably the one most key to your personal success in life.

Suppose, for instance, that you work 9 to 5, and you have many friends but you do not have anybody in the company in which you are employed to give you particular guidance about how to succeed. That is, no one is interested in bringing you up to the top. Added to this, you have a family which has no interest in your success. This does not mean it is against you; it may mean the family just wants you to be happy in life, and offers you no guidance. In this case, you probably do not have strong support or mentors.

Tom Stevens and His Father

Here is an incredible example of family support that worked. One of our Trustees met Dr. Stevens in 1984 and asked him how it was he became a surgeon. He reported his father was a medical doctor and guided him to take the right classes throughout high school and college. When Dr. Stevens was asked if he ever resented his father's taking control of his life, Dr. Stevens replied he never had any particular idea in mind about what he wanted to do anyway, so his father's guidance was accepted and appreciated. Becoming a doctor was as natural as breathing. At the time the Trustee knew him, Dr. Tom Stevens was the Chairman of the Surgery Department of a Chicago, Illinois hospital.

He proved to be fascinating with his marvelous stories about the lives he saved.

Foundation Elements

If you do not have the father our good doctor had, then you need to create your own reality. First, strategically build your foundation by finding people interested in your goals. If you have a goal of beginning your own clothing-design business, you need to get the necessary education, and in that process find those with compatible goals. These others will share their ideas with you, and as long as you reciprocate and are generous with your time and enthusiasm, they will be part of your support network.

> Contrary to popular opinion, the cash flow comes from people. It is other people who create money. Money does not happen by itself, so you need to hook up with people who know how to create money to get a cash flow.

It always helps to have an encouraging family, and as the assets accumulate in your Trust, you will be able to acquire a "supportive family." So, how do you acquire the necessary "stuff" to gather around you those people to support you? To build your own reality you need to accumulate not only people, but also a sufficient cash flow. Contrary to popular opinion, the cash flow comes from people. Other people create money. Money does not happen by itself, so you need to hook up with people who know how to create money to get a cash flow. You will also need to take a risk. This risk could be a small investment in something as simple as "penny stocks," or joining a friend on a business venture where your hard labor generates cash. Whatever it takes, you can assume that a 9 to 5 job, in most cases, is just not going to get all that you need.

Connections

Like Sally, some people are lucky and may inherit the money. Without that magical mentor, though, the money dissipates quickly. Knowing what to invest in and what to avoid takes a good deal of experience. Few people have this background, and so it takes "connections" to know what to do with an inheritance.

Some may win the lottery. As mentioned, after winning the lottery the statistics show that 299 out of 300 people lose their friends and money at the end of a couple years. And why is this? It is because they did not have that magical mentor who knew how to steer them through the extraordinarily difficult and tricky financial world and tell them how to handle relationships.

You need to trust that you can change. If you want to have any sway in this world, you need to have backing that is viable in an ever-changing and complicated society.

Let us explore what a perfect support network might look like. Your mother is loving and your father attentive. Your brothers and sisters may be mischievous, but you can trust them. Your mother has connections to financial organizations willing to have you work for them so you can "learn the ropes." Your father has international connections, and this allows you to spend summers and some of your high school years in foreign countries learning to speak other languages. Your father's uncle is an ambassador for the United States to China. He takes you to China a couple of times a year. When your family sits down at dinner, both your mother and father tell you from time to time the true history of the world according to the family's interaction with various governments. Also, you go to school with the future heirs of fortunes. In other words, you are born into a network in which you are well connected, and from which you are likely to have many mentors.

If this is not how you were raised, then you need to reassess your life and get better positioned. Of course, we are not expecting the average person to be able to accumulate the kinds of wealth and power just described, as that took generations. We do expect the ordinary person, though, to hold a vision of the family's future and to realize that perhaps the third or fourth generation from this date could possibly have a life described like this. We realize thinking this way is unfamiliar and perhaps even scary, but those in power have held this vision for several generations, so why cannot you? Maybe it is that you simply did not know.

So, let us assume that this person who is born into this incredible support network is in a position to make a difference in the world. Could he or she have gotten there without great grandfather's having set up an Irrevocable Trust?

Find the Mentor

Few people will take another person under their wing to guide them through life. To get the vision and achieve the long-range goal for the family, you will need to find not only one but two or three magical mentors to get you there. Unless you know what you are looking for, though, you may inadvertently overlook the person or persons with the needed information. Thus, the first step in finding these magical mentors is to recognize their qualities. These are people who have substantial experience in life, and who also have the motivation to want you to succeed. Like the swashbuckling pirate captain who shares his loot with his rowdy men, you will have to realize that whatever you gain needs to have an upside for those around you who helped you achieve your ambitions. You need to be generous with your time, your information and perhaps even practice being a mentor to others.

If you look around, you may find that not many people have mentors. In fact, it might be a good exercise to do a quick survey among your friends and associates to find out who has taken the time to assist each of them to move forward in life.

Mentor Qualifications

Mentors are natural teachers; they also understand something about the psychology of pain. For a person to rise to the point where he or she feels confident to guide others, it is usually necessary for the mentor to have lost in some way.

Good mentors are those who are not afraid of getting deeply involved; they are familiar with starting from the bottom or having hardship in which they have been thrown off their own paths.

Perhaps one of the most important things good mentors should have is tough love—the ability to tell you in a strong, but caring way, that you must change. You, on the other hand, must have enough brains to comprehend the message and do something about it. Your ability to humbly accept correction without undue upset will earn you respect.

Mentors are aware of the bigger picture. They can see your potential and know that if they support you, you can stand up and make a difference for others. Mentorship is about sharing hard-won knowledge, know-how and skills.

Built-In Mentor System

The Private Trust is more likely to have a built-in mentor. To form a Trust, the Grantor must find two other people willing to take on the responsibility of the assets of the Trust. If your grandmother decides to create a Private Trust, she chooses one person who is not a family member, and perhaps the other person would be a family member.

The Cotrustee, who may or may not be a family member, is selected to ensure it takes two signatures for all the financial documents. This is a built-in safeguard. If your grandmother chooses these two people to be the Trustees, though, they automatically become her mentors. Because of retained powers allowed by the Internal Revenue Code, your grandmother can continue making beneficial and investment decisions and so will be working closely with the Trustees. Trusts need Beneficiaries, so now she names her children and her grandchildren to reap the rewards of strategic investment planning. As the Trust builds its assets and is able to make a beneficial or gift distribution, the Beneficiaries become rewarded and now have a vested interest in the success of the Trust. What you see is a strong group forming composed of people motivated to assist the process via a vested interest in a common goal. This, in most cases, brings the family together.

To ensure there is sufficient communication among all players, meetings of the Board of Trustees should be held no less than semiannually. Meetings focus on educating all members of the Trust, including Beneficiaries, about the invest-ments, the welfare of each other, the long-range goals of the Trust and the social functions of the group.

In the beginning stages of the Trust, the Trustees may not possess any particu-lar great wisdom about finances or legal matters. Each Trustee, though, needs to be willing to get involved to understand them. As the Trust evolves, the Trustees become both more educated and more valuable.

In the long run, Trustees can develop into parental figures to the Beneficiaries, teachers to the Trust group, advisors and legal councilors to the Grantor and the Beneficiaries, function as accountants or have a good grasp of the finances of the Trust, and with experience gain a smattering of psychology to counsel with Trust members. So Trustees become, over time, broad-based persons who have the best interest of all members of the Trust in mind, and thus are among the first qualified to become magical mentors.

Buy a Family

We mentioned, though, that a person could buy a family. So instead of having the great-grandmother set up the Trust, you set up the Trust and pack it with your favorite people. Over time, this group becomes vested in the interests of the Trust and forms a family. All you need to do is take that risk to find the initial funds to gather magical mentors with connections around you. You may find your forte in real estate, environmental cleanup, or a variety of other areas where risk taking allows great gain. But first of all, you must realize it can happen, know how it can be created and want to do it.

Yes, it takes money, connections, friends, trust and the right environment; you also need to become involved in understanding ways that promote vested interest. A corporation, as well as other business forms, promotes this type of interlocking commitment where there is ample reward for all the participants.

Leadership

And if you are going to pull off your dreams and build a new family, or support your current one, you need to develop leadership abilities. This includes consistency, dedication to the goal and, most of all, patience.

Evolution

One of the most valuable attributes of the Irrevocable Common-Law Trust is it provides a strong structure through which a family evolves and grows. Consider for a minute the fractured family that we have today. Brothers and sisters scatter; they are in different states, even countries, and have diverse businesses and priorities. In some families, there is only the excuse of holidays to come together, and in other situations families do not meet even then. What if the entire family were part of a business, though, and that business was the vested interest of the financial growth of each individual and the family's future? What if, instead of coming together for only holidays, now the family comes together four times a year to discuss the Trust finances and the education of the future generation? What if one of the brothers starts a new business and it flourishes? Because the Trust funded the business to start, now some of the proceeds go back into the Trust and are redistributed to the Trust members. The same applies to Trust members who are aspiring artists or musicians who may be worthy of support. If they become famous, the entire Trust membership gains. What if the famous artist, Vincent Van Gogh, was your brother? If this was your family, how interested would you be in the success of your brother's business? Yes, you would be extraordinarily supportive of him. So, let us say he had an assistant who became ill. Suddenly, your brother can turn to the

Trust group and any member who has some of the qualifications can temporarily take the place of the assistant. Your brother has a resource to ensure his success. Van Gogh never received this support during his entire lifetime.

And if this is a family that you "bought," you have many people with vested interest in your success as you need.

Army of Support

It may take many years, perhaps even into the next generation, to have a mature Irrevocable Common-Law Trust with built-in mentors, teachers and a pool of unlimited talent.

Here is another example. You are a member of a strong Trust group, functioning for more than 20 years. Your sister has just gone through a terrible divorce. Her inheritance is secure, though, because it has been held in the Family Trust since she was born. Her husband could not get one dime. Further, she not only has Trustees who came to help her, but she also has access to legal counsel and an entire family (army) which supports her.

> It may take many years, perhaps even into the next generation, to have a mature Irrevocable Common-Law Trust with built-in mentors, teachers and a pool of unlimited talent.

The same could be true for the male members of the family. If the relationship is financially unequal, though, a separate Trust may be set up for the wife so she receives a distribution whether or not she remains married. Otherwise, the financial imbalance in the marriage may eventually create an overt long-range harm. Either the spouse hangs onto a bad marriage for the money, deceiving the partner, or becomes bitter because he or she feels trapped.

Glue

What makes Trusts so powerful? It is something called "glue." Glue keeps people together—trust and a vested interest in the success of the group are the basic elements. The tighter we are bound together in supporting each other, the better our own chances for survival. In fact, the motive to stay together is the top priority, and financial gain should be second or third. There are many ways to get your needs met that do not involve money. How many people in the trades, such as carpenters, painters, and gardeners, exchange services with each other? How many people who are hands-on healers, acupuncturists, or have a healing talent in another modality trade services with each other? In fact, if you delete money from the system, everything else goes to barter and trade. Barter and trade are what operated our world for thousands of years before the "almighty dollar" was invented. You might even say that riches lie in what assets others hold and are willing to share with us. When evolving support, these other values need to be incorporated regularly and consistently.

We hope that we can inspire you to understand that committed relationships, with vested interest, form some of the greatest advantages a person could have.

Choose your mentors wisely; you have a big dream to capture.

Chapter 4

Rethinking Ownership

T he greatest deterrent to putting assets in an Irrevocable Trust is giving up control. This chapter gives you an entirely different perspective about ownership.

It Belongs to Me, Right?

Getting the goods of the world can be a wonderful experience. Further, strutting your stuff in ways ranging from subtle to blatant is considered proper, laudable, or even mandatory. Being the "Joneses" instead of trying to keep up with them is often a secret wish. It means being in control of your life, instead of at the mercy of others—or is this an illusion? Whether it be a shopping spree, a new car, or getting a mortgage for a home, the lust to have is considered normal—but is it?

There is a different way to look at ownership. As a lawyer told us, "The only reason they let you have anything at all is so, if you do not obey, it can be taken away from you." What? You do not believe it?

If you do not pay your income taxes you can lose your home, your car and anything else the IRS decides it wants to place a lien against. If you do not pay your county property taxes, your home disappears into the black hole of forfeiture. As a homeowner, you live with the threat—the constant reminder— that if that if you step out of line it may cost you everything. Lose your job, become involved in an unfortunate divorce, and all your hard-earned equity in the property can be claimed by the ex-spouse, the bank, the state, or the IRS. You owned it. You lost it. In fact, if you ask people around you about the state of affairs of their finances, you will probably discover some of them have lost "it" at one time or another.

Here is another hard truth. According to a friend of ours who became closely associated with an ex-judge, the judge told her, "People never own their home: that is why the state can take it when they do not pay their property taxes. Property only belongs to the state, never to the individual." We would like to give you a footnote on that, but for the safety of the judge, we cannot. We quote it here though, because we have heard it several times, and even from a real estate agent we met at a spa while we were steaming in a mineral bath. In an astounding confession, she revealed this fact to several others in that hot pool. Some homeowners flatly did not believe her, and others were so shocked they fled from the pool in dismay.

A hint the statement is true is found in the definition of land held in allodial title, "Free; not holden of any lord or superior; owned without obligation of vassalage or fealty; the opposite of feudal."[15] Do you own your home in allodial title? No, you own it in fee simple.

Although these people who shared their knowledge about the true ownership status of property must remain unknown, we can send you to any law dictio-

---

[15]   *Black's Law Dictionary, Second Edition*, 1910

nary to look up the term "fee simple." Property transferred in fee simple allows it to be inherited, not owned.

You may wonder what the mysterious difference is between allodial title and fee simple. By answering a few questions and learning some obscure history, you can more fully understand.

Do you want to pay for all the benefits of the county services? We mean, do you want to dig your own water well, supply your own electricity, provide your own fire and police protection? Probably not; therefore, when you elect to pay county taxes, you also forfeit full ownership of your property. Obviously, allodial title is not practical. Unless you are ultra rich, fee simple is for you.

This state-owned property fact is becoming more and more known, and if you ask around, it will be revealed to you by those who know.

Why Ownership Can Be Bad

Taking the responsibility to pay off a home loan, or to buy a car on installment payments, is something of which to be proud. We agree, except in the current corrupt climate of government and tax organizations, ownership could be a greater liability than most people realize.

The politically savvy kings of ancient times knew all about this. They bribed the ordinary person by offering him a title and some land if he served in the king's army. As a bonus, he would see exotic foreign countries and find hard-won glory in distant battles. There was always, though, that sly little royal trick. For a commoner, now a knight, to hold the land took an army, and without the strength to battle the raiding bands of encroaching nations, this new little fiefdom was doomed. Now that same honorable knight must ask the clever king for help to defend his tiny plot of land and his family. For that, he had to pay a price. Whatever the price was, it involved some pledge that enslaved him to both king and land, and that hard-earned title became tainted with a different noble slavery. The serf on the land may have had a better arrangement than the hapless knight—obligated, laden with responsibilities and political schemes that complicated his life.

Although this paints a dark picture, and is perhaps dramatic to make the point, ownership can be leverage others use against you. If you take this leverage out of the hands of others, could you find a new freedom?

But, you argue that without the mortgage, you would not have the present equity in your home against which you could borrow. Delighted that it turned out to be a forced savings program, you believe it is a blessing to you.

Not only were you lucky that you did not lose your home, but fortunate that you bought it where and when the real estate prices increased. Maybe you even paid off your home, continue to pay your taxes on time, and spend enough funds for home improvements and repairs. This is the upside of your dream, but would you like to keep that home in the family? Or, perhaps, would you like to use your amassed equity in someway to benefit your family members?

Why Use Is Better Than Ownership

Ownership is stranger than fiction. If you form an Irrevocable Trust, and transfer assets into it, such as residential property, the ownership becomes split. The Beneficiaries have equitable interest, and the Trustees hold legal title. Now recorded at the county, the residential property is owned by the Trust, and the Trustees' names are listed as the responsible parties.

As mentioned in Chapter 2, this is known in law as *divided title*, and no one actually "owns" the assets. The Trustees are legally responsible for the assets in the Trust and take care of the property, but only hold it for the benefit of the Beneficiaries. A Trust removes direct ownership. It takes money and property out of your hands, where it can be used against you. Now in the hands of people removed from a direct involvement in enterprises, legal and financial complications are less likely. Property is safer.

In other words, if you own a home, have a bad automobile accident where you destroy another's property, the car insurance may not cover the damage. Usually, the claim may require your home to be sold to pay off the debt. If you do not own a home, though, it cannot be forfeited. There is no asset for the plaintiff to claim.

You say this is twisted? This makes no one responsible? This, though, is how most politically protected politicians configure their assets. They put them into what is known as a Blind Trust. These high officials in government cannot be sued for anything substantial. They have little in their name—perhaps a personal checking account and an old car. Since we cannot infuse morals and ethics into a society, we can only see to it that people are protected from frivolous lawsuits over which they have no control. For example, if you lose your job, your home can be lost and then the IRS can hound you for years for back taxes.

This is not true when you place "your" home in an Irrevocable Trust. It is removed from you, providing there are more than eighteen months between the event and when you put the home into Trust. The only time the Trust which holds the property could be involved in a claim is if the Trust, acting as a Trust, causes the damage. For example, the Board of Trustees holds a function at a person's home. The Trustees sign an agreement the facility is to be used for five hours. During that time, the party gets rowdy, and furniture and windows are damaged. Now, the Trust is clearly responsible for the harm and is responsible for paying the facility owners.

What about marriage? Assets in a Trust before the marriage remain in Trust, as they belong to neither the groom nor the bride, but to the Trustees held for named Beneficiaries. Assets gained after a marriage can be community property, unless the Trust buys them and keeps them for the children of the newly married couple. The couple can also put new assets in Trust for the children. We have one circumstance where a person had all his assets in Trust, and he wanted to marry a fine woman. He explained to her that he owned nothing as all his asserts were in Trust. She fled the relationship. One could say she was after him for his money, or maybe he did not offer to initially fund a Trust for her.

Gullible But Rich

There is also the not-so-uncommon event where assets are in Trust, and the gullible, not-so-beautiful Beneficiary marries the dazzling princely rogue. If Trustees are doing their job, the cunning husband wastes oodles of time and money going to court trying to get the well-protected wife's assets. He will eventually discover that she does not own them, and the Trustees do not care about his plight.

As a reminder, please do not confuse the word Trust with a Statutory Living Trust. In a Living Trust, property remains in the name of the original owner, and is not removed into the names of the Trustees. Therefore, a Living Trust offers no asset protection, and only limited probate protection.

This chapter exposures you to the potentially huge economic, peace-of-mind, legal and tax advantages of having the use of property in an Irrevocable Trust without the headaches and legal exposures of ownership. Now for a deeper understanding, it is time to share with you the history and evolution of Trusts.

Chapter 5

Trusts Down Through the Ages

Armed now with at least a basic understanding of what a Trust is and how it works, we turn to a historical survey of Trusts. We address their antiquity, long tradition of use and the reasons they came into being and have endured since.

The earliest known writings are tax documents, and Trusts date back to at least the time of the Egyptian pharaohs. The Bible documents the issue of inheritance when Esau sold his birthright to Jacob.[16] This implies a formal arrangement existed in those days. We do not have details about these contracts, though. Around 400 B.C., Plato used a Trust to form a sovereign university in Greece.

In ancient Rome, only citizens inherited property. When a Roman chose a foreigner for his heir, though, he could sidestep the citizenship need through a legal instrument known as a *fidei-commissum* similar to today's Common-Law Trust.[17]

---

[16]   Genesis 25:29 33

[17]   George Gleason Bogert, *The Law of Trusts and Trustees*, Section 2, West Publishing Co, St. Paul, MN (1984) p. 15

This *fidei-commissum* served one purpose and lasted only long enough to help the transfer of property. It shows the need of a landowner to have trust in another person to carry out the landowner's will after his death.

Many examples of this procedure are in Roman judicial records.

Church vs. King

As early as the 11th century, English knights found Trusts to be effective in safeguarding their property while they were away at the Crusades. Without this legal protection, they soon found the king was all too willing to confiscate their property to finance wars and other projects of his own. In response to this royal thievery, the warriors installed the Church as Trustee of their property during their absence. Only the emissaries of Heaven had power enough to block the king's conniving. The sophisticated legacy of case law governing the conduct and responsibilities of Trustees we find in our courts today grew as a result. The Royal Courts of Chancery enforced the laws of Trusts.

The Mortmain Acts of 1279 A.D,[18] also known as the *Statutum de viris relig iosis*, forbade the Church from owning land, and certain orders had taken vows of poverty. Those who wanted to give land to the Church could do so only through the "use." Thus, a third-party held title and served under bond to handle land. Today this third-party is known as a Trustee.

Medieval England provides excellent examples of the "use." It was a way to "enfeoff," or transfer the legal title of land, to one person or group, while holding the use of the land for the "*cestui que use*" (the "feoffor" or another person or group, known in modern language as a Beneficiary). Holding (lease) title to land under English Common-Law carried with it many obligations. The

---

[18] " . . . religious men should not enter into the fees of any without the will and licence of the lords in chief of whom these fees are held immediately."
http://www.yale.edu/lawweb/avalon/medieval/mortmain.htm

lord of the land could claim a "relief," or money payment, when the land descended to an heir of full age. If the heir was a minor, the landowner had the rights of "wardship" and "marriage." When a daughter of a tenant married, or a son knighted or the tenant held for ransom, the lord became entitled to "aids" (that is, more money). A "use" avoided these extractions while still letting the *cestui que use* enjoy the benefits of the land. To avoid the feudal burdens and obligations to care for the land that came with the death of a single feoffee, (see Glossary) several feoffees could serve as joint tenants.[19]

Scholars of medieval English land law note the religious bodies were among the first to employ the "use" extensively.

Massachusetts Trust

When the English colonized North America, the "use" changed into the Trust and the colonists brought the idea with them. They further developed the idea by devising the "Massachusetts Trust," which is almost synonymous with "Business Trust." They did this in part because it literally took a special act of Parliament to secure a corporate charter to acquire and develop real estate. The Trust gave them a way to pool their resources without having to deal with state-imposed controls and burdens.

Some Trusts currently in the United States have existed longer than the country itself. They provide benefits to countless Heirs Beneficiary (see Glossary), as well as many communities. By using a Common-Law Trust and not a government granted charter, a Trust operates with greater freedom and far more privacy. By providing a common vehicle for the self-interests of its Beneficiaries, a Trust teaches the lessons of interdependence, cooperation and working together for the common good.

---

[19]   Bogert, ibid., p. 15

The Privy Seal and the Queen

Queen Elizabeth I was notorious for robbing her subjects of their money. Whenever her spies discovered a merchant made a profit, she immediately sent agents to borrow it through an agreement known as "the privy seal." She never paid back any of her debts.[20] Historians note that this practice contributed to keeping the feudal system in place during her entire reign. Those subjects who had the ability to create riches either hid them well or left England.[21] Thus, this monarch unintentionally contributed to developing Trusts among rich, private citizens and to protecting assets by the clergy.

> "John D. Rockefeller established more than 270 *Pure Equity Trusts* which kept his vast empire sovereign . . ."

Early American Trusts

Later in Pennsylvania, Governor Robert Morris of the Virginia Colony, an English-born Philadelphia banker, a member of Congress and the "financier of the American Revolution,"[22] set up a

---

[20]   Agnes Strickland, *Lives of The Queens of England from the Norman Conquest*, Volume XVI, Chapter viii, p. 208, George Barrie & Sons, Philadelphia, 1903.

[21]   Strickland . . . Throughout the many successive reigning monarchs, English subjects also learned to stay out of the way of the king or queen's progress through the countryside, as the royal armies had the habit of raping and pillaging both land and people. When residents of towns close to the ruler discovered the retinue was traveling, they fled before the ravaging armies.

[22]   *Columbia Encyclopedia, Second Edition*, Columbia University Press, New York, 1950, p. 1326.

Trust named The North American Land Company,[23] which remains in existence today. Similarly, Patrick Henry[24] also set up several Trusts which are now more than 250 years old.

The descendants of these famous patriots, some of them still in leadership roles, achieved durability for their Family Trusts by carefully training each successive generation to understand and apply sound legal and financial principles to Trust management.

As reported in the *Chicago Tribune*, March 22, 1947, the Chicago Merchandise Mart is a *Pure Trust* established by Joseph P. Kennedy.

John D. Rockefeller established more than 270 *Pure Equity Trusts* which kept his vast empire sovereign and beyond the reach of inheritance taxes and other government intrusions.

The U.S. government itself allegedly created thousands of Trusts, including the U.S. Constitution, Medicare and federal highway programs–the latter fact posted on highway signs along Interstates, especially during times of construction.

We know that administration skills allow a Trust to continue. We devote many pages in Volume II to this subject.

[23] *Capital Strategies,* "Brief History of Pure Trusts", http://www.wealth4freedom.com/wns/trusthistory.htm

[24] (". . . Give me liberty or give me death"), Revolutionary War-era governor of Virginia, passionate opponent of the U.S. Constitution, advocate of the Bill of Rights and a wealthy speculator in land.

Dark Side

We would be seriously lax, though, if in our discussion of Trusts, we failed to discuss their other, darker side. This is a story not only of relentless, multigenerational self-aggrandizement, but of the manipulation and direct involvement of the U.S. Government in support of that agenda.

The resultant chapter in this nation's history became so black that learning about it is compulsory for the U.S. schoolchildren to this day. Further, it would be fair to say that, to many, this is what the word "Trust" means at a visceral/emotional level.

In the late 1800s, certain major American industrialists developed the practice of concentrating their assets into associations or "combinations" in restraint of trade. Unfortunately for the reputation of Trusts, these individuals twisted the long-established Trust methods into a new shape to reach their goals. Though termed "Trusts" and outwardly imitating the traditional pattern, in reality the conglomerates they created violated the basic ethical purpose of Trusts—to care for the family. They poured their immense resources into the petty games of self-protection and self-aggrandizement at the expense of their other people. These brilliant but shortsighted industrialists fixed monopolies, manipulated material costs and product prices, nullified free market competition, corrupted the media and dominated Congress.[25]

As we have seen, before that period Trusts were used by the private sector as a shield against the abuses of kings, queens and legislatures, not as a cudgel to smash business rivals.

Yet, as Industrial Age technologies concentrated increasing amounts of power in the hands of ever fewer men and corporations, Lord Acton's maxim "power corrupts" took a new turn. Instead of consolidating their power in the private sector to stabilize families and provide better service to their customers and the

---

[25]   Hon. E.R. Ridgely, (D-Kans.), *AntiShyster News Magazine*, "Title Wars," Vol. 8, No. 2, p. 20.

community, they abused their positions, crushing competitive initiative and reducing service quality to end users.

Clearly, government intervention was justified, and it had to come from the federal level. The shift of power out of statehouses and into boardrooms was carried out by several of these associations, whose influence now crossed not only state borders but national ones as well. Increasingly independent of local markets, regulations and boundaries, these would-be masters of the universe gave the time-honored techniques of Trusts new roles never intended by their predecessors. Seemingly over the financiers' objections and despite their ability to buy votes, Congress passed the "Antitrust" laws banning monopolies. Predictably, the executive branch failed to carry through and enforce them, as shown by the fact we still have an oil cartel, and few industries show true competitive pricing. In large cities, the overall trend is that mom and pop stores have been driven out of business by larger chains whose volume buying power results in pricing significantly lower than individual stores can offer.

On their face, these laws appear straightforward, genuine examples of the democratic process at work, embodying the masses' demand to curb big money's abuses of power. Public outrage was present, doubtless further inflamed by the hired pens of William Randolph Hearst and other "yellow journalists"[26]. At least some of the members of Congress who proposed and passed the "Trust-busting" legislation had a different motivation from the voters, though. (Like lawmakers in other eras of democratic government, they followed the theme, "Government is the art of extracting votes from the poor and wealth from the rich by promising to protect each from the other.") The attention made lawmakers take seriously their duties as public servants. They took action against the real danger posed by the giant industrial "Trusts" to the economy and the nation (thus winning the vote of the little man). In reality, they provided those same wealthy captains of industry with the federal firepower to blow their competitors out of the water. Even though it appears the separate companies became different oil companies, they have not competed. Do they fight among themselves? We think not!

---

[26]   See Glossary.

As Michael Parenti notes in *Democracy for the Few:*

Progressive Repression

In the twentieth century, as in the centuries before, the men of wealth looked to the central government to do for them what they could not do for themselves; to repress democratic forces, limit competition, regulate the market to their advantage, and in other ways bolster the process of capital accumulation.

Contrary to the view the giant Trusts controlled everything, price competition with small companies in 1900 was vigorous enough to cut into the profits of various industries. Suffering from an inability to regulate prices, expand profits, and free themselves from the "vex-atious" reformist laws of state and local governments, big business began demanding action by the national government. <u>As the utilities magnate Samuel Insull said, it was better to "help shape the right kind of regulation than to have the wrong kind forced upon [us].</u>[27] (Emphasis added.)

While the billionaire bankers and manufacturers who owned representatives in Congress, drafted the laws supposedly aimed at busting Trusts, the obvious targets of those laws simply changed their tactics. They restructured their complex Trusts into "holding corporations" and carried on much as before. As usual, the competition was left to its own devices, first to discover the new game and then how to play it.[28]

The public stigma which became attached to the term "Trust" at the beginning of the last century explains why the public has not searched out the techniques of wealth building used by these past masters. Like masters of PSYOPS,[29] the

---

[27]   Michael Parenti, *Democracy for the Few,* St. Martin's Press, Inc., NY, 1983, p. 80.

[28]   See *Black's Law Dictionary, Sixth Edition* definition of Trust for a further description of these "Trusts."

[29]   Psychological operations.

rich may well have anticipated their reverse-psychology campaign which funded both sides of the debates. This is now Standard Operating Procedure (SOP) for pushing controversial legislation through Congress. By making it uncomfortable for people to use Trusts, they will never learn the secrets. Genuine or not, the drama, sensationalist press campaigns, political cartoons and flowery oratory of the era turned the American public strongly against this artificial entity. Even now, most ordinary folks have a hard time seeing themselves associated with a Trust, let alone creating one.

Nonetheless, students of Trusts who can keep an emotional distance from the events of yesteryear stand to gain a precious lesson. The instrument used by Rockefeller, Carnegie, Morgan and others to amass their monopolistic power (upheld and expanded by their Beneficiaries) has precisely the same shape (although not the same purpose or contents) as the one we examine in this book.

That fact, perhaps more than any other, may help you understand why rich private interests, and the government agencies which claim to curb them, keep such secrecy about the uses of this powerful device—and why it is not taught in the schools they fund.

Some assume the reason attorneys lack information about Common-Law Trusts is the wealthy, who control the curriculums, have no motive to share their strategies.

We do not favor or support monopolies or abuses of power by private interests anymore than we do tyrannies or dictatorships by caesars, kings or congresses of the people. Having and using a Trust will neither ensure that your own behavior is ethical nor make up for any other flaws of character, intelligence, experience or training. We would be lax in our duty as educators and members of the community, though, if we downplayed or ignored the enormous potential for power which remains in this family business. This is precisely because it encourages those who care most about you to support your dreams and supplement your strengths with their own.

The knights of Old England used their Trusts defensively, as impenetrable shields against the king. The robber barons of Wall Street turned theirs, though, into weapons to clobber the competition. How you develop and use the power of the Trusts you create largely depends on the scope and purity of your purpose, and neither of those is a known nor a fixed quantity.

One fact is certain, though, just as surely as nature loathes a vacuum, if you fail to explore and exploit the blessings which life gives you, someone else will take them away. You can hide from them, bury them, surrender them, abuse them, ignore them, waste them, cry over them or laugh at them. Or you can nurture them (and those who contribute to them), develop them, protect them, add to them, share them, explore them and maybe someday even grow to understand them.

Tribal Power

Tribal power exists in current Trusts today, especially through the Du Pont Family, which has a shared interest in not only Trusts but corporations, partnerships, and limited liability companies all across the world. Even though the Du Ponts are not registered as holding a majority of stock, the family votes in blocks. This is how it controls many of the Boards of Trustees and Boards of Directors in various organizations throughout the world. Cataloged in a book titled *The Rich and the Super-Rich*[30], the Du Pont family is similar to the Rockefeller and all the other major families. These power dynasties long ago discovered that voting as a unit is where political leverage remains, in other words, the tribal strength of agreement.

Contrary to our belief that rugged individualism is almighty and desirable, the opposites is the truth—collective agreements are what controls this world. A handful of conclaves developed and matured to take the leadership of our planet. Unfortunately, most such groups are not strictly focused on the welfare of the People. They use financial leverage through group agreement, and this is the great power of the Irrevocable Common-Law Trust, a force not available

---

[30]   Frederick Lundberg, *The Rich and The Super-Rich*,
Lyle Stuart, Inc., New York (1968), out of print.

through the average Statutory Trust. The leverage of a united family available through the Common-Law Trust is what provides its unique place in the world. And, as long as the United States Constitution and the state constitutions secure our right to contract, the Irrevocable Common-Law Trust stays, also giving the average middle-class family collective leverage.

The Feudal System and the Common-Law Trust

Although we cannot quote an exact source about the term "Common-Law," we can assume that common means to share, as in "common good." In feudal England the common people equally shared the land. Both the freeborn and the serfs cultivated strips of land, known as "selions," which were 220 yards long by 5½ yards wide. Researchers believe there was an effort to give each household an equal chance to cultivate some of the good land of the township with the poor, and thus these selions were scattered. Because they were scattered, the land became common to the people.[31]

The Common-Law is based on shared resources. We have all heard the term, "feudal overlord," that is the leader, or the overall landowner. The term landlord comes from this tradition. In that time, though, the feudal lord cared about the get the better deal, and in the fair distribution of the resources.[32] The people worked the land. Although, considered little better than animals, to the feudal lord, his serfs were an asset, without which the land could not become productive. Thus, while there were taxes, it was not the norm to abuse the serfs. There is an idea that if a person is tied to the land he is enslaved. This also allowed them, though, to be secure in their homes. The idea they could not leave to work some other land may or may not have been a matter of concern. In viewing the feudal age through our modern sensibilities, we may not see reality as the serfs saw it.

---

[31] Arthur R. Hogue, *Origins of the Common-Law*, Liberty Press, Indianapolis, Indiana (1966), p. 126-127

[32] Ibid., p 93

Even in America, eventually the slaveowners came to realize that if the slave was well-kept, he or she not only lived longer, but became more cooperative.

> By the 1850s many slave holders had become more aware of the need to increase food allotments, maintain more sanitary living conditions, and provide adequate clothing and shelter for their slaves.[33]

Although this effort became greater after more than 150 years of slavery, we only bring your attention to this matter to compare it, not to excuse it, and to broaden the definition and idea of what slavery might be.

This is in contrast to today where corporate management disassociates itself from the "worker," and takes no personal responsibility for his or her welfare. People are discarded when of use no longer. This may be through downsizing or retirement. The "worker" is then supported by the State in the form of unemployment and medical benefits. Instead of an overlord who has an interest in the worker's welfare, we have a near machinelike mechanism that handles people with indifference, and sometimes downright neglect, for example, welfare programs and child services.

As society evolved, the idea of sharing became less centralized, until shared resources is mainly within the family. Without the support of the family, members do not have a firm foundation in life to carry them into new adventures, and to give them the courage to learn and take the necessary risks to grow.

The idea of any Trust is to provide the financial basis so the family members can contribute to society from a position of security, instead of uncertainty. When you must focus on gathering enough to simply make it through a week or a month, there is not much time to devote to helping others, contributing to the community, or to developing yourself.

Those who have built up this family power base for generations are those who are in power today. For generations to come to be in a position to manage to

---

[33]   Jack Salzman, David Lionel Smith, *Encyclopedia of African-American Culture and History,* Cornel West, Editors, Volume 5, Simon & Schuster and Prentice Hall International, New York, "Slavery," p. 2464

the common good, families must set the foundation now to have enough leverage in the future to be of benefit to this world.

The Ulterior Motive

Besides addressing the mundane, legal and philosophical reasons for creating a Trust, we are taking a massive departure from the familiar. The presumably safe tradition of legal and historical facts will now segue into what many of you will find "out there." Rest assured, though, there is a good reason for our doing so.

Found hidden in the antiquity of history is one of the hottest political footballs of all time. This subject remains questionable, even today. Without bringing it to your attention, though, you would miss the background of what compels the Super-Rich to use Trusts.

Beneficiaries be damned; the real purpose of the Trust for the Super-Rich is to accumulate and protect assets for themselves! Ancient rulers who literally took their servants and treasures to the grave with them could, were they here, but look in awe and envy at the boldness of the scheme.

The rich are motivated to create wealth so they can reincarnate back into their own bloodline and thus inherit their resource structure. They not only keep their material comfort, but also their leverage.

Because of the controversial nature of the subjects of reincarnation and other esoteric themes in general, we feel that we should address these beliefs more fully in Appendix H. Here you will find the more amazing details of some of the rituals of the major organizations and leaders of our world, and understand more thoroughly why they have such an intense motive to accumulate wealth. This one area is probably the demarcation line between those who seek power and those who choose to live their lives to the fullest capacity without concern about how or when they come back, or even if they do.

In bringing this point of view to light, we are not offering or suggesting it is correct, only it is probably a strong motivator for some.

Chapter 6

Wealth Retention: Tactics of the Rich

B efore we take you into some of the details of setting up a Trust, you should understand some broader concepts about wealth. In this chapter you will enter into an awesome world of power, and get an in-depth look at vested interest and the cohesiveness of the elite.

This chapter embodies the discussions at the dinner table, or with your mentors if you grew up in the stratum of society where deals and manipulations occur to make political moves.

The Eternal Loop

A properly run Trust comes into being, lives and dies for the Beneficiaries. Indeed, the first test of whether an entity is in fact a Trust and not a scam of some sort is whether it has at least one real Beneficiary. And, this Beneficiary cannot be the Grantor who set up the Trust. A viable Trust is one which is set up for the benefit of someone other than the Grantor.

Beneficiaries are the basis of Trusts, for Trusts are simply specialized legal vehicles to provide for and care for Beneficiaries, and to ensure that not even the marriage partners, or anyone else, gets the funds or assets. Although in many Statutory Trusts, the duration may be just long enough to liquidate the estate and parcel out the proceeds, as in certain Living Trusts, it may also renewably run for many generations, as in the private contracts known as the Irrevocable Common-Law Trusts.

> Because of an Irrevocable Trusts's ability to hold assets in its name, and not in the name of a person who will die, it allows wealth to be retained and passed down the genetic line (progeny).

To prevent Beneficiaries from thwarting long-range plans, the rich discourage any misconduct through the way Trusts have been sent up: you cause trouble, you are disinherited. This is better known as the No Contest Clause.

Because of an Irrevocable Trusts's ability to hold assets in its name, and not in the name of a person who will die, it allows wealth to be retained and passed down the genetic line (progeny). Thus, the legal matter of having Beneficiaries allows wealth to be kept generation after generation. The Super-Rich, the dynastic families who run this planet for their private benefit, thanks to generations of intermarriage and despite amounting to less than 3% of the population, control at least 95% of all the known wealth on Earth.

The Business of Hoarding

Even if you do not think that 3% is a real number, you must remember, these Super-Rich families have been hoarding since before William the Conqueror ascended to the English throne in 1066 A.D.

Railroad Leases

Further, great sections of the land in America are still owned by royal families. For example, the railroad leases are part of an intricate network originally set up through the Lewis Cass Payseur Trust, a scheme devised by the English Crown on behalf of Marie Antoinette's surviving son.[34] Through the railroad network, the mineral and water rights of America are owned. You may remember the leases were in a 10-mile square checkerboard pattern on either side of the railroad lines–prime land where towns would soon flourish. Consider the accumulation of wealth from just from this scheme alone. The documentation of the Assets of the Lewis Cass Payseur Trust is found on page 321 of *Pandora's Box*. They include:

> **Through the railroad network, the mineral and water rights of America are owned.**

> Railway, Railroad and Related Companies; Banks and Related Companies, Cotton Mills, Thread and Sewing Machine Companies; Electric and Power Companies, Gold and Silver Companies, Iron and Steel (and other metals) Companies; Motor Vehicle Companies; Insurance Companies, Tobacco and Related Companies, Watch Companies, Land and Real Estate Companies, Food and Other Household Goods and a long list of miscellaneous companies.

If this, alone, does not astound you, then to further convince you, the 1913 *Report of the Pujo Committee* listed in the U.S. 62d Congress, 3rd Session, House Report No. 1593, Chapter III. The above list of assets is carefully reported in detail in the Pujo Committee Report. This underscores the power of those who have held the riches of this world for thousands of years. Multiply this effort by the number of dynasties over the past 1,000 years, and you will get the true picture of who owns what.

---

[34]   Alex Christopher, *Pandora's Box*, Pandora's Box Publishing, Spokane, Washington, 1993, p. 50

Welfare: The Double Standard

An old adage holds that children who do not work for a living become spoiled, cannot handle money, and that money ruins many lives. True, people who suddenly inherit sums which far exceed their previous income may find their new fortune leads to misfortune.[35] Yet, those who live all their lives in riches, do not have such problems.

Consider, for example, this statement from a respected study of wealth, *The Rich and the Super-Rich*:

> In requiring reports of a beneficiary interest in trust funds and of holdings as a trustee, the law reveals a large portion of the social security system of the rich. It is an excellent system, and provides much security for its beneficiaries. But in considering it, one wonders about the oft-heard thesis of many conservative and ultraconservative spokesmen and newspapers the federal Social Security System, the Family Welfare System and the trade-union system all carry great danger of destroying the characters of the participants. They might, among other things, become mercenary or lazy.
>
> The rich themselves very evidently do not believe that being the beneficiaries of huge trust funds has undermined their characters, or that establishing trust funds for their children will distort the children's characters. No case has come to light where the children of the wealthy have been left penniless for their own benefit. All known cases of disinheritance are punitive, where the children have displeased the parents. Why, if drawing benefits without labor from a big trust fund does not destroy character, will drawing benefits in old age from Social Security or a pension system do so? Why would a true Welfare State be injurious of the general public when a private

---

[35]   *People Magazine*, "Payday or Mayday?" May 17, 1999, p.128.

welfare system of trust funds is not apparently injurious to its limited number of beneficiary heirs?"[36]

If you still believe that giving your children financial support is harmful, you might want to examine how you formed that idea. Was it suggested by indoctrination you received through the mass media, owned and operated by people who have more interest in obtaining your family legacy for themselves than in seeing you pass it on to your heirs?

Who Are the Real Welfare Recipients?

Consider the real welfare state erected and run for the benefit of the rich through such grand enterprises as:

- Private banks designed to appear and sound as if they have been conceived for the public good, yet are privately owned, e.g., the Federal Reserve Bank.[37]

- Agricultural subsidies in the U.S. alone were 15.2 billion dollars in 2002[38], with most of the benefits inuring to a handful of vertically

---

[36] Lundberg, *The Rich and the Super-Rich*, p. 210

[37] The Federal Reserve Bank document of major stockholders lists the following who own 100% of the primary stock: Rothschild Bank of London and Berlin, Lazard Freres Bank of Paris, Israel Moses Seif Bank of Italy, Warburg Bank of Hamburg and Amsterdam, Lehman Brothers Bank of New York, Kuhn Loeb of New York, Chase Manhattan Bank of New York.

[38] Jeffrey Sparshott, *The Washington Times,* "Agricultural Subsidies Targeted," December 08, 2003, http://www.washtimes.com/business20031207-114046-8545R.htm

integrated multinational agribusinesses.[39] Well-fed contractors who manipulate events and governments to stay at the public trough, all aided by a network of public laws passed for private profit and paid for with unending bribes, gifts, graft and corruption.[40] The Boeing bribery scandal and the billions paid time and again to the super-connected Halliburton,[41] [42] Bechtel et al.,[43] are but a few examples of how the ruling elite keep the money in their pocket.[44]

- Trade policies, such as those embodied by NAFTA and GATT, whereby long-standing tariffs have been removed to allow industry jobs to flee overseas. This provides record profits to owners through cheap

---

[39] Timothy A. Wise, "Identifying the Real Winners From U.S. Agricultural Policies," GDAE Working Paper No. 050-07 (Updated June 2006), The Global Development And Environment Institute (GDAE), Tufts University, Medford, Massachusetts.

[40] *AFL-CIO News,* "Bush Buddies Get No-Bid Contracts While Workers Get the Shaft," September 14, 2006, http://www.aflcio.org/aboutus/ns09142005a.cfm

[41] *Common Dreams News Center*, "Halliburton Handed No-Bid Iraqi Oil Firefighting Contract," March 25, 2003, http://www.commondreams.org/headlines03/0325-11.htm

[42] Michael Dobbs, *Washington Post,* "Halliburton's Deal Greater Than Thought, August 28, 2003, http://www.truthout.org/docs_03/082903B.shtml

[43] Pat Gerber, *Common Dreams News Center*, "Another Scandalous No-Bid Contract Makes Us Look Like Fools," May 23, 2003, http://www.commondreams.org/views 03/0526-07

[44] Yochi J. Dreazen, *The Wall Street Journal*, "US: No-Bid Contracts Win Katrina Work," September 12, 2005 http://www.corpwatch.org/article.php?id=12620

foreign labor, and reduced or nil regulatory overhead without charging less for products in the United States.[45] [46]

That is the real welfare state—an entire nation's resources and people bound over to serve a privileged few!

This may be upsetting to some of you, but we are not here to coddle you in your carefully instilled, constantly reinforced delusions. Rather, we are here to wake you up, and to show you what you have been taught to believe about how the system works is simply not true. It extracts as much as possible from you. Stop being the victim!

Life in the Matrix

You might not think it, but this rather "out there" notion turns out to be directly applicable to what we are discussing. How? American business is the Matrix. Instead of running on our basic life force, though, it harvests the distilled essence, in the form of our money and property, not to mention irreplaceable time, energy and effort.

> The Federal Reserve System created a private central bank which looks governmental but is not.

[45] Sarah Anderson and John Cavanagh, *Policy In Focus, Policy Brief*, "Outsourcing: A Policy Agenda," Volume 9, Number 2, April 2004: http://www.fpif.org/briefs/vol9/v9n02outsource_body.html

[46] Bill Moyers, *NOW on-line magazine*, "America and Jobs,", Politics & Economy, May 7, 2004: http://www.pbs.org/now/politics/outsource.html

The Federal Reserve and the IRS

The robber barons made their stupendous fortunes at the turn of the Twentieth Century, in a climate of practically zero regulation and no federal income tax. They then sought to protect their privileged positions by erecting impregnable defenses around them.

The solutions adopted were simple, practically invisible despite operating in plain sight, and diabolically effective. The first, the Federal Reserve System, created a private central bank which looks governmental but is not. That entity, through controlling the borrowed-into-existence money supply (the interest on which forms the vast majority of the national debt), can literally bring about boom and bust at will.

The second, the IRS, is also a faux governmental entity and acts as the money collector, data collector and enforcement arm for the owners of the privately owned Federal Reserve Bank. Worse, since these same people have *de facto* control of the government, they have long been using its full weight and power to systematically lie to the people and trick them into surrendering their rights and property. For example, there is the issue of the term "nonresident alien." It means one who is a citizen of one of the several states and not a U.S. Citizen, who is a taxable entity. This requires a lengthy legal discussion but seems to be one of the main points of the IRC §861 argument, which is beyond the scope of this book.[47]

We do not advocate any tax battles. The information, though, is essential to make correct financial decisions. For example, knowing that the planet is run

---

[47]   The entire definition of "engaged in a trade or business within the United States" becomes a game of words. "Within the United States" refers to federal territories and not to any activity in the 50 states. See Appendix for a definition of the United States and the United States of America per the terms of the IRC and case law; Internal Revenue Districts outside of the District of Columbia were abolished as a result of the *IRS Restructuring and Reform Act of 1998*, 112 Stat. 685.

by those heavily invested in oil, makes you think twice before heavily investing in free energy. Trying to take on the "system" needs a deep understanding and no Board of Trustees should try it.

This, though, constitutes merely the microcosm the American Business Matrix (ABM). And remember, the money being issued, contrary to the Constitution, is backed by neither gold nor silver, hence is called fiat money—decreed into existence. If the American economy collapses, other countries will not value the U.S. Dollar–which is a Federal Reserve (promissory) Note and has no backing.

Of Banks and Suppliers

The same interests which own the Federal Reserve Bank also own the banks, financial institutions, credit bureaus, telephone companies and manufacturers, as well as service suppliers of every stripe, to name but some. All of them profit by convincing you to invest your hard-earned money and property into a business. Judging from the official small business failure rates of 85% the first year and 95% within five years, you would be much better off going to Las Vegas and playing the slots, which pay off sometimes as high as 90%.

And guess what? These same interests are the real impetus behind "bankruptcy reform" laws which make it hard for Americans ensnared in carefully crafted debt traps to get out and start afresh.

Remember our fiat money discussion? That is what a business loan is. A ledger entry is made, a worthless check is issued, then off you go on your statistically doomed business venture, generally with your house and other property as loan collateral and your blood, toil and sweat to enrich the bankers.

Everywhere you turn for items and assistance you need to do business, the ABM awaits, not just as business entities, but as governmental ones, too: taxes, permits, licenses, inspectors, user fees, special tags and more.

If you succeed, the ABM makes money at every step both before and during. If you fail, your business assets are seized and sold to some other sap as the great con continues, your collateral is forfeited, and you may well wind up saddled with a lifetime of debt.

What if there were a better way, though, a way in which the potential not just for failure but the consequences of that failure were minimized, while at the same time, the likelihood of success was greatly increased?

Because an entire family can put its assets together, either the Private or Statutory Trust offers great financial leverage. The substantial backing thus engendered immediately acts to counter such major causes of business failure as undercapitalization, inadequate knowledge, poor accounting and internal theft. To do this, though, means first dispelling the ABM promulgated myth of the entrepreneur.

The Myth of Making It in the World

The American propaganda machine constantly reinforces the belief that the entrepreneur is one of this country's most valuable assets. Further, we are told that America is the "land of opportunity." Here, we can succeed beyond our wildest expectations and dreams. *The Wall Street Journal* reports many such successes, as do several other high-class magazines, such as *Fortune,* and *Inc*.

> The average person can tilt the odds of success much to his or her favor by being better informed and organized when new ventures are attempted.

What if statistics and generational records prove otherwise? What if the entire concept of the entrepreneur fails in the face of reality? If the concept is faulty, then what will you do when you discover what does work?

The premise that, contrary to what the public has long been told, inherited wealth owns the political structure, controls the money supply and controls our lives has been proven through extensive research. We again refer to *The Rich and Super-Rich.* The author, Ferdinand Lundberg, demonstrates through numerous examples the rags to riches concept is false. Even if the first generation has great financial success, the resulting financial leverage, when compared to inherited wealth, is nil. Further, inherited wealth controls the success or failure of the rest of us by manipulating the money supply, the politicians, and the flow of money.

The average person can tilt the odds of success much to his or her favor by being better informed and organized when new ventures are attempted. Through a group endeavor, such as one offered through a Trust group, the likelihood of success in business is greatly increased. Why? Because the entrepreneur is no longer working alone. The specific goal of creating assets for Beneficiaries changes the emphasis and perspective, too. Careful planning, and understanding strategic money management, require broader-based decisions, and a hand-picked Board of Trustees highly likely to give sound advice. Further, when you operate through a properly structured Irrevocable Trust, you gain many astonishing tax advantages. This is one of the great keys to asset multiplication.

This is why this book stresses the creation and proper administration of a Trust. The powers that rule the world are in Trust. We do not expect the first generation to have the financial leverage of the great "old money" families, but we do expect generations which follow to be in a much better position to have a positive effect on the world.

Earlier in this book, we presented the bizarre notion the planetary elite believed they could concentrate even more wealth and power for themselves via successive reincarnations into elite bloodlines, but matters can go the other way, too. Here is a remarkable past life memory of one of our associates. Notice how beautifully it shows the matters we have been discussing–and the money did stay in the Trust, no matter what he did:

> Destined to be born into the lap of luxury, the Beneficiary of a Trust, I took it upon myself to be rebellious—I was one of those children who got the money and did not get the love. Although my father gave me the best, it was not what I needed, and so fast women, booze and all the forbidden

were my preference—anything to get my father to see me. He was so busy making the money, though, that he apparently did not know how to spend it.

In the unspoken reality that often happens between father and son, it seemed that he delegated spending to me. I did not have an instruction book, or knowledge of his intentions and motivation to accumulate wealth, or, especially, what he expected of me. So I gleefully "threw the money to the wind." This only resulted in arguments, neither of us addressing the unvoiced issue of our relationship. How to invest or build a fortune was not my interest. Running from my emotional pain thwarted any attempts to find satisfaction.

Off to Harvard I went, getting there through bribery, I am sure, for I never applied myself enough to master the art of anything, except, of course the fast things, airplanes and cars. Japan invaded China, and I planned to volunteer my talents as a pilot. The thrill seeker part of me was sure an adventure awaited that would satisfy my need for substantial excitement, a thrill pill to assuage my quest for constant challenge and adventure.

Perhaps it was not my path, or maybe I was just too fed up with all the money, as obviously, I was not succeeding in getting the attention I desperately needed. Heck, I do not even remember my mother—what did money do to her?

So, too much booze, and the daring acceleration of my shiny, red LaSalle convertible on a hot summer's night, ended my life in China. I left all amazing opportunities behind to get it straight then—the war's excitement vanished before I even got to fly an airplane there.

Now, I am back, in a new life, with a different set of circumstances, and the memory of my foolishness. I study the art of Trusts, because I now know that I did not do it right the first time. Perhaps this time, I can influence people to pay attention to their children, as well as give them vast financial opportunities, so they will not do what I did.

So, you might say, I am "doing time." I got born in the 1940s into a lower-middle-class family, and my father did not seem to care too much for me. I got to experience what I could have avoided, if I had not been so hot-headed. This time, I have done my life the hard way. The limits this financial deprivation place on my dreams and ambitions are frustrating, for I would truly like to help the people of the world, far more than I am able to do having been born into near poverty, and into a family that was more interested in fighting than succeeding at anything. A true reflection of my own state of mind—the last time.

So, if you think money is bad, or you worry about giving too much to your children—that is not the issue. Children need support, and money is only one avenue. I suggest you teach your children leadership skills, and to value the people of this world, to help and assist others to succeed, and to create job opportunities, as well as all ways possible to expand the potential of our fellow citizens.

Encourage and support children's creative endeavors. You never know. You might have a potential Rembrandt or Einstein looking for your help and mentorship.

Establishing an End

The rich who have ascended to positions of dominance are vested in the notion no one else should be allowed into their nest of power. To thwart those who would disturb or even usurp their cozy place, they ensure the ignorant remain so. Thus, they invented various ways to make it appear to the rest of us they allow inheritance, but they have put a cap on it. The Statutory Irrevocable Trust permits the transfer of wealth from one generation to the next, but it does not sanction it to accumulate beyond the third or fourth generation. Excerpted from an actual Trust Indenture is this paragraph. It demonstrates the principle of "Remoteness of Vesting," or the "Rule Against Perpetuities":[48]

> THE TRUST shall expire at 12:00 noon on the day before the end of the running of twenty-one years after the death of the last survivor of one of the following: the Grantor, the initial trustees, and the children and grandchildren of said parties, which survivor must have been alive on the date of the creation of this trust, unless this trust is sooner terminated in accordance with the provisions of this trust instrument. If this trust is reviewed by a court with respect to the issue of remoteness of vesting, undue duration, or a similar rule and the applicable state law has shorter requirements than the rule against perpetuities, that a shorter requirement shall be the intent of the Grantor.

Working 9 to 5

The rich encourage a strong work ethic, and we concur that work is good, especially the experience of working with others to learn new skills. Here again, though, is another myth. While we are kept working, those with the time are designing our greater enslavement. By keeping us in survival mode, we cannot realize our true potential.

Besides, most middle-class Grantors may unwittingly pass along to their children the attitude that being a contributing member of society necessarily includes working a 9 to 5 job or an equivalent. The concept of having no other condition for obtaining one's money than walking to the mailbox is foreign to most people. When the cash flow pours into the Trust, the Trustees must distribute it, and that means trips to the mailbox for all Beneficiaries.

We have nothing against working 9 to 5, but it should be purposeful and limited. To remain engaged in manifesting another's dreams does not help your life unfold. To turn your 9 to 5 into a meaningful experience where you can

---

[48] See Glossary for further definition of the Rule Against Perpetuities.

establish your own goals within the framework of another, we refer to you the book *Rich Dad, Poor Dad*.[49] From this vantage point you can even start young to build assets and acquire the financial skills which you will later pass on to the next generation.

Power Groups

Any group of people can misuse power. In a white paper written by Ted Nace titled *Gangs of America*[50], he outlines the unholy ability of corporations to amass power. There can be any name, form or scheme to take advantage of others. The problem lies in the lack of inherent appreciation and understanding that each person who lives is not only a miracle, but holds an unfathomable amount of unique knowledge. Nurture others; gain innate potential and power. People are an unlimited resource, so why diminish them or, for that matter, even fear them?

Powerful group influence can be used to benefit society, or, sadly, to degrade it. That is why, when setting up a Trust structure you hope will enhance the lives of many people yet unborn, you must also take care to build into it provisions for strong ethics and morals. You might even set up guidelines for the Trustees and certain tests for the successors within the Trust, to ensure as much as possible that only those with good intentions will wield the power the assets will provide.

---

[49] Robert T. Kiyosaki, *Rich Dad, Poor Dad*, TechPress, 1998

[50] Ted Nace, *Gangs of America, the Rise of Corporate Power and the Disabling of Democracy*, May 2003 draft, Berkeley, CA 94707 (510) 527-6363, © 2003.

Chapter 7

The Application of Wills and Trusts

E ven though the previous chapters have given you the broad strokes of wealth and the philosophy of riches, we now want to bring you back to Chapter 1, where lack of foresight caused great grief. It is a cautionary tale concerning a common situation that results in the careless dissipation of wealth, one we deliberately placed prominently up front to shatter your complacency and seize your attention. Now that you have seen the long-range results of how a Trust can work for the good of a group, you can see the true cost of failing to plan properly for your family. It is too late to do anything once you are gone. Now that you have a vision of possibilities, it is time to lay in your dreams, but what to do and what not to do?

Will Deficiencies

The typical solution to pass along your wealth has long been a Will. Some financial reports advise that annually as much as 53% of Americans die intestate (without a Will), leaving their estates, and thus their descendants, to the not-so-tender mercies of the Probate Court. This is where blood is only sometimes more important than marriage, where the state and federal tax authorities get to take big bites, where creditors get their money, where fees get paid for court-appointed executors and the like. Asset payout comes only after a great deal of time and according to a state-mandated, prioritized list of recipients.

Sadly, even having a Will does not solve the problem. All it takes to contest even the most carefully drafted Will is one aggrieved person or another party, such as a charity named in the Will, to dispute anything from a minor clause to whether or not you were even sane when you wrote it. This challenge puts your estate into Probate Court, where the wrangling can continue for years, sometimes to the limits of human and legal bill-paying endurance.

The Living Trust is not exempt from this flaw. Although it can get around probate, it is treated the same as a Will if contested. Meanwhile, your estate's assets remain frozen (also true if you died intestate), leaving your descendants with nothing until matters are finally resolved. It was precisely to address this and other problems that Trusts were created. When properly constructed and administered, they provide you with maximum say over to whom your estate goes and how, while maximizing privacy, protecting the estate, and minimizing the tax bite. Some forms of Trusts are more effective in providing these benefits than others, but all offer major advantages over the usual Will.

If you did not read all of Chapter 2, this is probably a good time to go back and read Divided Title and the U.S. Constitution, along with the legal definitions given concerning Trusts in general.

What More Do I Need to Know About a Trust?

In its simplest form, a Trust is a legal entity created when you, known as the Grantor, transfer **ownership** of personal property to a Trustee or Trustees, for the benefit and support of a named party or parties (the Beneficiary or Beneficiaries), according to the terms set forth by you in the legally binding Trust Indenture.

There are two basic types of Trusts: Revocable and Irrevocable, with many variations on each.

As explained in Chapter 2, in a Revocable Trust, you become the Trustee and the main Beneficiary. You can change the provisions in the Indenture until you die, but whatever the final version becomes, unless there is some gross legal defect, it is cast in concrete upon your death. It cannot be changed thereafter. Thus, a Revocable Trust becomes Irrevocable. There is a big tax catch here, too. If ownership of your estate does not change until you die, then while alive, you bear the burden for all the requisite taxes. In other words, personal control equals personal tax liability.

Cast In Stone

In an Irrevocable Trust, though, as soon as you sign and witness the carefully thought out Trust Indenture, for good or ill not only are you committed, but likewise your Trustee or Trustees and the Beneficiary or Beneficiaries. Once the Trust is funded, there is no turning back, and from this point on, while you have the **use** of some or many of the assets, you will not **own** them, and **cannot be taxed** for them, either. Why? They no longer belong to you! They not only belong to the Trust but are insured, maintained and, if necessary, guarded by funds generated from the Trust. While alive, you can enjoy some of the benefits of

> In other words, personal control equals personal tax liability.

ownership with none of the hassles–while saving big on taxes and safe in the knowledge your estate will never be tied up in Probate Court. Why? Probate Court has no jurisdiction[51] over an Irrevocable Trust if it is properly drawn. Since the assets do not belong to you, when you die, you have no assets to pass on. The assets are part of the Trust, and the Trustees continue to administer them whether or not you are alive. Probate is about death, and an Irrevocable Trust lives much longer than you.

------

[51]   In Appendix A the history of the word "jurisdiction" is presented to mean the place where one has sworn allegiance. In our current political atmosphere it generally means the place where one agrees to the laws.

Figure 2 in Chapter 2 depicts a generalized Irrevocable Trust structure. It shows the key players, together with just a few of the many potential income streams available to it. The permitted income streams in your Trust, though, will be a function of what you specify in your Trust Indenture.

Breaking It Down

Your Trust begins with you, the Grantor. For this example, we assume the initial corpus (literally the body of the Trust) consists of $250,000.00 plus your $250,000.00 whole life policy and, say, another $100,000.00 in mutual funds.

Depending upon the Trust type, the corpus which forms the assets of your Trust can come into being during your lifetime or through a Will that automatically comes into being when you die. This is a Testamentary Trust.

Either way, the Trustees administer the corpus and must:

- Increase the value of the Trust.

- Follow the terms of your Trust Indenture.

- Determine investments (where to put Trust money and/or assets to generate revenue).

- Administer distribution: how much of the profits can be shared with Beneficiaries.

- Properly handle accounting to retain enough funds to:

  o   Cover expected administration expenses.

  o   Keep enough funds to increase investments.

- Meet and converse with the Beneficiaries to ensure their needs are met in accordance with your wishes.

This emphasis on generating revenue from investments is no accident; diligent Trustees are all about growing the corpus, the more the Trust makes, the more they make.

Trustees, with the exception of the Grantor who usually acts as a Trustee of a Revocable Trust, are paid a fiduciary fee based on a percentage of distribution. Through receiving a fiduciary fee, a Trustee makes money if the Trust makes money. If the Trust loses money, the Trustee receives either no money, or much less money. The idea is to motivate the Trustee to bring in a sufficient cash flow for the Beneficiaries.

There are many issues, though, about what is considered acceptable risk, and what Trustees should and should not do. These are addressed in the Probate Code. This body of case law can be an excuse for Trustees to be fearful to take risks. Recently, laws were passed to encourage Trustees to increase the value of the Trust for the Beneficiaries. There are Private Trust contracts that can encourage Trustees to take greater risks, but those will be handled later in this book.

Remember, your Trust Indenture must be written to provide not just your Trustees but their successors with clear-cut guidance on, a) your intent and b) what are and are not acceptable investments.

It may seem a little spooky, but in a sense you eventually reach a point where you speak from the grave to those entrusted with caring for those dear to you and advancing the causes you cared about during your lifetime.

Chapter 8

Trusts—Not for Everyone

Y ou may be looking for answers because you are involved or embroiled in the issue of inheritance as a Beneficiary or as a Grantor. If you are thinking of setting up a Trust, this chapter defines qualifications with the emphasis on who should **not** put assets into a Trust.

If you are a Beneficiary, you will learn some of the intricacies in setting up a legacy for future generations.

Granted, the chapter title *is* provocative, but it nicely carries a key idea, that as marvelous as Trusts may be for some, certain types of Trust may be ill-advised, harmful to and even illegal for others. The more complex and legally demanding the Trust type chosen, the greater and more serious the funding restrictions and administration protocols. The Irrevocable Trust is by far the most demanding and restrictive, but in such rigors lie benefits attainable nowhere else.

Often managed by lawyers, CPAs or other professionals, the Irrevocable Statutory Trust is compatible with current financial methodologies. If not managed by those licensed, then the Trustee may be an untrained family member who relies heavily on legal counsel. There also may be a court-appointed Trustee.

The Irrevocable Statutory Trust is different from a Private Trust. At this point, we distinguish between the two.

The Irrevocable Statutory Trust comes in many different forms; see Appendix B for a list. Among legal professionals who specialize in Trusts, the various kinds listed are complex and involve sophisticated expertise. This book will not go into detail on each of the applications listed, as it is in your best interest to speak with a Trust professional.

At this point we simply want you to understand the Irrevocable Common-Law Trust is the most fully realized form of Trust when set up correctly. Further, until about 100 years ago, it was the most common Trust used. We use it as a background and a point of comparison. Later in this book we discuss the Irrevocable Common-Law Trust in detail because we feel that all other types of Trusts **devolved** from this one.

Once you understand this original, ancient and sophisticated Trust, you can more easily decide how to arrange your affairs.

The following applies mostly to Irrevocable Trusts and especially to the Common-Law Trust.

When Not to Get a Trust

Just about everyone is eligible to get a Living Trust. Managed by the Grantor, who becomes the Trustee, you can put funds from any source into the bank account. After all, you are taxed on all the income that comes in your name, so the source needs only be legal.

Not everyone needs to have an Irrevocable Trust, and few are qualified.

We will spend a significant amount of time throughout this book explaining the advantages of a Trust, but sometimes an individual's circumstances or capacity is not conducive to putting funds into an Irrevocable Trust. This is because funds coming into the Trust must only be under the control of the Trustees. The following conditions compromise the Trustees, or create a complex tax - position.

Some of the hindering reasons include: government wages, IRAs, W-2 wages, some retirement funds, professional licenses, doubters, excessive greed, and the criminally minded.

Government Wages

Government wages cannot be assigned to an Irrevocable Trust because when you have a contract with the government, you receive proceeds from the government. The government must write the check only to you as an individual. Some researchers believe this is because the federal government is itself a Trust, and the People are the Beneficiaries. If this is the case, then only the named Beneficiary may receive the funds distributed.

> Usually, one of the significant motivators to assign assets to a third party is to reduce taxation.

The correct way to put assets into a Trust is by filling out proper assignment documents, and the entity (business, corporation, partnership) which pays the funds recognizes the assignment and writes the check per the assignment.

The government does not acknowledge any such assignment. Also, the Trust is not the individual "entitled" to the funds. This is because the government taxes the funds, and if the funds by assignment go to another entity, it is not likely to be taxed it at the same steep rate as for an individual. Usually, one of the significant motivators to assign assets to a third party is to reduce taxation, and to protect against lawsuits.

If the government wrote a check to you for any benefits, this also cannot be assigned to an Irrevocable Trust.

Independent and Private Contracts

Sometimes, people have independent contracts with the government. Even these independent contracts cannot be rewritten and assigned to another entity. For example, Peter, a friend of yours, is an independent contractor. He repairs military Hummers. He then decides to get an Irrevocable Trust. Peter goes to the person with whom he created the contract and asks to renegotiate it to put it under a different name—the name of the Trust. The government does not recognize this change, especially if the same person is doing the same work. The government might acknowledge the change if the contract were to be rewritten to a company, and Peter was not part of the company.

Oddly enough, the same rule applies to a contract with a corporation. The IRS challenges a change of a contract from an individual to a Family Trust.

Retirement Programs

IRA programs defer the taxes until funds are paid out. Such IRAs cannot be transferred into a Trust, but the Beneficiary can be changed to a Trust.

Roth IRA plans, though, deduct taxes before the funds go into the retirement program. Therefore, these funds can be transferred to a Trust.

Some private retirement programs are Trusts themselves and cannot transfer funds to another Trust unless the program has survivor benefits. This means if the main Beneficiary dies and benefits accrued to him, the benefits may go to his heirs or to a named Trust.

W-2 Wages

The employer deducts taxes from the employee and reports them on Form W-2. These wages cannot be assigned to an Irrevocable Trust. The employer pays taxes linked to a Social Security Number. What the employee does with the funds is up to him or her. These funds can be received into a Revocable Trust, but not an Irrevocable Trust. An Irrevocable Trust must produce its own funds, and the Trustees need to be solely in control of these funds. If the Grantor of the Trust puts his or her wages into the Trust, then the Grantor remains in control. The Trust's status changes from Irrevocable to Revocable, and the Grantor becomes responsible for all the taxes in the Trust!

The proper way to arrange funds into an Irrevocable Trust is if, for example, Mary, a schoolteacher, wants to put money into a Trust. She assigns her stock portfolio to the Trust. By assigning the stock portfolio, the profits go directly from the stock account, now owned by the Trust, into the Trust checking account. Mary has no control over the money. Thus, she is not taxed. If Mary does not have an investment account, but stills wants to start a Trust, she can use her paycheck to invest into various opportunities, even offering a 10% APR loan to a friend. The friend then pays the Trust. For an Irrevocable Trust to be independent and properly legally positioned, the Grantor cannot control the Trustees. Because of this, there is no advantage to putting W-2 wages directly into the Trust.

Professional Licenses

Doctors, dentists, CPAs and lawyers in some states can only work through corporations, LLCs or partnerships. This particular ruling applies to California. When you use a corporation, you owe taxes to the state, and sometimes there is double taxation. When licensed professionals work through a Trust, the Beneficiaries pay the tax, often at a much lower bracket.

Professionals can get a corporation, though, and a Trust can own some corporate stock.

Disorganized and Confused?

Sometimes, unorganized people want to get an Irrevocable Common-Law Trust. Unfortunately, the disorganization and continual loss of significant paperwork arise after the Trust is set up. Although this is a workable condition, these people must learn to become more organized. Because they work with a group of people who share a common goal, the chaos caused unsettles the entire group. If you are not paper oriented, and not in a position to devote time to understanding the legal realities of this more sophisticated Trust, then it may not be for you. Although, if you just want to give funds to a Trust and walk away, not be involved, then this arrangement works to your advantage.

Poverty

People who live hand-to-mouth and do not have any savings are not candidates for any Trust, though contrary to popular opinion, you do not need to be wealthy. Those who are mostly without reserves and assets, though, make incredible Beneficiaries, for they have great need, and usually have gratitude which those born to kinder circumstances may not have.

The Responsibility of Privacy

Privacy is a core feature of many Trusts, and demanding privacy and asserting your rights are learned behaviors. These simply do not come naturally to most people. Only through mentoring can people learn to say "No" to a terrifying, skilled interrogator. You will find more on this in chapters to come.

If the most innocuous meeting with officialdom makes you break out in a sweat, and you are so spineless that you let people use you as a doormat, how are you **ever** going to stand your ground to keep your Trust safe? You need to keep your composure and guard your tongue if confronted with professionally trained government intimidators, a.k.a. agents. After all, they fully expect you to offer no resistance whatever. Their "requests" are to be obeyed. Therefore, you should tamely accept whatever documents they may wish to give (serve) you as well as invite them in and show them whatever they may wish to see.

The answer is obvious. You cannot! Therefore, if your natural instinct when confronted is to cower, roll over and bare your throat, then even a Revocable Living Trust may not be for you.

You must get beyond your own fears and think of the future of your Beneficiaries. If you are not willing to do that, then do not get a Trust.

Some wonder why it is important to resist unwarranted searches and inquiries. People think that if there is nothing to hide, there is no reason to keep your private affairs.

Pretend for a moment you are fifteen years old and your father rifled through your bedroom while you were out on a date. Even if you had nothing to hide, this is a violation of your person, your space and displays a lack of trust. It is insulting and degrading.

Your own paperwork can be used against you. Endless questioning can wear you down in your attempt to explain any little thing. Anyone associated with you now may become a target. If there is no evidence of criminal conduct, there is no reason to subject yourself to invasion of strangers. Trained in trickery, agents can make you feel guilty even if you have done nothing wrong.

Why subject yourself to it? Make them get a search warrant. If they do not have enough evidence to a convince a judge, then they have nowhere to go. They must leave you alone, or continue to harass in hopes you surrender some morsel. Of course, that leads to another morsel . . .

Privacy is a major issue. From individuals to partnerships, corporations and Trusts, all privacy issues are sacred only if you know how to stop illegal inquiries. Stopping illegal inquiries requires individuals and business officers to know their rights. People who do not know them, have none.

There is only one way to stop an illegal search and seizure. You must have enough knowledge to gain the confidence to say "No." As assets collect in a Trust, privacy becomes more of a major issue. What others do not know you have, they cannot covet. Those people who live in fear of the IRS and are afraid to step forward to take responsibility should not be Trustees.

Trusting strangers and being open about our personal affairs leaves you vulnerable to government officials and scam artists alike. Both count on our misplaced trust and openness to make their tasks easier.

Identity theft is a big problem. People have begun to "get religion" on protecting passwords, account numbers and the like. This makes opportunities tougher on the con artists and grifters of the world; but how many people know a) they can protect their privacy when, say, the IRS comes calling or b) what specific actions to take when so confronted? Taking these last two stands needs education, training, and plain old guts. It is possible to avoid surrendering significant information that can be damaging to you. Your resistance prevents others from being dragged into the muck and mire of accusations.

Doubters and Skeptics

These are people who are indoctrinated to accept the idea of a Will or Living Trust. When presented with a more sophisticated Trust, they are not interested in listening to the advantages of the Irrevocable Trust, whether Statutory or Common-Law.

Their own fears of surrendering power or assets to others immediately cause them to panic and warn you of all the evils in the world. They usually do not have enough information to make a rational judgment about the subject and believe that all Trusts are bogus. Sometimes, there is great fear they will get in trouble if they get involved in a Trust group. They do not believe the advantages, and some believe it is just a trick. Some trick, since the rich created the game! Should you happen to be one of these doubters, you will need to either educate yourself or forget about having an Irrevocable Trust.

The White Man's Disease

This particular issue does not apply to a Living Trust, where the Grantor becomes the Trustee. In considering any Irrevocable Trust, though, we may find difficulties because of our social upbringing. Many are afraid to rely on and trust one another.

Often, people are not in a social position where they have enough friends to be able to create a Trust. This is what we call, "The White Man's Disease," as opposed to ancient tribal social support. This disease is rampant throughout society—the inability to trust others and make deep long-lasting, committed friendships. Because of this, many people cannot find a Trustee, someone whom they feel they can trust. After all, it takes much trust to place hard-earned assets into the hands of another. Without at least one Trustee who can be trusted, there is no way a Grantor can move personal and family funds into an Irrevocable Trust.

There is often no intent to share holdings with family or anyone else. What makes an Irrevocable Trust work, though, is passthrough accounting. This allows the Trust profits to pass through to the Beneficiaries, who are generally in a lower tax bracket than the Trust. Passthrough accounting creates further options which we discuss later in this book and in Volume II.

Greedy people intent on not giving any of their wealth to others miss the bigger picture—that by sharing, they can multiply their funds, as a Trust is designed to do.

Do you suffer from this pernicious disease, or are you blessed with close, deeply respected friends and willing to share your wealth with them?

Bogus Trust Scams

Con artists feed on the fear of trusting. Of all the Trusts that exist, the one used most by scam artists is the Irrevocable Common-Law Trust. Many people caught in Trust scams are honest people who do want their assets to go to their Beneficiaries; Scam Trust Artists have continuously existed for at least 100 years and prey on the ignorant. They sell their version of an "Irrevocable Common-Law Trust," by telling people they can be the Grantor and the Trustee, and thus, avoid taxes. The details of this game will be explored in far greater detail in Volume II. In fact, one of our many motivations for writing about this subject is to ensure that most people will not fall for this old trick.

> People who want only to hide their assets and avoid taxes never think about their Beneficiaries.

People who want only to hide their assets and avoid taxes never think about their Beneficiaries. When presented with false information about the possibilities of an Irrevocable Common-Law Trust, they think they can put assets, for example, in the

Cayman Islands under the name of the Trust and thus avoid taxes. This is not the proper use of a Trust, and the authorities are well aware of this game.

This is why bogus Trust scams have become rampant. The sales pitch is, "You can put your funds through a Trust, and still control them. You will be the only signer on the checks, you don't get taxed on the Trust income, and the Trustees will be arms' length; they will not interfere." This sounds too good to be true, and it does not make sense. Often in this game, the ideas of protecting assets and avoiding probate are tantalizing, and even honest people get trapped in this con game. These Trust scam participants know nothing of passthrough accounting, or passing assets to their Beneficiaries or other Trusts.

> A Trust is a sacred document. It is used to make wealth for a group of people and to share material goods—a true tribal situation.

Others knowingly try to scam the IRS via improperly constructed Trusts, and suffer accordingly.

A Trust is a sacred document. It is used to make wealth for a group of people and to share material goods—a true tribal opportunity. A Trust can benefit many. When a Grantor wants to have total control over all the funds, the government is happy to give such an arrangement its blessing. That Trust is called a Grantor Trust, and the person who sets it up pays taxes on the income of the Trust.

In an Irrevocable Trust, though, the person who sets it up properly is never taxed on the Trust income. Using various techniques which benefit the entire group (tribe), the income is processed through the Trust. Those people who amassed assets for generations and centuries know how to set up their own empire to benefit their progeny. Both the Irrevocable Statutory Trust and the Irrevocable Common-Law Trust are set up under these long-term methods and procedures.

Tax Issues

Just because funds are "offshore" does not mean a U.S. Citizen does not owe taxes. When funds come onshore, taxes may be due. Anyone who tells you otherwise is lying to you. Check with tax professionals about correct rates.

We recommend Trusts be set up only for the Beneficiaries. To set up a Trust for the tax benefits is a demonstration of shortsightedness, and shows a lack of appreciation for the true intent of a Trust.

For those who are interested in tax information about Trusts, we refer you to a book titled *The Trust Bible.*[52]

Criminals

The criminally minded are not interested in managing this Trust format because it is based on shared profits. Those who use the Common-Law Trust for illegal purposes are shortsighted and usually of the emotional maturity of a two-year-old who only wants his or her own stuff (it's **MINE!**).

Spouses

Married people need to separate joint property before it is put into an Irrevocable Trust, since community property law supercedes an Irrevocable Trust agreement. If the spouse will not surrender assets, there can be no legal transfer into a Trust.

In a Living Trust, it is common for both the husband and wife to become the Grantors, and there is then no need to have a separation of joint property.

---

[52]   Clifton Beal, *The Trust Bible: a Quick Guide and Preliminary Understanding of Estate Planning*, Xlibris Corporation, 2003, www.Xlibris.com

In some marriages, the husband or the wife may be more passive, expecting the other to handle the finances. Even if your spouse signs any documents in blind trust, this is not one of those times when the signature should be gained without full, conscious consent.

Also, if one of the members of a marriage is dominated by parents, or there are other outside influences impinging on the marriage, it may not be a good idea to continue. There are times where the wealthy parents will oppose any effort for one of their "children" to put assets into a Trust. The lawyers get rich, the marriage is torn apart, and the new Trustees start their jobs embattled.

Also, children can be horrified to discover their assets now belong to a Board of Trustees, or to a Trustee. These reactions by close family members can last for years. Thus, it is best to tell those affected about the change **before** assets are transferred.

Only clear, conscious intent with the support of family allows the smooth transition of assets into an Irrevocable Trust of any type.

Chapter 9

Parenting and Perpetual Wealth

With more of the basics now understood, it becomes possible to look, in greater detail, at how important proper parenting is to the success of your Trust. Your actions can have almost everything to do with whether your Trust becomes a smooth running cash cow or a raging battlefield driving Beneficiaries and your Trustees to despair or worse.

Until the last few hundred years, average people were too poor to even consider getting a Trust for their heirs. Many families today lack experience in this little known financial area.

Seeding the Future vs. Ceding the Future

Since prospective donors of an inheritance are seldom inheritors themselves, they may not know what it is like to receive a large bequest. Thus, they are less likely to be familiar with the emotional, legal, financial and tax aspects when an estate passes to the heirs. The prospective recipients are also in the dark about these issues, and bear the extra load of the responsibility to know how to take proper care of willed investments, income property, land, etc. The result can be not only confusion, suspicion and fear, but also when the actual event comes to pass, the heirs can be quite overwhelmed.

This situation is further compounded by our society's phobia about death and dying, resulting in little connection between the intention of the Trust's creator and the inheritors. Instead of clear, specific instructions regarding the who, what, when, where and why of the bequest, we may find innuendo and hearsay until it is too late and the Grantor is dead. It would be far better to know who gets what portion of the rental property or other assets and what that means to the recipient while the Grantor is around to question and debate, and especially to learn his or her "tricks" of administration and process of decision making. This is even more true if the Grantor has a complex financial portfolio.

Young Minds Meet

It might be a good idea to consider preparing children for their eventual responsibilities. To properly create and perpetuate wealth, though, we suggest people start when children are young, by including them in meetings about the family finances, or discussing investment strategies at the dinner table. People may also want to ensure children have skills in some financial arena, such as bookkeeping, accounting or investment counseling.

Preparing children for eventual wealth management requires them to feel secure. Therefore, we strongly suggest avoiding the not-so-uncommon mistake of using a pending inheritance to manipulate the would-be heirs, or pitting one child against the other for bonuses and benefits passed out at some future date.

We also find it curious that some may favor males or females in deciding which child is to receive how large a share. Although parents may have favorites, it is best to leave the results of the inheritance to be shared based on merit. The emotional issues associated with inheritance can be harsh and violent, as shown by the sordid stories about those who force a relative into an early grave. The roots of emotional issues are not in the money gained, but rather from whether the inheritor feels loved or not loved. Parents may shower a child with money, and neglect the child's feelings, ignore the child outright, or simply favor another child. Shunned, a child never feels good enough. He or she may well turn into the child whose outbursts rip the entire family apart when the Will is read to the grieving survivors. In general, children who are secure

> There has to be a place of stability, sanity, support and love for your children while they go through the incredible and even chaotic process of becoming young adults.

about themselves in their early years have the potential to be the stable members of the family, and be a huge help in making a smooth financial transition when a significant family member dies.

Because of the incredible flexibility of administration of Trust assets, the solution to many of the inheritance difficulties described here can be achieved through an Irrevocable Common-Law Trust. Beneficiaries can even be involved in the Trust administration process by working for the Trust in a clerical or advisory capacity. When the family assets become the family business, there is a greater opportunity to open communication channels that are not available through other types of business entities and Trust structures.

Teenagers

Sometimes, no matter how good the plans, how careful the parenting, the task can become impossible. It is not unusual, for example, for a long well-behaved child to become rebellious on entering puberty.

Teenagers' bodies are positively awash in hormones and all that go with them. We now know, because of brain chemistry research and the portion of the brain used, the way they think is fundamentally different from the way adults do. Indeed, the differences are so extraordinary and pronounced that more and more researchers are coming to think of puberty as a temporary form of insanity lasting years! Teenagers' brains not only process data differently than do adult brains, but they do it in a much more primitive, visceral part. It is any wonder, then, that teenagers often seem intensely tribal, emotionally volatile, even alien and alienated, sometimes all at once?

This is why it is vital to them and you that boundaries and roles are properly defined. Firm rules, laid down with love, must also be enforced. There has to be a place of stability, sanity, support and love for your children while they go through the incredible and even chaotic process of becoming young adults. If you cannot or will not provide these needs, your children's friends, gangs and predators of every stripe will.

By providing proper parenting, though, you teach your children not just facts, figures and procedures, but a philosophy of life, instilling your values and providing your children with benchmarks to which they can internally refer as long as they live.

Healthy Participants

This obviously is not a book on the psychology of child rearing, but it is nevertheless important that we show how this applies to Trusts. Emotionally healthy, stable Beneficiaries make for a smoother transition when you pass. Your well-oiled, competently supervised Trust remains intact, whereas "crippled birds" and their bottomless pits of need ever crying out for attention can affect your Trust at levels ranging from endless irritants to hamstringing Trust management. Just as coaches have their playbooks and commanders and executives have their Standard Operating Procedures (SOPs) and plans, so too do Grantors and Trustees have their own methods for dealing with problem Beneficiaries. Tried-and-true procedures, developed over the centuries, are readily available. They have been tested in the legal fires of courts high and low both here and abroad. Some of this knowledge is in Volume II, for there are ways to handle problem Beneficiaries.

Predictable Loveless Lives

We have all heard examples of children who are the Beneficiaries of great wealth, and yet, their behavior is destructive. Here is an experience, written by one of our Trustees, that takes us through one of those rich-kid scenarios, and we now have added information about how to avoid this. Having money has nothing to do with getting out of being a parent as follows.

In the Right Coin

Good Beneficiaries are not born. To the contrary, they are reared. While there will always be a few twisted ones out there, we believe that all manner of self-destructive and destructive behavior by those who will become Beneficiaries is largely preventable. It requires what the military calls command emphasis, especially in the critical formative years. What follows is a look at what children need, coupled with some true-life searing examples of what can happen when their real needs, not passing wants, go unmet.

> Children need a stable, loving, disciplined environment in which to safely develop and grow, to test themselves, learn about themselves and the world around them.

Command Emphasis Defined

What is command emphasis? It is the direct, continuing involvement of whomever is responsible for the physical, emotional, financial and spiritual support of the child or children. Hint: not the nanny, *au pair* or housekeeper! What is significant is that lines of loving communication be built, repaired as needed and expanded over time. Communication must be bidirectional. Developing these takes time, but it is a wise investment, one which yields vast dividends in all areas as the years march on. Failure to invest properly here usually yields broken children, who then become dysfunctional adults ill suited to life in general, let alone proper stewardship of your legacy.

Children need a stable, loving, disciplined environment in which to develop safely and grow, to test themselves, learn about themselves and the world around them. Without this, children become more and more damaged and then act out in a largely subconscious cry for help, designed to force the parents or guardians to intervene and pay attention to them. Sadly, this often has the opposite effect, causing further alienation and estrangement on both sides. Granted, the high divorce rate and resultant single parent families are not helping, but then, neither are "intact" families where substance abuse, physical abuse, sexual abuse, emotional abuse or abandonment occur. Nevertheless, it is imperative to provide the necessary ingredients for children's healthy development somehow, including proper same sex role models. If children do not get their basic needs met, they self-destruct. Based on the writer's direct experience in junior high school, not high school, we share with you an unusual perspective.

Junior High with the Upper Crust

Junior high for me in Greenville, South Carolina came as a shock. It was there that I had my first sustained encounter with the upper class. In this case, the progeny of the people who owned, presided over, and had upper management jobs in the fabric mills—a key part of the region's economy— or in law offices, accountant firms, suppliers and the like which supported them. I soon discovered that not only were they far better dressed than I was (firstborn son of six children of a defense engineer) and wired differently, but they did not operate in familiar ways. The girls were always immaculately turned out, complete with makeup, carefully styled and cut hair, the latest fashions, and looked like junior versions of "The Stepford Wives". The boys, naturally rougher and more boisterous, nevertheless wore expensive monogrammed sweaters, slacks, shirts and penny loafers. The usual acne problems plagued some, and smoking seemed to be alarmingly common, especially among the girls. What was pervasive, though, was an atmosphere of class distinction, elitism and outright snobbery, with some only mildly that way, and others blatantly so. These people ruled the roost, held all the important student positions, and lorded it over the other students. There were a few work arounds, notably academic excellence, by which you could gain some small status with them, and this, as we will see, ultimately worked to my advantage.

An Undisciplined Lot

I grew up in a strict, and by my lights, over disciplined home, but the scions of the wealthy signally lacked in discipline to a shocking degree. The son of a local barbecue magnate was a juvenile delinquent (repeatedly saved by his doting father) with an arrest record as long as my arm and, unfortunately for me, was the former Seattle Golden Gloves boxing champion. He was inches taller than I , long of limb, strong and a bully. Worse, he had a friend effectively his twin. I was then smallish, pudgy, weak and uncoordinated. Ring day, when we got our class rings, was sad and painful. On another occasion I got bounced off a bunch of built-in combination locks on student lockers by the two, then wound up almost expelled for simply defending myself. Another undisciplined one was small, cut class a lot, smoked, was flunking several subjects, but was of such social prominence that his name was in the society pages as having attended the midnight pancake breakfast. It got downright surreal when this kid showed up one day at school, face barely visible over the dashboard of a brand-new, huge, powerful Oldsmobile Tornado. He had to sit on a phone book to see at all! Parental largesse gone wild! And for what achievements? It was not uncommon to see yawning kids in class who were prominently featured as guests at the midnight cotillion the preceding night. Up until the wee hours on a school night? Brilliant!

Because South Carolina's Tricentennial was coming, we had to do a Civics class project on our state's history. Everyone save me in my group was from the upper crust, and I got a bad feeling about my likely project grade because of this. My Civics teacher, Mr. Reed, was African-American and a good and wise man, and it was to him I repaired after a disastrous first weekend meeting which could easily have gotten me killed en route. Why?

One of my project partners, a short, chubby boy, gave me a ride in his grandfather's Cadillac. Yes, another too short driver in a big, powerful car with only marginal road vision! What followed was terrifying. Ever been the helpless bystander while doing eighty over a succession of blind hills?

It went so fast I hit the roof a few times! There were no seat belts back then.

The neighborhood in which I eventually arrived was full of mansions. They were vast, sprawling homes and grounds which made my typical middle class house seem both shabby and tiny by comparison. Once there, we did manage to agree on what we would build, but it was downhill then as work was instantly abandoned for an impromptu sock hop. I think I got a glimpse of a parent while there, but would not swear to it. We were left alone after we arrived. A repeat attempt a week later was equally unproductive, which is why I sought out Mr. Reed a second time. I had to tell him the only person willing to work in my group was me. He told me to forget them, do the project myself, and that he'd take care of the rest. Did he ever! First prize was ten dollars from him. My brother Ed and I tried one idea, swiftly discarded it, then designed and built an impressive model of Fort Sumter, whose bombardment by the Confederates is considered to be the start of the Civil War. Hands down it was the best project in my Civics class, and it won first prize. Even better were the grades. I got an "A+." The privileged do nothings in my original group all got "F" and richly deserved it. Were they ever shocked!

I learned an important lesson from that experience and carry it with me to this day. These days, though, I feel sorry for those kids. It is now clear to me they were high-end latchkey children, children whose parents were so immersed in careers, themselves and high profile socializing they effectively abandoned their offspring. To appease their own guilt they threw money at their kids instead of providing the love, discipline and stability their kids so obviously both needed and craved. The results confronted me every day I was in that school, a condition alleviated only when I went to a new high school, Southside High, in my area and they left to attend Greenville High. I have not followed their careers, but behaviorally speaking, the handwriting was already on the wall and it was bleak. The list was long.

Smoking was common, but some were already into marijuana. I gather a lot of drinking was going on, too, but I never saw it at school. A notable amount of sexual activity occurred, judging from events I heard and saw, plus some incredibly provocative and revealing outfits certain girls wore to class and, frankly, flaunted themselves in. These are junior high girls, recall, running around daily in full makeup. Many of these kids had cars or plainly, unsupervised access to one. As noted, there were severe safety issues involved. Many of these kids socialized at night, skipped classes, and were not focused even when in class. Work ethics were marked by their absence, though there were some who somehow managed to be social gadabouts and good students. There were several budding career criminals, a path fostered by parents unable or unwilling to provide a firm hand and a steady course to their out of control progeny.

Summing Up

Which would you rather have as Beneficiaries, the sad, undisciplined wastrels described immediately above, kids who knew the price of everything and the value of nothing, or Beneficiaries who grew up in a loving, stable, supportive, and properly disciplined environment?

Do you want Beneficiaries with faux self-esteem via sycophancy and manufactured achievement? Or rather, Beneficiaries with real self-esteem gained by doing something, by striving for the mark and either falling short and trying again or hitting it by dint of hard work, belief in self and sheer dogged persistence? Do you want your legacy in the hands of people who have solid characters or layabouts who *are* characters? Whom would you entrust with such weighty responsibilities while you were still around?

Before deciding, consider that many top leaders started at the bottom, working in the mail room and the like before reaching the heights. Consider also that many who have made it failed as many as six times running before hitting it big. Finally, it might be well to take a look at the Bundeswehr, the Federal German Army. Officer cadets in the Bundeswehr go through an accelerated period starting as privates, spend time as noncommissioned officers, and only then, if they work out, become officers. This gives them a much-needed perspective on how the other half lives, on the needs and problems of the soldiers they will one day command and potentially commit to combat.

The choice is yours. Choose wisely. We recommend that you pay your children in the right coin, the coin of love, if you want healthy, sane, functional, Beneficiaries to carry on after your departure from this world.

Properly nurtured and supported people do not need to create drama to get attention, whether from their parents or others. Nor do they need to destroy the lives of others, being whole persons themselves.

Chapter 10

The Power of Distribution

We often hear that communism is evil. Sharing equally when not everyone puts in the same effort is abhorrent to the western mind. The family unit, though, is based on shared wealth. The family wage earner or earners bring home the paycheck and share the buying power with the entire family. What could possibly be wrong with that?

The argument against communism is that those who work harder should be more rewarded. We agree. This chapter includes rewards and incentives in a shared-wealth environment.

We take the same family principles and apply them to a larger group, for example, several families, and we now have a greater financial leverage. Shared resources have greater buying power and thus get the better deal.

Bringing the idea up one more level, we have collective wealth distributed through the government programs, for example, Social Security and other federal benefits. When applied to the government though, it seems the group power may be limited or even limiting. Benefits often have strings attached.

For example, if you accept welfare, then a warrantless search can be used against you.[53]

When accepting payments from any source, there may be conditions. This also applies to accepting funds from any Trust. Limits created by the Grantor often state they cannot be used against activities of the Trust. In the Standard Oil empire, for example, Beneficiaries cannot invest in any enterprise that might decrease the oil domination.

Building an Army

The Board of Trustees learns quickly that those who get a dole from the Trust are beholden to it. This leverage can marshal Beneficiaries into a united group whose vested interest protects the Trust. Experience shows the mere investigation of a Charitable Trust produces a strong reaction from the Beneficiaries, generally in the form of lawyers for the affected charities.

Impoverished Relatives

Often the bane of better-off family members, needy relatives who just cannot make it on their own, can through the Trust, receive a regular stipend. This gets them both off your back and off your fret list. Should their needs increase, they must then go to the Board of Trustees, rather than you, to argue their case.

If you struggle with your conscience because you believe if you help them, you make them more lazy and the challenges of life are for them as well as you, get out of denial. Some people are not cut out for "making it" in the world. It is

---

[53]   *Sanchez v. County of San Diego, No. 04-55122 D.C.,
         CV 001-01467* JTM Opinion. Appeal from the United
         States District Court for the Southern District of
         California, Filed September 19, 2006.

best if they are put into a place where they can work for the greater good of either humanity or the family. The Trust picks up the bill–even if the only cash flow to them is a couple hundred dollars a month. Besides that, with a constant cash flow, even that little, they may just get on their feet. After all, it is less for them to worry about, and life just may take care of the rest.

We suggest that people take a different look at the potential of family members and perhaps use them as assets. Even if the only talent is housecleaning, it is of value to any family to remove the load of the mundane.

The Anxious and Jealous

Because we review Trust documents, we note that death sometimes presents an ugly issue about who will inherit, and we have even reviewed Trust documents created when the Grantor wished to disinherit relatives.

What is astonishing about these documents is they set up a dark scenario. The entertainment industry writes grand scripts based on this one premise. People are generally aware that how a Will or Trust is written can determine who lives or dies. Thus, this aspect of distribution needs to be more thoroughly looked at. If you are better off dead to others, maybe you should redraft your plans to distribute your wealth. Some now, with more later would be a good beginning. Of course, if you do not have much to begin with, this solution does not apply.

This is one of the reasons some choose to use an Irrevocable Trust, since death has no effect on the Trust. In fact, death and distribution of wealth are transparent in a properly structured Irrevocable Trust, whether Statutory or Common-Law.

In an Irrevocable Trust, whether someone dies or does not die is irrelevant. It does not change the status of the invested principal, nor does it necessarily change the income distribution to the Beneficiaries, as the assets are legally under the control of a perpetual Board of Trustees, not an individual.

Too many times we have seen families where one member has the talent to make the money and becomes hated by disgruntled relatives who are needy and jealous. It only makes sense, that if one member of the family has a gift, there must be a way to harness it for the benefit of all. Of course, in our social structure, if you cannot take care of yourself you are considered inferior, while he or she who brings home the bucks is revered, even if it is through envy. The idea here is to get everyone to win by working together. That should be the underlying motive for a plan to distribute wealth.

Talents and Application

In a Trust situation, not all Trustees are talented in the financial arena. Some have more expertise in the legal field, and others in bookkeeping and accounting. Those who are known as the "bean counters" are often too timid when it comes to taking monetary risks. Better in the back room, they can do wonders with various financial reports. Even in this scenario, we can see that we all have our gifts and need not chide those who cannot cut it in the business world by making millions.

> Too many times we have seen families where one member has the talent to make the money and becomes burdened or hated by disgruntled relatives who are needy and jealous. It only makes sense, that if one member of the family has a gift, there must be a way to harness it for the benefit of all.

There seems to be a sixth sense for those who accumulate millions, and not everyone has it. When a Trust group finds that magic man or woman who can multiply the assets, at least part of his or her ability to enlarge principal should be shared with the entire family.

Here is a distribution event that did occur, although it was not within the context of an Irrevocable Trust:

In one family, the husband died, and the wife inherited thousands, and maybe even millions. She took her entire family on a world cruise, creating long-lasting memories and deepening the bond between them. Do you want to build a fortune or keep it? Or do you want to hoard it for yourself? Do you want to build an army of support? What more could you do if you had powerful support? That is exactly what distribution procedures do.

You may be grumbling about all of this and say "Not everyone deserves such a break." Well, those who are ungrateful just do not get as much, do they? That is why the Trust Capital Units are distributed minimally at the beginning of a Trust. Let the Beneficiaries prove themselves. In fact, you can make up all kinds of challenges for them. For those younger, they can earn Trust Capital Units by getting better grades or devoting time to Trust business. For those older, they can make some overall contribution to the family, or provide services to other members.

For the rebellious, we have all sorts of ways to straighten them up. A perusal through IRS Publication 17[54] lets you know that a distribution can be given to a Beneficiary without any money included–the Beneficiary pays the taxes anyway. That usually sobers up the more unwilling to comply. Let the IRS hound the disobedient for a while. Just the mere threat of it should get the desired results. We know of no other agency that can cause the heart to stop in fear—we might as well make good use of such talents.

We discuss broad spectrum distribution in Chapter 25, where wealth is distributed not only to one's immediate family, but to another Trust. That Trust in turn shares the wealth with a different Trust. A diagram can be found in Appendix D.

For those who are interested in getting into the nuts and bolts of distribution, we devote an entire chapter in Volume II to the Trust Certificate Register and the TCU process found only in the Common-Law Trust structure. Although it may be a "mind fry" to grasp this more esoteric way of handling shared wealth, it will be to your great advantage if you choose to go down this path. Also,

---

[54]   *Your Federal Income Tax For Individuals*, Publication 17, Catalog Number 10311G, Part Two, Income, Section 13 Other Income, Estate and trust income, Current Income required to be distributed, " . . . you must report your share of the distributable net income whether or not you have actually received it."

since this is the first time something of this depth and nature has ever been published, we hope this information serves as a foundation point.

Control of Beneficiaries

With distribution comes control. Where cash flow makes a significant impact on the recipient, the power or its misuse follows. Because a Board of Trustees is made up of more than just one person who could take advantage of the situation, we hope to prevent domination games. Should the distribution be the major financial support of the Beneficiary, then the Trustees may elect to use gentle guidance and incentives to encourage greater involvement in education, healing modalities or spiritual endeavors.

In most cases, the Board of Trustees does not get involved in any type of inter-ference with someone's life. The funds received can be used as the Beneficiary chooses, except where the use may be contrary to the Trust Indenture. In a Common-Law Trust situation, though, inviting Beneficiaries to a Board of Trustees meeting can be much to everyone's advantage. Here is where a great bonding among Trust members can occur.

One More Thing

There is the situation where distribution may support the lazy, deter their taking on challenges, or make them complacent about life. Putting aside for the moment the possibility such inability to self-actualize may stem from a dys-functional family, there are those who just may not be aggressive enough to even try. We have a situation where a Beneficiary received only $100 a month–enough to help her pay her rent. Unfortunately, the Trust giving the $100 fell upon hard times, and even this small amount was stopped.

Over time, it may have been the Beneficiary had gotten herself into an overall better situation where she felt supported, or perhaps the loss of the $100 pro-vided a keen incentive. Forced by this new circumstance and desperate to keep her apartment, she went to her boss to explain the loss of the $100 made it impossible for her to remain where she lived. In response, he made other ar-rangements at work and reorganized her commission structure. In a month she was offered a promotion. By her own words she reported, "I have always avoided responsibility; I have been fearful of taking on new challenges. It scares me to accept this position, but I am going to do it."

During the five years in which she received the beneficial distribution, she changed jobs. Being in a better place to make this move, coupled with the removal of the $100 a month extra cash, allowed her to be willing to meet this new challenge.

We would not say the $100 a month prevented her from taking on additional responsibility; we would say the $100 a month provided her the time she needed to make the right connections. Would she have accepted the promotion without the loss of the $100? Although the upset provided by the new situation became highly motivating, she may have done it anyway because she trusted the management structure. We will never know.

The Board of Trustees always felt honored to help her, even with just this small amount, and she had been grateful. In a situation like this, it is always up to the Board of Trustees to make the judgment call as to how much, when and if a beneficial distribution should be given, or a gift from the Trust should be offered.

Chapter 11

What Can You Put into Trust?

L egally speaking, any lawful item may be put into a Private Trust. Long experience has shown, that just because you can, does not necessarily mean you should. Practical considerations must apply, since otherwise Trustees waste time, energy and money cataloging, managing and accounting for worthless junk.

Naturally, correctly identifying what is and is not suitable takes both judgment and discernment. To help you, we provide the series of decision criteria set forth below.

First Criterion

Does it have intrinsic value?

This applies whether the item is a tangible, such as a house, or an intangible, such as a patent, copyright or a trade secret.

You may not know its true value, but that need not concern us now. We are merely discovering whether the item has value. The definition of value can be how useful it is to the Trust and its convertibility to cash.

Second Criterion

Will it keep, or better still, increase in value?

While market values rise and fall over time, certain factors remain true. The supplies of gold, silver, prime real estate, high-grade antiques, good art, key mineral rights, copyrights to timeless songs, etc., are finite. Thus, they are likely to hold their value.

Van Gogh never sold a painting in his lifetime, but one recently sold for $46,000,000.00. The songs "Happy Birthday" and "Rudolph the Red-Nosed Reindeer" may be so familiar to you to be obnoxious, but they are cash cows to those who hold the copyrights.

Copyrights and patents were established, under Article I, Section 8, Clause 8 of the Constitution. ". . . to promote the progress of science and useful arts, by securing *for limited times* (emphasis added) to authors and inventors the exclusive rights to their discoveries . . ." The original intent has, over time, been deliberately and consciously perverted. Consequently works done for hire now one under copyright for a staggering ninety-five (95) years, with the FBI in charge of enforcement.. This is how it is now, but when the First Congress passed the Copyright Act of 1790, the law made sense.

Since passing the first U.S. copyright law in 1790, there has been a clear trend toward changing what Congress intended as a time limited incentive for authors into endlessly extended market rights for corporate interests. This is why insiders called the now-dreaded DMCA (Digital Millennium Copyright Act) the "Mouse Act," referring to Disney's hottest property and iconic symbol.

While patents may have great value for the Trust, they expire. Trademarks will, in the long run, have more value for the Trust, since they may be extended *ad infinitum.*

Trust Implications

Since copyright law now protects works of all sorts (books, articles, data bases, computer programs, music, CDs, DVDs, paintings, sculpture, etc), smart Grantors and Trustees will immediately grasp the great value and longevity as assets of useful copyrights. What would the rights to, say, the songs of Elvis, the Dr. Seuss books, the Harry Potter books, or something like Windows be worth to your Trust? What about Peanuts or The Simpsons?

Every year, these and other properties bring in tens of millions to hundreds of millions, maybe even more, both directly and through licensing arrangements. You well may have something similar in your own family circle. Know any writers, producers, artists, cartoonists and the like? How about someone with "points" (profit percentage) in a hit film? These and many more can form valuable assets for your Trust. Be sure to consider such offbeat, even macabre to some, possibilities as licensing the use of the images and likenesses of any famous departed. Every time people like Elvis, John Wayne, Marilyn Monroe, Humphrey Bogart, Frank Sinatra, etc., appear commercially, someone makes money. Indeed, there are whole firms which do nothing but license such uses and go after those who seek the benefits of such use without permission or paying licensing fees. Copies of artwork, songs, books, designs, etc., have the same stipulations attached.

We give you these examples to show you that assets can and do come in forms well beyond what many people think of, and to help you to not overlook what could well be treasure beneath your feet.

Third Criterion

Do I want to sell it before I die?

Depending on the asset and the particular nature of those who will inherit from you, it may make sense to take a valuable, potentially awkward asset and convert it into cash, placing the money thus gained into Trust. There need to be tax considerations. An asset placed into Trust is accepted at fair market value[55], and selling it after it has been in Trust for a while may be much to the advantage of the Grantor's Beneficiaries. The question is whether the asset should be put in Trust at all. What is the tax bite if it is sold before putting it into Trust, and what are the tax advantages after it is sold by the Trust? Further, if the Trust gains the asset and sells it, the Grantor will not get the cash, but a portion of the gain. Trust profit is shared with the Beneficiaries.

There are two other considerations. Is there a place where the Trustee can keep the asset safely, and will the Beneficiaries fight over it? It is usually not feasible to put furniture into a Trust because it will not last longer than the Trust, and because it is more likely to be sold or moved because the Grantor dies. If furniture or china is put into a Trust, though, the Trust must have a home in which it is kept, and of course, the Trustees need to inventory it and handle the maintenance and insurance.

For example, say the asset is a beautiful matched set of fine china. Perhaps no Beneficiaries want it, but it has great value and so there is a dispute about whom should have it. Trivial as it sounds, this has torn families apart. We know, having seen it ourselves. People may not be thrilled if you step in and sell such an item, but it beats tearing the family apart. In this situation, where are the Trustees going to keep the china? How are the Trustees going to settle who gets it? If it is transferred into Trust, and there is no separate home in which for it to stay, then it needs to be sold quickly. If funds gained from its sale are large enough, then they are likely to be invested, increasing the principal held in Trust for investments. If the dispute with the Beneficiaries is loud enough, the Trustees will simply pay them off. By the way, the Beneficiaries will then need to pay any tax due.

[55] *American National Bank of St. Joseph v. United States,* 92 F. Supp.403

Fourth Criterion

Does it create a positive cash flow?

A strong cash flow is the fuel that makes your Trust perform, for from it come the funds for new investments, payouts to the Beneficiaries, and of course, salaries and overhead to run your Trust.

Property put into Trust may be income producing, such as rental or commercial units that do have a sufficient cash flow, or it may be residential property that can be converted to cash and invested to jump start the Trust.

Fifth Criterion

Is it a valuable collectible?

To discover the value of coins, jewelry, art and similar collections, an expert appraisal settles the fair market value. This sets the initial corpus—the basis for proving the value of the Trust Corpus. The first corpus is essential to maintain correct accounting procedures.

Even if the collectible is of value, the wisdom, or lack thereof in placing it into Trust, has much to do with your purposes in setting up the Trust. Is your prized collection only an interest of yours, or do any of your future inheritors share the same passion? If yes, then you may want to give the collection as a gift. If it is valuable, historically significant, etc., you may wish to place the collection into Trust, with the condition that it be kept in one or two designated places. The Trust bears insurance, maintenance and security expenses. As Grantor, you may also decide what you want done is to keep a painstakingly assembled collection and even build on it after your death. This is why we have the massively endowed Getty Museum in Southern California, which is a Trust. You may have a collection of antique dolls which you probably would like properly housed and cared for so the public can enjoy them. You may have one of the best collections of drivable antique cars in the world, as Jay Leno does, and cannot bear the thought of its piecemeal dismantlement after you pass. If so, you may wish to set up a Trust to house and protect your collection of history on wheels, or perhaps create your own museum for it.

In this case, the cash flow in the Trust must be substantial to care for the cars, with enough left over for Beneficiaries; otherwise, they will demand the assets be sold so they can get their fair share.

As an alternative, the Trust could loan the collection to a museum. This could result in a tax deduction for the Trust, and transfers the insurance expense to the museum.

Sixth Criterion

Do my Beneficiaries want to use it?

Prime examples of assets meeting this criterion are: recreational property (ski lodge, beach house, ranch, etc.), planes, helicopters, cars, even motorcycles and hang gliders. Assuming the cash flow supports keeping these assets, the cost of maintenance now becomes the Trustees' responsibility. Nonownership provides legal protections: For example, you do not own it, it cannot be seized, and you are not responsible for the taxes. Neither are the Beneficiaries. Here is a more specific example.

The Kennedys have long had a fabulous family compound in Hyannis Port, Massachusetts, held in Trust for the family's use. This became important after the Chappaquiddick Bridge incident. According to Brent Johnson of *American Sovereign Magazine*, Ted Kennedy was sued by the parents[56] of the drowned Mary Jo Kopechne. The established facts are that Ted Kennedy owned neither Hyannis Port, his home, nor his personal car. In Brent Johnson's account of a settlement, he states the parents received $30,000.00. In another account of the

---

[56]   Brent Johnson, *American Sovereign*, "Pure Trust Organizations":
http://www.americansovereign.com/article/article31.htm

settlement, it is stated at $1,000,000.00.[57] Whatever the truth, the result was, the major Kennedy family assets were protected.

We do not have the exact details of how the Trust is structured, but it is most likely Senator Kennedy drove a leased car, and the homes were each held in a separate Trust. With nothing to gain, any lawsuit resolved itself quietly.

Ted Kennedy is said to have taken an Oath of Poverty, and it is on file. "Legally speaking, he is a pauper!"[58]

Seventh Criterion

Can the asset be converted to cash, or does the asset produce a cash flow?

Rental property meets this criterion and is one of the favorite items to put into Trust. The problem with this lies in managing the property. Will the Trustees now be responsible, or will the Grantor stay on and work the property? Will a management company take on the task?

It is another matter, though, if the rental property, bought at market peak, used an adjustable rate mortgage and the demand tanked while interest rates soared. Can the rental payments still cover any mortgage taxes and fees due while leaving enough for maintenance and improvement costs? If it seems the property may become costly, or is running in the red, it is best not to put it into Trust unless a financial or tax adviser tells you otherwise.

Good art, though, be it paintings, sculpture, drawings, folk primitive, tribal or what-have-you, belongs in Trust, to be both enjoyed by your successors or, if needed, sold to care for your Beneficiaries and their needs.

---

[57] David Horowitz, *FrontPageMagazine.com*, May 15, 2000, "March of the Racketeers": http://www.frontpagemag.com/Articles/Printable.asp?ID 2995

[58] Brent Johnson, Ibid.

Registered assets

When goods registered with the state (for example, vehicles) are subsequently exchanged into a Trust, it holds the registration in its name.

Usually, property transfers easily into a Trust. Once placed there, though, we do not advise taking out a second mortgage. If you plan to refinance your home continually, do not place it into a Trust. Unless the Trustees own the mortgage, the property will need to be taken out of Trust and put back in the Grantor's name to refinance. This takes time to take the property out of trust and place it back in his or her name. Sometimes there is often a time crunch, the complications of taking property in and out of Trust sometimes make it impossible to do within the window available.

Chapter 12

Types of Trusts

For those of you interested in using a Trust to protect assets for your Beneficiaries, this section offers a smorgasbord of choices. For those of you already involved in a Trust, this will show you a panorama of possibilities in the Trust world. Because we do not claim to know every Trust type, we can only hope that this section gives you a working knowledge of the subject.

Much like a tailor helps you select fabric, measures and fits you for a fine garment, the next three chapters will help you discover what Trust most suits your particular set of needs. Each Trust has its advantages and disadvantages, and all are **not** equal!

The differences among the types are real and significant. Also, certain decisions, once made, cannot be undone. Whether from ignorance, by design, or a little of both, the users of Trusts have crossbred them over the years to such a degree the field is now overgrown with a tangle of dozens of different species.[59] Many of them vary only in the slightest shape or shade of color from others. You probably will never have a use for most of the major categories

---

[59] The Sixth edition of *Black's Law Dictionary* lists more than 90 different types of Trusts.

found in Appendix B, but knowing something about them may help you to decide what you need. Also, having another item to compare to the one you are studying can help your understanding dawn sooner and more brightly.

The Motive for a Trust: The Issue of Title

To review the basics, all Trusts shift the issue of title. To avoid probate, title must vest into another person or entity either at death or before without the need of a judge's approval. This is done by putting another's name on financial documents while the Grantor is alive. This successor Trustee can "go to the bank and get the money" when the Grantor dies. Also, the Trustees can gain full authority before death. In other words, the Trustees either become co-owners of assets or the owners, and thus have signature power.

So, why doesn't everyone do this? Because the other person has to be trustworthy. Without recourse to recover funds, you are vulnerable. This is why a Trust Indenture is necessary. It is a contract with those other people who have signature power limiting them to what they can and cannot do with the funds.

The Set Up and Administration

The listed Trusts in Appendix B all involve legal documentation. For Living Trusts, forms can be bought easily through the Internet, or at some office supply stores. It is much more reliable, though, to go to a lawyer who is familiar with estate planning issues.

For certain complex Trust schemes, some companies offer seminars about how good their product is, and how it can protect a family. If you attend a seminar, you will get an amazing education. Putting into action the ideas and system presented, though, is a different issue.

The documents which create a Trust organization are only about 25% of what is needed to make the organization succeed. Paper does **not** equal success.

Organizations grow or decrease based on the people who make the day-to-day decisions and are responsible for the success. Do not think that buying documents which form a business entity, including a Trust, is enough. Only knowledge, administrative ability and connections with the right financial, accounting and legal people will allow your organization to succeed. What you want to buy is backup support comprised of knowledgeable people. They can either take the responsibility to provide correct legal and accounting advice, or train you so your organization has the best advantages possible in this complex world.

Statutory Trusts

The term "statutory" identifies the laws which apply to these Trusts, and the Trusts themselves, are designed with guidelines by the state. What the state makes, it can also change or revoke. Also, on a day-to-day human level, many Statutory Trusts are created or managed (or both) by individuals *licensed* by the state (lawyers, banks, CPAs, and others.) who are subject to state-imposed limits on their operation. Usually, these limits are determined by their allegiance to the state and a fear of state and federal taxing authorities. Trustees who are lawyers or accountants who do not follow the mandates of state authorities risk having their licenses revoked. Sometimes this can be good, as there are many necessary laws about Trusts. The other side is they owe their loyalty to the state, and at times there can be a conflict between what the Trust needs and their priorities.

Testamentary Trust

A Will can set up a Trust. The Will states the names of the Trustees and the assets, with a description of the purpose of the Trust. Usually a Testamentary Trust is not too complex and the directions to the Trustees simple. After probate, the court approves the Trustees selected, or appoints a Trustee. Funds then are distributed or invested by the Trustees for the Beneficiaries, who can be the blood relations of the person setting up the Trust, or another organization.

Living Trust

Probably the best known, garden-variety Trust is the living Trust. Its name comes from the Latin *inter vivos* ("between the living") and means that, unlike a Testamentary Trust, it takes effect while both the Grantor and Beneficiary are alive. Usually, the Grantor is also the Trustee.

As shown in Chapter 1, Figure 1, the Grantor creates a Living Trust when he or she transfers financial accounts and assets to the Trust's name, and authorizes signature power for the person who will take over the administration on the Grantor's death. For example, if on the bank account for the Living Trust, the Grantor's name is J.B. Watkins and the Trust name is J.B. Watkins Family Trust, he or she allows the son or daughter to co-sign on the account. When J.B. Watkins dies, the successor Trustee already has signature power, and so there is no need to go to Probate Court to get a judge to give permission to the bank or other financial institutions to release the funds.

After the death of the Grantor, the Trustee gets an Employer Identification Number (EIN) or Trust Identification Number (TIN) or the Trust and assumes responsibility for the taxes. At this point, it becomes an Irrevocable Trust.

You may be surprised to learn that, in the United States, this most common of all Trusts is available only to U.S. citizens.

Despite the Living Trust's name and seeming difference from the Testamentary Trust, each of them distributes its assets after the Grantor/Trustee's death.

As a Grantor Trust, the Living Trust is revocable, that is, the Grantor may change his or her mind and change or revoke the Indenture. For that reason, it does not protect the Grantor from tax liability on his or her income. A Living Trust *could* be written as though it is irrevocable, though common use does not follow that pattern. We mean, except for where the Grantor can be or change a Trustee, the details of a Living Trust should consider while the Grantor is alive, the irrevocable nature of the Living Trust after the passing of the Grantor.

The following is a summary of the Living Trust:

• This form affords no asset protection against liabilities incurred by the Grantor. If sued, all the assets can be seized as the result of a judgment or tax lien.

• Beneficiaries can be liable for income taxes on distributions made at the termination of a Living Trust, unless its final Beneficiary is a state-approved charity.

• It is a large step up over a Will, since it protects the Beneficiaries from the time, expense and vagaries of Probate Court, but only if its terms are not challenged by any Beneficiaries or other potential heirs.

• Unlike the Irrevocable Trust, a Living Trust is not considered a business and cannot operate one. Assets from a business can be put into this Trust, though. For example, a printing press could be put into a Living Trust to be sold as part of the Trust assets after the Grantor's death.

• Filed in the county, descriptions of its assets and identification of its Beneficiaries are matters of public record. Thus, con artists can target the Beneficiaries.

The Revocable or "Simple" Trust

Although Revocable and Living Trusts are the same, we separate them for clarity. One of the few major differences is that Revocable Trusts can be managed by Trustees, while Living Trusts are assumed (by taxing authorities) to be run by the Grantors.

Created by a Grantor, Revocable Trusts hold legal title and the assets placed with a Trustee under the name of the Trust. The Trustee administers the estate. The Grantor may be a Cotrustee. If the Trustee is not the Grantor, the Grantor retains the right to terminate the Trustee and change the Indenture.

Through the Trust Indenture, the Beneficiary receives equitable title to benefits from the Trust that may or may not be exercisable during the life of the Grantor. This means the Beneficiary has the right to petition a court of equity for redress, should the Trustees fail to perform as needed after the death of the Grantor.

Some Revocable Trusts require the Beneficiary to agree to termination before the Trust can be ended.

Despite the obvious disadvantages of the Revocable Trust, it does allow an owner of real or personal property to pass legal title to someone else. The second person then assumes responsibility for protecting and expanding the assets, relieving the Grantor of management duties and liabilities. This single fact alone justifies its existence and offers some people increased peace of mind. Clearly, though, its benefits bear little likeness to those available from an irrevocable instrument.

By the way, for all Revocable Trusts, the Beneficiaries have a right to see the accounting records back to the beginning of the Trust, when the Grantor handled the paperwork. The successor Trustee who takes over the Trust on the death of the Grantor, is responsible to produce the accounting records on request of the Beneficiaries.[60]

Irrevocable Statutory Trust

The tax benefits can be impressive, and the asset liability protection is noteworthy for any Irrevocable Trust. Because you, as the Grantor, give a percentage of your personal assets to either a Trustee or a Board of Trustees, this Trust needs to be seriously considered before moving forward.

You may think that a wife or brother can become a Trustee of a Irrevocable Statutory Trust. Thus, you the Grantor, believe you remain in control of the funds because of this close relationship; in §672 of the Internal Revenue Code, though, there are strict rules concerning who can and cannot be a Trustee. The rules are designed to prevent close family members from acting solely on your behalf. It is assumed they are more likely to neglect the Beneficiaries–the people they are hired to represent and protect–in favor of your wishes. There

---

[60] *Evangelho v. Presoto* (1998) 67 Cal.App. 4th 615 , 79 Cal.Rptr.2d 146.

are some circumstances where this close relationship is allowed. We address these in Volume II.

One Irrevocable Statutory Trust, known by some as the Term Trust, can be used for a 10-year period to divert income from you to your child. Because your child is in a much lower tax bracket than you, this can often be a great tax advantage. Just with this information alone, it is easy to see why there is interest in this estate planning vehicle. For an extensive list of Irrevocable Trusts, see Appendix B.

All Irrevocable Statutory Trusts can allow other family members to put their assets into the same Trust. For example, perhaps the grandparents would like to transfer a mutual fund into the Irrevocable Trust set up by their son-in-law for their grandchildren.

With Irrevocable Statutory Trusts there are complex issues about taxation and gifts which the Board of Trustees must handle. You need to consult with professionals if you feel this is a better way to handle your finances.

Irrevocable Common Law Trust

The Irrevocable Common-Law Trust has the same properties as the above Trust, but when you exchange goods into the Trust, you receive Trust Certificates identifying the number of Trust Capital Units received in exchange. A percentage of the Trust Capital Units equals a portion of the corpus (the "stuff" in the Trust) of the estate.

You can do the same process with a corporation, such as exchanging a mutual fund into a corporation and receiving shares of the corporation in return. Taxes are paid when corporate shares are cashed out. The same applies to a properly set up Irrevocable Common-Law Trust, the taxes are due when the Trust Certificates are cashed out.[61]

Many people can exchange goods into the same Trust. This means once the Trust is set up, other people (usually in the family) can exchange their assets for Trust Capital Units. The Common-Law Trust is, thus, a more complex system. There is also greater flexibility to allow for asset separation.

The Trust Certificates have value when the corpus of the Trust is sold. If you hold 30% of the Trust value at the time the Trust is dissolved, then you will receive 30% of the payout of the Trust. If the Trustees use the initial corpus to multiply the assets, the Trust can be worth millions. This means the value of the Trust Capital Units increase.

Further, Trust Capital Units control the share of profit when the Board of Trustees decides distribution.

Charitable Trust

Once passthrough of profits to Beneficiaries provides for the needs of the immediate family, the Trustees can then set up a Charitable Trust to help those other individuals or groups identified in the Trust Indenture. A Charitable Trust needs to have a specific theme or purpose, and the money thus distributed to organizations cannot be used to benefit the Grantor or his or her family. These Trusts are passthrough organizations like the Domestic Trust, set up in one of the several states.

---

[61] *Commissioner of Internal Revenue v. Logan* 283 U.S. 404 (1931)." No tax is assessed on the conveyance of property to a corporation because the exchange constitutes a tax-free trade and exchange for an unknown realized gain or loss."

Tax Exempt Status

This Charitable Trust can generate funds through its own investments and then distribute profits to various organizations. To receive funds from other organizations and contributors, this Charitable Private Trust needs to have a recognized tax-exempt status,[62] so its donors can receive tax credits.

The Charitable Trust can receive a distribution from other Trusts, and pass the funds onto other organizations. If the Family Trust adds to its certificate register the name of the Charitable Trust, then it receives a K-1 distribution along with all the other Trust Capital Unit Holders. In this case, the tax-exempt status is not needed, as the Family Trust is a passthrough organization.

Charitable Remainder Trusts

Do not confuse the Charitable Trust with the *Charitable Remainder Trust*. There are two types of Remainder Trusts: the *annuity* and *unitrust*.[63] In both cases, the Grantor is the Beneficiary, and on his or her death , the income from the principal of the estate goes first to the named Beneficiaries and then to a charitable organization. Since both types fall under the heading of *Grantor Trusts* (the Grantor being also the Beneficiary), no income tax benefits derive from their use. For more details about these Trusts, check with your accountant or other financial advisers.

Now and again, people believe that a Trust must contain a charitable element to qualify for tax advantages. These clients have heard that a Trust or foundation has just made a donation to a cause, for example, a university, hospital, Public Broadcasting Systems (PBS), etc., and assume that everyone must. We have not found any requirement like this except for the Charitable Remainder Trust.

---

[62]   See IRC § 501(c)(3).

[63]   Steve Maple, *The Complete Idiot's Guide to Wills and Estates*, Alpha Books, p. 208.

Among a family's highest priorities is the care of its members. When you and your family gain far more than is needed to live comfortably, you may choose to set up a Charitable Trust or Charitable Remainder Trust. All of humanity will then applaud you.

Do not stress yourself (or your initial store of assets!) about charity at too early a date. Engaging in "socially conscious" activities is wonderful and rewarding when you can well afford it, but it is not necessary to prove that you have enough interest in others. Simply do the basics well. Create a self-sufficient Trust cash flow to support your Trust staff and Beneficiaries. In turn, this supports their families and supplies your customers/clients/patients with high quality goods or services. Further, this trains your family members in their responsibilities to be prudent, self-controlled, law-abiding and industrious. Finally, it ensures the Trustees have a strong incentive to make beneficial distributions.

Perform just these few, simple actions with grace, humility and persistence in the face of all the challenges modern life has to offer and you will find yourself a long way toward carrying out any duty you may feel you owe society. Such a civic responsibility is enough to qualify a Trust for tax benefits. Courts will support your mandate to your Trustees to carry out your plans as stated in the Indenture. The implicit primary purpose for any Trust is that it looks out for the Beneficiaries.

Educational Trust

A Trust can specifically address the educational needs of the family and/or in such a way the Beneficiaries are named educational institutions. As with other Trusts, the Beneficiaries are responsible for any taxes due on the funds they receive.

Estate planning often involves various schemes to support both the family and its descendants, as well as to gain the advantage of the best tax strategies. The Educational Trust is an Irrevocable Trust designed to set aside specific funds dedicated to various educational opportunities. Tax professionals can advise you regarding the advantages.

Somewhat similar to a Charitable Trust, where funds are invested, and the income produced is distributed to various charitable enterprises, the Educational Trust is set up to support learning institutions, as well as family members and the Board of Trustees.

The Educational Trust is based on the qualifications of the Beneficiary to receive the funding. These qualifications are determined either by the Grantor, or by the standards of our society, such as, if the Beneficiary is accepted to an accredited institution, then the Trust benefits apply.

The funds can be given, not just for tuition and books, but to support various aspects of campus living. This includes fraternity or sorority fees, a living expense allowance, room and board, transportation, and/or travel involving education, as well as supporting the Beneficiary until he or she finds suitable work.

Several guidelines can be written into the Educational Trust to define when the Trust funds stop, or when restrictions on the Trust funds apply. For example, if the Beneficiary becomes emotionally unstable, acquires a substance abuse problem or a physical disability which prevents him or her from continuing an education. In the latter, there can be other provisions in an overall estate plan, such as a medical policy, or another Trust fund comes to a Beneficiary's aid.

The Grantor has ample room for creativity when designing an overall educational plan for his or her or her family, such as:

- Trust support stops at a certain age, to prevent the "professional student."

- Grade point averages determine amount of Beneficiary support.

- Defining the age at which a Beneficiary can name children as Beneficiaries of the Educational Trust.

- Requiring that once a Beneficiary accepts the educational benefits, the Beneficiary contributes to the Trust to support future generations.

- After establishing a career, the Beneficiary gives back to the Trust a percentage of earnings to contribute to the next generation.

Chapter 13

Trustee Differences

Not all Trustees are the same. There are four classifications. Each Trustee serves a different purpose and is applicable to different Trusts. The last one is a danger.

1.   Grantor Trustee

2.   Independent Trustee

3.   Adverse Trustee

4.   Dummy Trustee

Grantor Trustee

As mentioned before, the Grantor and spouse usually become the Trustees as well as the main Beneficiaries in a Living Trust. He or she has enough motive to increase the assets for the Trust because the Grantor enjoys them. Placing assets into a Trust assumes consideration for the contingent Beneficiaries. Because control equals taxes, the Grantor pays the income taxes on the Trust profits.

Independent Trustee

The Independent Trustee is often a Bank represented by lawyers who act as Trustees for the Bank. The Bank then receives a percentage of the Trust distribution to the Beneficiaries.

An individual can be an Independent Trustee who receives remuneration or a percentage. He or she will not have a substantial adverse interest.

Adverse Trustee

The adverse Trustee, though, takes on a different responsibility than either the Grantor Trustee, or the Independent Trustee. The adverse Trustee has a greater vested interest in the Trust than the Grantor and cannot be removed by the Grantor. The adverse Trustee functions in some Irrevocable Statutory Trusts and must qualify in all Private Trusts, also known as Common-Law Trusts. His or her role is more aggressive, and an adverse Trustee has broader powers than an Independent Trustee.

> The adverse Trustee functions in some Irrevocable Statutory Trusts and must qualify in all Private Trusts, also known as Common-Law Trusts.

The term adverse means the Trustee can be adverse to the wishes of the Grantor. This would occur if the Grantor wants to use the Trust funds contrary to the best interests of the Beneficiaries.

Standard Oil Trust

The need for a definition of an adverse Trustee came through lawsuits against the Standard Oil Trust.[64] Because John D. Rockefeller had total control over the Trustees, who were employees of Standard Oil, he could fire them. This proved the Standard Oil Trust was a Grantor Trust, and not an Irrevocable Trust.

Substantial Adverse Interest

To prove the assets belong to the Board of Trustees and not to the Grantor, there needs to be an adverse Trustee with substantial adverse interest. This means the Trustee holds a greater percentage of the Trust than the Grantor. This Trustee has a vested right under the Trust, insists on performance of the Indenture and cannot be compelled to surrender control.[65]

Of course, none of this makes sense without some background. To accomplish this inequality between the Grantor and the Trustee , the Trustee needs to put assets into the Trust of greater value than the Grantor. Because that is not likely, the alternative becomes the Trustee's holding a greater percentage of the Trust than the Grantor holds. This essentially creates a reversal of roles. The Grantor, who placed most of assets into the Trust, is now subservient to the Trustee, who may or may not have put assets into the Trust, yet holds more Trust Capital Units than the Grantor.

This seemingly contradictory statement may have lost the reader. How can the Trustee hold a greater percentage than the Grantor if the Trustee does not put funds into the Trust?

This is where Trust structuring becomes essential. In Common-Law Trusts the Trust Certificates identify Trust Capital Units held by each member of the

---

[64] *Rice v. Rockefeller*, 134 NY 174, 31 NE 907 and State ex rel., *Watson v. Standard Oil Co.*, 49 Ohio St 137, 30 NE 279.

[65] *Commissioner of Internal Revenue v. Betts*, C.C.A. 123 F.2d 534 (1941).

Trust group. The Units held equal a percentage of the value of the Trust held by the Beneficiaries and by the officers of the Trust. The adverse Trustee gets more Trust Capital Units than the Grantor, and thus should the Trust ever "cash out," the Trustee gets the majority of Funds. Without this technique, it is not possible to understand how an adverse Trustee is created, because only occasionally will any

> **If the Irrevocable Trust dissolves, the adverse Trustee gets the greater percentage of the current Trust value.**

Trustee put personal funds into a family Trust when there is no blood relationship. The great deterrent is that legally the profits of the assets added by the nonrelated Trustee accede to the Trust Beneficiaries, and not to the Trustee's Beneficiaries. Because the blood relationship between the Trustee and the Grantor is discouraged, it seems the adverse Trustee is not inclined to share in the Trust.[66]

If the Irrevocable Trust dissolves, the adverse Trustee gets the greater percentage of the current Trust value. It becomes unlikely the Grantor would end the Trust under these circumstances.

In Trusts holding assets worth millions, the Trustee position is bought. That is, the Trustee gains the position by buying a portion of the Trust Capital Units.

Once an adverse Trustee can be proven, the Grantor is no longer taxable for the increase of the assets. As you can imagine, this one issue becomes key to establishing the legal status of the Trust in reference to its tax standing.

Also you can add a Trustee's Beneficiary to the Trust complex. Not being blood related to the Grantor's family, the Trustee's Beneficiary cannot pass on the Trust Capital Units.

---

[66] The blood relationship can be allowed in some cases. We cover this in Volume II. An understanding of Trust Certificates is required before a decision to put either a brother or a spouse in as a Trustee can be considered.

Scam Trusts

In a scam Trust, the promoter tells the Trust package buyer that he or she can be both the Grantor and the Trustee without any tax consequences. This shady deal has been going on for more than 100 years and fills the coffers of the IRS with ample extra funds. Once it is proven that a Trust is incorrectly structured and administered, the Grantor becomes taxable for all the years the Trust operated. This large dollar amount often requires assets to be sold, and the proceeds become IRS property. This proves to be a rich and lucrative con artist game giving IRS Agents great motivation to find these poorly structured Trusts. Several scam Trust court cases are included in Volume II.

Both the IRS and the courts recognize the issue of legal title held by an adverse Trustee. The legal system is clear about the difference between a Grantor interested in getting major tax benefits and liability protection to build the assets for the Beneficiaries, and one who wants to use the scam Common-Law Trust to avoid taxes. Unfortunately, innocent people still get caught in this scheme.

Motivation

In comparison, the Independent Trustee often lacks sufficient motivation, because there is no substantial adverse interest. This Trustee gets a percentage of distribution, but does not reap the benefits of additional funds because of owning a percentage of the Trust. Corporate banks who act as Trustee do not hold substantial adverse interest[67], and have a reputation for making only safe investments without the motivation to increase the profits. When the Trustee is adverse, aggressive investment activity is more likely.

An Independent Trustee is more often a stranger to the Beneficiaries and some-times even to the Grantor. This Trustee, chiefly interested in ensuring the accounting and legalities of the Trust, is not attentive to the personal interests of the Beneficiaries. There may be little or no communication between the provider and receiver of funds, so the Beneficiaries do not have the advantage

---

[67]   *Morton v. Commissioner of Internal Revenue*, 109 F2nd 47, Jan 9, 1940.

of a mentor. Wisdom passed on to the Beneficiaries from the Grantor is lost, as is the family history, which can easily be kept in a Private Trust.

After Death

After the Grantor dies, the sticky issue of an adverse Trustee is moot. Any blood relation can become the Trustee as long as the person named qualifies under the Trust Indenture. For a functional family, this should be an easy transition, but if the family is dysfunctional, it is better the adverse Trustee remain in place.

Because death does not displace an adverse Trustee, the Trustee may remain as Trustee for as long as he or she feels it is necessary. Should the Trustee's remuneration be ample, we can assure you the Trustee is not likely to step down simply because the Grantor passed.

It is often a wise move to keep an adverse Trustee in place. Not burdened with the more common emotional issues and history of the family, this Trustee can be unbiased when the volatile issues of investments and distribution come into focus. In contrast, should a son or daughter become the Trustee, the undercurrent of jealousy and competitiveness may cause an otherwise smoothly running Trust to become chaotic.

> It is often a wise move to keep an adverse Trustee in place since he or she is not loaded down with the more common emotional issues and past history of the family, and can be impartial when the highly volatile issues of investments and distribution come into focus.

When the Grantor sets up the Trust, he or she may want to specify in the Indenture qualifications for being a Trustee. Depending on the family issues, the Grantor may want to ensure that an adverse Trustee remains on the Board of Trustees.

The events that frequently happen prior to death include the issue of the Grantor changing his or her mind. We handle that issue in Volume II.

Because of the emotional issues surrounding death, the adverse Trustee proves to be one of the greatest assets of the Trust. Dedicated to the Beneficiaries, the adverse Trustee is not subject to the caprices of the Grantor.

Definition

The Internal Revenue Code (IRC), has the best and most thorough definition of an adverse Trustee [68]. This Trustee cannot be subservient to the Grantor; that is, not blood related, not an employee, and there is no other condition under which the Grantor can dominate the Trustee. Although sometimes it is hard to follow the wording, we include this section so you can see the complete definition:

A) Adverse Party

For purposes of this subpart, the term "adverse party" means any person having a substantial beneficial interest in the trust which would be adversely affected by the exercise or nonexercise of the power which he possesses respecting the trust. A person having a general power which he possesses respecting the trust. A person having a general power of appointment over the trust property shall be deemed to have a beneficial interest in the trust.

B) Nonadverse Party

For purposes of this subpart, the term "nonadverse party" means any person who is not an adverse party.

C) Related Or Subordinate Party

For purposes of this subpart, the term "related or subordinate party" means any nonadverse party who is -

(1) the grantor's spouse if living with the grantor;

---

[68]   IRC § 672 (a) through (d).

(2) any of the following: The grantor's father, mother, issue, brother or sister; an employee of the grantor; a corporation or any employee of a corporation in which the stockholdings of the grantor and the trust are significant from the viewpoint of voting control; a subordinate employee of a corporation in which the grantor is an executive.

For purposes of subsection (f) and sections 674 and 675, a related or subordinate party shall be presumed to be subservient to the grantor in respect of the exercise or nonexercise of the powers conferred on him unless such party is shown not to be subservient by a preponderance of the evidence.

D) Rule where power is subject to condition precedent

A person shall be considered to have a power described in this subpart even though the exercise of the power is subject to a precedent giving of notice or takes effect only on the expiration of a certain period after the exercise of the power.

Dummy Trustee

There is one more classification of a Trustee. He or she functions in an Irrevocable Trust in name only. Signing checks and other papers may be the Dummy Trustee's only obligations while the Grantor runs the Trust. The problem here is that this Trustee cannot participate in any business, as he or she has nothing to contribute. Not trained or motivated, clearly a lackey for the Grantor, this Trustee is not of any value to the Beneficiaries. Usually, a Trustee of this nature is disinclined to get involved, and the first words to an IRS Agent are, "I just do what I am told." Immediately upon hearing this, you no longer have an Irrevocable Trust, and all profits are now taxable to you, the Grantor.

Payment for Services Rendered

The presence of a Trustee allows the Trust to meet legal and tax qualifications, giving the Trust an advantage. Because of this, a Trustee of an Irrevocable Trust is valuable. Any fiduciary services should be rewarded, and the more interested a Trustee becomes in the welfare of the Trust group, the more reward that Trustee should receive. The Trust belongs to the Trustees, and reasonable funds they receive for their services should not be questioned.

Custodian Issues in Probate Court[69]

Now that you have an understanding of an adverse Trustee, we share with you a problem that has occurred so often the courts determined who cannot receive funds from an estate.

This article is about who cannot get your "stuff." We quote Mr. Oldman from the *Los Angeles Daily Journal*:

> Those who draft or transcribe Wills, Trusts or other instruments to pass on wealth are excluded from receiving gifts from the Grantors or Testators because of the temptation to misguide those in their care. In September the Supreme Court [of California] has made the following decision:
>
> Under Section 21350 [of the Probate Code], gifts or bequests to people who stand in a particular relationship with the testator are presumptively disqualified from receiving the benefits provided by a will, trust or other instrument. . .
>
> Later, care custodians were added to the list of disqualified people. To create this situation, the instrument must have been executed by a testator who is defined as a dependent adult under Section 15610.23, and the

---

[69]   Marshall A. Oldman, *High Court Resolves Care Custodian Issues in Probate Code,* Los Angeles Daily Journal, Focus, September 28, 2006, p. 7.

beneficiary must be a person defined as a care custodian of a dependent adult under Section 15610.17 of the Welfare and Institutional Codes.

. . .Section 15610 of the Welfare and Institutions Code includes anyone who provided medical and social services to a dependent adult, whether or not the relationship began as a care giving relationship or as a friendship.

Anyone feeling helpless is tempted to "bribe" those who care for them. It is not always the fault of caregivers. Here again, the Trust assets cannot be given away if they are under the care of the Board of Trustees whose responsibility it is to take care of those who feel helpless. An adverse Trustee has the authority to stop the Grantor from giving away assets belonging to the Beneficiaries.

Chapter 14

On Trusting

We previously discussed what some call the "White Man's Disease," a culturally based inability to trust others. The causes of mistrust stem from or consist of:

- Too much mobility that disconnects bonding and long-term relationships

- Personal isolation because of entertainment deriving from television, computers and other modalities not requiring direct human contact.

- Lack of genuine community.

- Apparent social upheaval.

- The constant barrage of negative information from the media.

The Why

It is understandable we have become a distrustful society, since ripoff artists abound, people steal identities and strangers assault by e-mail offering us African riches in return for front money. Worse, our kids cannot be kids, considering the mass housing of registered sex offenders near schools. Sexual predators work teen chat rooms constantly, and children are enticed at the mall and even from their own yards into lives of prostitution. Throw in drugs, available 24/7, with deadly diseases, and it becomes enough to make people want to throw in the towel by opting out.

This is not the way to go, though. Fundamentally, we must trust, for it is how we are wired as humans, and it is one of our greatest strengths. Nature intended it that way. We innately know that our belief in one another, and backing each other up, are two of the most powerful survival weapons we have.

Failure to trust not only has its own inherent downside, but unless we install countermeasures, it becomes ever more self-reinforcing, eventually making us high-tech hermits. If your next door neighbor mistook your friendly greeting as a prelude to an assault or the woman down the hall thinks you just escaped from San Quentin State Prison, you still need to trust someone or a group of people. Having your back covered, as the vernacular goes, is imperative to your existence.

> Failure to trust not only has its own inherent downside, but unless we install countermeasures, it becomes ever more self-reinforcing, eventually making us high-tech hermits.

White Americans have forgotten the hard-won lessons of trust learned by our immigrant forebears in a strange land where they did not know the language. Others in the ghetto, the barrio, Chinatown, etc., know and practice these lessons daily: cooperation, mutual protection, fierce group identity and community pride. Even when the neighborhoods look and feel like war zones, you will find these factors at work, often with a strong religious content as well. And it is precisely this banding together that got children educations, allowing them to enter the professions, and bought homes for many people who could not have done it on their own. Meanwhile, many of us lead lives of "splendid isolation." If you are going to have a viable Trust, though, you need to rethink that notion. You cannot do it alone.

The Who

Who has been there for you through thick and thin? Who offered wise counsel in the worst of times? Who has a good head for business and at least some grasp of the law? Who genuinely cherishes you and yours? Who has a knack for making money–legally? Who has a spine and the will to stand his or her ground if challenged? Who is naturally curious and willing to learn? Above all, who has genuine character, is emotionally mature, is of the highest personal integrity? Who would you trust with your life?

That may seem extreme, but that is what a good Trustee does—looks after the welfare of others to ensure their well-being according to your wishes. We realize that this list of qualities occurs not in just one person. This is why we recommend you choose two people as Trustees. Even in this combination, only some of these traits exist. The solution to this is found in their willingness to consult with professionals in areas where they may be lacking.

It is from people who have these characteristics, who are not blood relatives, that you will find your Trustees for your Private Trust, or for your Living Trust that will eventually be Irrevocable on your death. The Trustees serve under sworn oath and are bound by the terms of the Trust Indenture that you have so carefully crafted. Your Trustees are in legal control of all that you choose to put into your Trust, for the care, protection and advancement of those dear to you and the causes in which you believe.

"What is the next step?" you ask.

Details Save the Future

To ensure the Trust is managed correctly, create a detailed Trust Indenture. Clear rules, procedures and guidelines do much to assuage your fears. Of course, this implies that you, the Grantor, have enough knowledge about Trust matters to be clear about what information you need.

The more exact and detailed the Indenture, the better. If it leaves basic matters open to question or contains contradictory statements, parts of the Indenture may be nullified, or the entire Trust may be rendered void. You, the Grantor, must be involved in the early draft of the document, and you have full authority to change it however you see fit—until you sign it. For the Irrevocable Trust, once the Trustees sign their acceptance, the specific terms and the document as a whole become *set in stone,* the fundamental law for the family, and will be upheld if challenged. In a Common-Law Trust, subsequent Minutes expand and further define the Indenture, but they must not alter the original intent of the Grantor.

> **Forming any Trust is the single furthest-reaching decision most people will make in a lifetime.**

The Grantor and the Trust Documents

Ideally, the Grantor and Trustees-to-be take active roles in creating the Trust Indenture. In reality, though, most people know so little about Trusts they are lost when offered the opportunity to create a contract providing them both maximum legal protection and maximum financial advantage. Therefore, some Trust firms created generic Indentures and make them available to the public. If you decide to use a one-size-fits-all form, we strongly suggest that you first study and compare the literature of several companies and meet with various representatives. Forming any Trust is the single furthest-reaching decision most people will make in a lifetime. Anyone starting down this road will be wise to gather and study as much information as possible before making a binding commitment.

In a Statutory Trust, Beneficiaries are named, and what they are to receive is specified. In a Common-Law Trust, the 'bloodline' can be named, and the first Beneficiaries named, while a list of other Beneficiaries who meet the specified criteria in the Indenture can be listed on the Trust Certificate Register. For example, the descriptions of whom will be eligible for Trust Certificates can be descendants of grandparents, or it can be descendants of only the Grantor and/or his or her spouse. This list of Beneficiaries is created by meetings of the

Board of Trustees of a Common-Law Trust. That is, the Beneficiaries are not a static matter but one of qualification. Their distribution can increase as they earn their way through life, or through spending time helping the Board of Trustees.

Removing Beneficiaries is not recommended except in extreme cases, with well-documented statements and reports. The procedure for removal must be outlined in the Trust Indenture. Beneficiaries can be added by a majority vote of the Board of Trustees, provided the Beneficiary qualifies under the rules of the Indenture. This decision is recorded in the Minutes.

> For those who would like a guarantee, the Trust Indenture can specify the Trustees be bonded.

Trustworthiness

We covered this in detail earlier in this chapter, but need to revisit it now, mainly in reference to a few points.

People who look at the possibility of placing their assets into an Irrevocable Trust often are hesitant or fearful the Trustees chosen will be dishonest. The most common reaction when you consider setting up a Trust is, "Whom can I trust?" A close friend is often suggested as the suitable person to be a Trustee. If the friend has no proper understanding or Trustee training, why would you want to trust the assets to a person with good intentions, but who has no knowledge of how to manage a Trust?

We found this to be a common problem, trusting property to those not qualified to know what to do if the IRS requests an audit, or the Trust is sued. We do not expect new Trustees to have this knowledge, but to be willing to learn. If new Trustees are terrified of authority, it is not likely they will eventually take the reins of the Trust.

For those who would like a guarantee, the Trust Indenture can specify the Trustees be bonded. This is similar to the FDIC insurance on your money in the bank.

So we are back to the question of "Whom can I trust?" The answer is easier when you understand the details.

In any Irrevocable Trust, giving the reins of financial control to another person is not so difficult when the limits are understood. It is even easier if the Grantor holds all or some of the seven powers of control[70] in the Trust:

- How the income of an Irrevocable Trust may be applied to support a dependent.[71]

- At termination of Trust, the corpus reverts back to the Grantor.

- How the income of the Trust is to be accumulated.[72]

- How the corpus is to be distributed.

- Temporary power to withhold income from a Beneficiary.

- Power to withhold income during the disability of a Beneficiary to accumulate and add to the income corpus.

- Power to allocate between corpus and income.

With the Grantor remaining as an adviser, he or she becomes a nonvoting member of the Board of Trustees. Now, the Trustees and the Grantor become a team to meet the long-term goals and to build the assets of the Trust for the benefit of the Beneficiaries. For those who are visionary, the Irrevocable Trust is a creative process. For example, if the idea of Disneyland had been only Walt Disney's vision, he would have entrusted the remaining scheme to the Trustees, who would incorporate his ideas as generations passed. This is pre-

---

[70]   IRC §674 (b) and (d)

[71]   IRC 677(b)

[72]   IRC 675(4)B

cisely what Randolph Hearst did to perpetuate his publishing empire. The court cases regarding this specific issue and the impact on the Beneficiaries are contained in Volume II.

In summary, the main responsibilities of the Trustee are to increase and protect the assets of the Trust. This is what the courts expect and why the Grantor chose the specific person for the job. With this in mind, it becomes clear that Trustees must have a grasp of finance and have some legal knowledge, or at least be interested enough to learn. This is not an easy combination to find in one person, and adding the quality of steadfastness makes finding the ideal Trustee nearly impossible. Since Trusts can have more than one Trustee, why not have on the Board of Trustees, one (1) friend and one (1) who is familiar with either accounting or who has interest in or access to legal information?

Lack of Trust and Abuse of Power

Although we have focused on the issue of trusting Trustees, the real problems often apply to family members, Grantors and conflicting power issues. If you are worried about trusting people with your assets, consider this case where an Irrevocable Trust and an adverse Trustee may have saved the day.

Health Care Agent

Although we cover the issue of the Durable Power of Attorney for Health Care (DPAHC) in Volume II, we need to touch on it here. The DPAHC is a document where you choose who can make health care decisions for you when you are unable to. This applies when you may be in a coma or near death. The DPAHC is a necessary step to ensure the assets in the Trust are not drained unnecessarily. In the following referenced article, an Irrevocable Trust is not used. The integrity of a family member, though, displays the care needed to choose people wisely.

Courts have recently dealt with the issue of Health Care Agents, also known as caregivers, who become recipients of generous gifts by those they serve. They cheat the family out of their inheritance. Also, a family member may take advantage of those unable to decide for themselves as we find in the following disturbing article.

In a letter written to Liz Pulliam Weston in the *Los Angeles Times*[73], we learn of an event where a daughter stole significant amounts of money while acting as Health Care Agent for her parents. She drained their savings accounts, and charged large balances on their credit cards. Not stopping there, she took out loans against the life insurance policies, leaving nothing to pay for even funeral expenses. She could have been prosecuted for these crimes, but she died before the theft was discovered by her daughter, who is the granddaughter.

The distraught granddaughter seeks legal advice from Ms. Pulliam who states:

> . . . Your mother's estate is responsible for these debts. If she left any assets—bank accounts, investment accounts, real estate, cars, whatever—those typically can be tapped to pay the debts after her funeral expenses and other necessary bills are covered. . .

> . . .if there simply are no assets to tap, . . .seek the advice of a bankruptcy attorney about filing a Chapter 7 case on your grandfather's behalf. That would eliminate the credit card debt . . .

The granddaughter is now bereft, for her mother took everything. If the grandfather had placed assets in an Irrevocable Trust, the daughter would not have had access.

---

[73] Liz Pulliam Weston, "Abuse of power of attorney drains grandfather's funds," *Los Angeles Times*, Money Talk Section C, page 3, October 29, 2006

Chapter 15

Trustees and the Law

With this groundwork laid, let us now turn to the law books to discover what experiences these mysterious Trustees are having, and what those who studied the subjects of Trusts have passed on to us.

Of course, we would all like our Trustees to have the wisdom of Solomon and be super heroes sitting on your Board. Exceptional talent is unnecessary. As one respected Trust expert, George Bogert, wrote, "Only ordinary care, skill and prudence are normally required of Trustees."[74] The primary guideline is that Trustees are bound in the management of all the matters of the Trust. They are to act in good faith and employ such vigilance, sagacity, diligence and prudence as, in general, prudent men of discretion and intelligence employ in their own affairs.

If an otherwise competent Trustee makes an error in judgment, the law generally will not hold him or her liable. On the other hand, if he or she fails to display reasonable skill (Appendix F) good intentions will likely prove no defense. To quote Bogert again, "Good intent will not relieve him from liability for negligent or improvident conduct." Should a Trustee claim some exceptional skill, such as the ability to rapidly increase the value of assets, the court tends to hold that Trustee to his or her word.

---

[74]   See Appendix F for a definition of "Reasonable Skill."

Trustees and Beneficiaries

Trustees must act solely for the Beneficiaries, so the former must never be dependent on the latter. Bogert explains:

> One of the most important duties of a trustee is that of undivided loyalty to the beneficiaries. While he is administering the trust he must refrain from placing himself in a position where his personal interest or that of a third person does or may conflict with the interest of the beneficiaries. All his conduct which has any bearing on the affairs of the trust must be actuated by consideration of the welfare of the beneficiaries and them alone. He is in a position of such intimacy with those he is representing and has such great control over their property that a higher standard is established by the court of equity than would prevail in the case of an ordinary business relation.[75]

Because Beneficiaries receive income or other benefits from the Trust, if the flow slows or is interrupted, they are the first to notice. Therefore, according to the courts, they stand as guardians of the Trust's well-being. Incidentally, a Trust without any Beneficiaries is no Trust.

Trustees are held to a far higher standard of understanding and competence in Trust affairs than the Beneficiaries. Because of this, a court presumes that an honest, capable Trustee can easily dispose of all but the Beneficiary's strongest allegations of improper conduct, by access to information and documents not possessed by the Beneficiary.

Should a court decide, despite these considerations, the allegation has merit, it is the Trustees who must prove themselves blameless, not the Beneficiary who

---

[75]   In re the Matter of The Honorable Grant L. Anderson, Pierce County Superior Court, State of Washington, No. 96-2179-F. Item 2. *Law Student Trust Law Hornbook.* [Excerpts from Bogert, *Trusts* (6th Ed., Hornbook Series, Student Edition, West 1987), § 95 entitled "Trustee's Duty of Loyalty":] Body Text, pgs. 341-344.

must prove a tort or criminal act was done. Recall, too, that Trustees are **personally liable for all willful violations of the Trust Indenture.**

Can the Grantor be a Trustee?

The proper application of Trust ethics and administration is intricate. On the surface, it appears that ordinary people can serve as Trustees, and that is true. No one is born a Trustee, and no Bar card, public accounting certificate or MBA can qualify someone who is mentally, ethically or emotionally unsuited for the responsibility. "Ordinary" people, though, must educate themselves and gain experience in how their Trust works. Few formal classes in Trustee training are available, and learning to be a Trustee takes personal study and practice. Sometimes when an Irrevocable Trust is created, the Grantor becomes its General Manager, since he or she is the most familiar with the daily financial affairs. Having the advantage of personal knowledge of the corpus, the Grantor is the logical choice to train Trustees in the mechanics of managing the affairs of the Trust. Any holes in the Trustee's knowledge of Trust administration can be filled by a professional Trust management company, which may also train the Trustees. Oddly, the ability to teach others is not an innate talent all have. Some Trustees need to drag the information from the Grantor by asking a multitude of questions.

The Grantor may assume a Trustee position under the following conditions:

- Once a Trust has been in operation for several years, and has made consistent Beneficiary distributions.

- The ebb and flow of cash and assets have significantly changed the original corpus.

- The Grantor has become thoroughly indoctrinated with Trust procedures.

Even if these criteria are met, should the Grantor become the sole Trustee, he or she may become responsible for the taxes of the trust. The Trust can revert to a Grantor Trust. The exception is, if the Grantor has never taken any funds from the Trust, or if he or she has taken funds, has declared them and paid any taxes due.

As a Cotrustee, the Grantor must continue to keep separate checking and financial accounts for personal expenses and ensure that both personal and Trust accounting procedures are meticulous. A Grantor who has chosen this course cannot ever act as a sole Trustee. He or she should, though, have a least one other Trustee and it is even better if there are two other Trustees. In Chapter 22 Protection and Support, we discuss the court case of Mr. Betts, who successfully became a Trustee of the Trust he set up. You will see the difficulties faced.

Specific Duties of a Trustee

The Trustees handle the Trust's finances and need to have Social Security Numbers which have not been compromised through bankruptcy or liens. If possible, at least one of the Trustees should own property. This proves much to the Trust's advantage when setting up merchant accounts, getting loans, credit cards, etc.

A Grantor, who becomes a General Manager, can be involved in decisions about many or all the items on the following list. To provide solid evidence of substance of transaction and "arm's length distance" (see Glossary), the Trustees, though, must take part in drafting and signing all documents connecting the Trust with the business world at large. Such activities include:

- Opening and closing all financial accounts:
    - savings
    - checking
    - investments
    - credit and debit cards

- ○ merchant accounts (to process customer/client credit cards)
- ○ offshore banking
- Signing/cosigning checks
- Opening accounts for private mailboxes, storage spaces, utilities, etc.
- Signing all leases, contracts or purchase agreements for:
  - ○ equipment, including Trust vehicles
  - ○ property
- Negotiating or joining in negotiations for construction, land development, easements, etc.
- Getting all needed licensing and insurance, such as:
  - ○ vehicle registration
  - ○ property owner's (or renter's) insurance
  - ○ business licenses
  - ○ Employer Identification Number
- Registering all relevant documents about real property with the county recorder
- handling or assisting with tax and legal matters

A well-written Trust Indenture clearly and thoroughly specifies assigned powers of the Trustees and the ones held by the Grantor.

Designing The Organization Structure

The Trustees are bound by the precepts set down in the Trust Indenture, this document contains instructions for setting up and organizing the Trust, a description of officers' responsibilities, limits on their powers, naming the Beneficiaries and directions for managing the assets for them. Working from a draft Indenture, the Grantor specifies his or her particular desires regarding the family's needs, acceptable investments, and generally, sets the tone for the entire Trust organization.

At this point, we must distinguish between a Common-Law Trust and a Statutory Trust.

Common-Law Trust

Once completed, the Indenture may only be expanded but not changed. A majority vote of the Trustees in a fully documented Board meetings may do this.

> Created under the right to contract, the Trust must have a definite end date, although it can be renewed by the Grantor, if alive, or the Beneficiaries.

Created under the right to contract, the Trust must have a definite end date, although it can be renewed by the Grantor, if alive, or the Beneficiaries. It is more likely, though, that because of significant changes in laws and circumstances, the Trust will either be dissolved, or assets will be put into a new Trust where the Indenture is more current.

Statutory Trust

Given that (or if) terms in the Indenture allow changes, they are more likely to happen through addenda. Again, the Grantor would need to expand on what has been set, not change it. Because this is an Irrevocable Trust, the Grantor has given up all control, so any changes must be made with the consent of the Trustees.

The Rule Against Perpetuities (see Glossary) requires all Indentures to set a definite end date when the principal of the Trust will be paid out to the Beneficiaries. Known as the remaindermen, they are usually the third or fourth-generation descendants of the Grantor.

A much more detailed list of information found in the Indenture is included in Volume II.

The Trustees may expand on the Indenture only to complete the Grantor's stated purposes: either to increase the assets for the sake of the Beneficiaries or to further protect them. They may never contradict or ignore the terms of the Indenture. In precisely the same way that laws repugnant to the Constitution are void *ab initio*, added policies which violate the spirit or letter of the Indenture are nullities. The Indenture should include strict rules limiting what may and may not be changed. The Minutes of the meetings or addenda in which revisions are discussed[76] or decided form a legal record of these supplements and may be subpoenaed in any court action challenging the Trustee.

---

[76] The discussion preceding the adoption of amendments to the Indenture can be as important as the amendments themselves, or even more so, since it reveals the Trustees' thought processes. There is a direct parallel here to *legislative history* in public law, i.e., "The background and events, including committee reports, hearings, and floor debates, leading up to enactment of a law. Such history is important to courts when they are required to determine the legislative intent of a particular statute. . . ." [**Legislative intent**: "Such is looked to when court attempts to construe or interpret a statute which is ambiguous or inconsistent."] (*Black's Law Dictionary, 6th*)

Functional and Reliable

Sometimes the only obstacle to setting up an Irrevocable Trust is finding reliable Trustees. Once that step is performed, the rest may be a walk in the park. As you have no doubt inferred by now, the Trustees form the keystone of the arch linking Grantor and Beneficiaries, both of whom hold Trust Certificates.[77] Trustees hold legal title to the assets, managed by them for the sake of all Trust members, including themselves, and defend the Trust before and during any legal challenges. Therefore, they should be (or show strong signs of maturing into) savvy, organized and experienced men and/or women, capable of holding their own in the face of opposition from other Trustees, Beneficiaries, government officials, and, yes, even the Grantor! Above all, of course, they should be *trustworthy*. If that list sounds a little like the Boy Scout or Girl Scout Oath, so be it.

> As mentioned before, Trustees are legally responsible for the assets of the Trust; one or another among them should have a business background, at least some interest in law and a grasp of accounting.

As mentioned before Trustees are legally responsible for the assets of the Trust; one or another among them should have a business background, at least some interest in law and a grasp of accounting. They need not be attorneys, but at least one of them should be willing to find his or her way around a law library, learn the basics of court and banking procedures. The two most important duties are:

- Protecting the assets by holding to a minimum the potential for legal challenges.

---

[77]   We will cover the subject of Trust Certificates more in following chapters and in Volume II.

●   Defending the Trust effectively if a conflict does arise. Of course, they may hire competent lawyers or other professionals if necessary.

Do not worry if you will never discover this blend of Henry and Richard (H&R) Block, Arthur Andersen, Donald Trump, Johnny Cochran, Matlock and Superman among your circle of friends and acquaintances. Remember, thanks to the large body of case law proving the legality of Trusts, few are ever challenged.

At the same time, your search for these individuals should be thorough, reasoned, careful and unemotional (beyond, perhaps, the "emotion" of trust or confidence). For that reason, prepare to create your Trust for the same reason you buy insurance, that is, well *before* the possible events you hope to avoid. Do not wait to start shopping for a Trust and recruiting Trustees after creditors or other troubles are sniffing at your heels or haunting your doorstep. Under pressure, you may make serious errors—such as selecting Trustees whom you later realize are still unqualified and may never be qualified. We do not mean, though, that you should expect to be blessed with someone who is fully prepared from day one; the first year or so of the Trust will be a trial-and-error period for all involved.

Many generations of successful families have refined the structure of the Irrevocable Trust to ensure that Trustees are well motivated to help their Trust Group family become millionaires many times over. Your job is simply to find "a few good men or women" who can both follow the program and understand it well enough to think on their feet when a new situation arises. The longer they work within this proven structure, the more comfortable they will be with it, and the more committed they will be to your combined success.

While it is important you understand the need of finding competent Trustees, in your enthusiasm for finding your collection of Mr. (or Ms.) Wonderfuls, do not overlook the power of training. Just find bright and honest people; a solid Trustee-training program run by a skilled Trust management firm can do the rest. Such a program includes how to prevent audits, lawsuits and seizure of assets. Again, prevention is the key, and it takes the form of reporting accurately and timely required information.

Controlling Your Trustees

There are several ways to keep your Trustees' performance on track while you preserve the "arm's length" (See Glossary) distance from the assets as needed by legal precedent and taxing authorities; the following three are interrelated. First, the Trust Indenture should clearly say that you divest yourself of all legal and equitable interest in the assets (arm's length). Equally clearly, it should spell out your purposes for the use of the assets, and the specific Trustees' duties. Second, you may involve yourself personally in Trust activities, either as Manager or (at least) as a remote (but not too distant) supervisor who needs frequent reporting in enough detail to keep yourself well-informed. Third, educating your Beneficiaries and personally keeping them up-to-date on Trust activities in reference to their potential involvement. This means that if you expect one of your Beneficiaries to eventually become a Trustee or a General manager, he or she should read the Indenture. This encourages them to keep watch over their own interests.

A fourth method, so obvious that it might be overlooked, is your choice of Trustees. Any Indenture, or written contract of any kind, is merely the record of a prior *meeting of the minds* between you and your original Trustees and, ideally, between every member of the Board of Trustees and the Successors. Only in this way can true continuity of your original intent be assured.

> If you create the Trust for your Beneficiaries, then you get to know the Trustees personally.

In a Private Trust, Trustees who stray from the Indenture may be challenged by the Protector. This is a person appointed by the Grantor to oversee the Trust functions, and who has the right to fire Trustees for violation of said Indenture. Volume II gives the details about the Protector.

The Beneficiaries' first recourse is with the Protector. This person stands between the Trust and a court of law, since he or she has the power to resolve issues without litigation.

If you create the Trust for your Beneficiaries, then you get to know the trustees personally. This allows you to give them your instructions about these Heirs Beneficiary, take the time to write the Trust Indenture correctly, and keep an eye on matters as they unfold.

Obviously, it is much easier to state the ideal than to bring it about in the face of a myriad of every-day challenges. Nevertheless, if you as Grantor take care to pass on your spiritual values to your Trustees and children, you will give them irreplaceable essentials of your own soul. This will help them to act as you would in circumstances and times that you cannot now imagine.

Despite there being no law requiring a Trust to have more than one Trustee, two is an ideal minimum (and three even better) for several reasons. Except the obvious benefit of added security for the assets and beneficial distributions, naming two or more Trustees at the beginning saves time, money and loss of control to the state. If you start out with only one, and the Trust Indenture does not provide for adding a second one, appointing a replacement in an emergency or additional ones for convenience may require a trip to court each time. This principle applies equally to Common-Law and Statutory Trusts. With two Trustees, one Trustee can always appoint another.

Trustee Replacement

A Private Trust may lose its Trustees. There may be no Trustees to take their place. This can be because of the following reasons:

- Successors are not available.

- Trust Protector is not functioning to prevent both Trustees from leaving.

- The terms in the Trust Indenture do not allow the Grantor to select other Trustees, or the Grantor has long passed.

If this occurs, there is no place to turn but to a court–and now your Private Trust just changed into a Statutory Trust.

Exchangers

In a Private Trust there is another name for those who exchange assets into the Trust for Trust Capital Units. Identified as "Exchangers," this classification is different from Beneficiaries who have given nothing to start the Trust and who have not contributed to any of the Trust funds. Exchangers are people or organizations, besides the Grantor, who have a reciprocal agreement with the Board of Trustees when they place assets into the Trust. Exchangers are typically family members. The Trust Capital Units received, identified on a Trust Certificate, allow Exchangers to become eligible for distribution with the Beneficiaries. The Grantor becomes an Exchanger when he or she places assets into the Trust.

The Grantor appoints the First Trustee, who in turn appoints the other Trustees and hires the Officers. At least the First Trustee should be unrelated by blood or marriage to any of the Exchangers, although certain specific exceptions to this rule exist. If you have two Trustees, though, the second one may be a member of an Exchanger's family, so long as the first is not. The purpose for this rule is, of course, to preserve the arm's-length distance between each Exchanger and the assets, quashing in advance the possible allegation by anyone unfriendly to the Trust (or Trustees) that an *undue influence* has been exerted on a Trustee to act improperly.

Again, the Trustees are legally responsible for the Trust property, and, if any asset or provision of the Trust is challenged, they *must* handle the matter. If the manager is also the Grantor, he or she needs to become comfortable with the Trustees' being legally responsible. What were formerly his or her private possessions, are no longer personal property.

Trustee Responsibilities and Powers Summarized

- The powers and participation of the Trustees of an Irrevocable Trust are greater than those of Trustees of other Trusts.

- Trustees must not be subordinate to or subject to the control of any other participant in the Trust; therefore, no Trustee should be an employee of the Grantor.[78]

- The Grantor of a Irrevocable Statutory Trust must never have more than a 5% *reversionary interest* in a Trust he or she creates of the Corpus or interest. Do not structure your Statutory Trust to have more than 5 percent ever revert (come back) to you, unless through certain clear exceptions defined in that section. If you do, you will have not only wrecked your Trust, but exposed you and your Trustees to legal sanctions and fines. This rule of Trust structuring is so basic that violating it, even while doing everything else right, will set you up to have the Trust annulled, exposing the Trustees to fines, and the corpus and profits to seizure. Because of the Trust Capital Units in a Private Trust, though, this particular rule does not seem to apply.

---

[78]   See Glossary, Nonadverse Party

Chapter 16

Privacy

In our experience with Trusts, one of the most misunderstood subjects is privacy. We live in a world where if you seek to keep information about yourself and your family private, you are suspected of being a terrorist. This chapter may shock some people, for we have taken a hardline position regarding your right to have privacy, and so some of these ideas may be quite a revelation.

Concern for privacy may not be as stressed in a Statutory Trust. The officers of the Trust may rely on lawyers, who are officers of the court and beholden to that system. New Trustees may also rely on CPAs who may be in a similar situation with the IRS. Banks and other types of large organizations which take the responsibilities of Trusteeship often assign the fiduciary responsibility to a lawyer. In a Private Trust, though, the Trustees are usually more diligent about the privacy of both the members and the investments, and thus can resist efforts of government agencies to delve into Trusts and identities of the Trust group.

Direct Access by the State

A corporation exists through permission of the state in which the corporation is placed. You need a Social Security Number to start a corporation. With double taxation, and the state's having direct access to corporate books,[79] privacy is doubtful.

A sole proprietorship is similar, since the entire business is under the owner's Social Security Number, and all assets can be seized, even if the owner does nothing wrong except unwittingly do business with the incorrigible.

The Right to Say "No"

Because a Private Trust does not exist by permission of the state, without a court order or a search warrant, its books are not open to the state for inspection. Unlike a Statutory Trust where the Beneficiaries are part of the public records, the Beneficiaries in a Common-Law Trust are kept confidential. This is to protect them from unscrupulous individuals who may target them.

Unless you have some knowledge of the law, you cannot understand the value of privacy. It comes from the simple fact that if someone does not know what belongs to you, then he or she cannot know how to get it. Why make yourself a target?

Further, in issues about taxes–without evidence to use against you through voluntary compliance–there is no evidence.

Privacy is an art form, and is most simply stated in the Fourth Amendment of the U.S. Constitution:

> The right of the people to be secure in their persons, houses, papers, and effects, against unreasonable searches and seizures, shall not be violated; and no Warrants shall issue but upon probable cause, supported by Oath

---

[79]   *Braswell v. United States, 487 U.S. 99 (1988); Curcio v. United States*, 354 U.S. 118 (1957

or affirmation, and particularly describing the place to be searched, and the persons or items to be seized.

Privacy is a sacred right, but you need to guard the right to have it. Without appropriate knowledge of how to handle privacy, you may unwittingly give up valuable information to the unscrupulous, aggressors, and unlicensed or unauthorized agents of any organization, including the government.

We can claim that placing assets into an Irrevocable Trust separates it from the original owner, but the assets are still only as safe as the Board of Trustees makes them.

In some Statutory Trusts, the Trustees may be untrained and thus rely on lawyers and CPAs for advice. You can only assume that these counselors are educated in the finer details of Trust law if they have experience dealing with Beneficiary and distribution issues.

A Grantor may, for example, ask his or her lawyer to be a Trustee. If the lawyer is familiar with estate planning and Trusts in general, this is probably a good choice, but just because one is a lawyer, does not make him or her a good Trustee. This is a specialty field, and the legal knowledge is only one part of a much larger picture.

Lawyers can also be compromised if they are Trustees, because as officers of the court, their first priority is to adhere to the wishes of the court. To keep his or her Bar card, the lawyer is beholden to the courts for the ongoing support given, and so may not, in the long run put up a consistent fight to keep the Trust private.

Lawyers can be excellent Trust Protectors, though. This is a subject we will delve into more in Volume II.

In our experience with lawyers with whom we have dealt on Trusts, we found, contrary to what you might expect, they often need as much training as the average person.

Tactical Resistance

Those people who have become members of any Board of Trustees need to be educated about how to handle warrants, investigations and unsolicited inquiries. This may sound scary to you because you have not been properly trained. The more knowledge you have, the better you can handle confrontations. After a while, Trustees become brave when they know the law, the rules, the procedures, and know how to have a conversation with inquisitive agents.

In our society, most people have been trained through the collective educational process (public school, news and entertainment media, etc.) to be naively open about their personal affairs. Fictional and "real TV" portrayals of police search-and-seizure operations show their barging into citizens' homes with little or no reference made by commentators to the Fourth Amendment protection against unauthorized entry into private homes. Because of omitted training about their rights, many people are unaware of the Fourth Amendment and other guards against invasions of privacy. This barrage of misinformation creates oppressed attitudes in the portions of the mind and psyche which should be filled with self-esteem and knowledge of the law.

> **Because of omitted training about their rights, many people are unaware of the Fourth Amendment and other guards against invasions of privacy.**

Like children parading their proud possessions before visitors and bragging about their accomplishments, too many adults flaunt their assets or discuss them openly with friends and other family members not involved in business with them. In general, people are too willing to share what should be kept confidential. These two beliefs, that one *should* and *must* be open about private business, are common among the American public at the moment. They create mental tendencies which make training a new Trust Officer to keep the records and documents private one of the toughest aspects of teaching him or her to perform Trustee duties competently in an Irrevocable Common-Law Trust.

Should you have some doubt about our claims that lawyers are beholden to the courts, you will find the below excerpt from the *Corpus Juris Secundum (CJS)*, most enlightening. This is from one of the most respected compendiums of American law and states:

> Thus, an attorney occupies a dual position which imposes dual obligations. His first duty is to the courts and the public, not to the client, and wherever the duties to his or her client conflict with those he owes as an officer of the court in the administration of justice, the former must yield to the latter.[80]

If you took offense to our characterizing as children those adults who make a show of their riches, you will not feel much better about how lawyers are trained to view their clients. The *CJS* goes on to say,

> A client is one who applies to a lawyer or counselor for advice and direction in a question of law, or commits his cause to his management in prosecuting a claim or defending against a suit in a court of justice; one who retains the attorney, is responsible to him for his fees, and to whom the attorney is responsible for the management of the suit; one who communicates facts to an attorney expecting professional advice. Clients are also called "wards of the court" *in regard to their relationship with their attorneys.*[81] (Emphasis added.)

Who are wards of the court? According to the most popular legal dictionary now in use by American lawyers, they are "infants and persons of unsound mind placed by the court under the care of a guardian!"[82]

---

[80]   Arnold O. Ginnow and George Gordon, *Corpus Juris Secundum, Complete Restatement of the Entire American Law*, West Law Publishing, Volume 7, §4 (1980).

[81]   Ibid., Volume 7, §4, paragraph 2.

[82]   *Black's Law Dictionary, Fifth Edition.*

Attorneys depend on the courts for their livelihood, and, let us face it, courts are run by judges, all of whom must be members of the Bar. Like anyone else whose "right" to work depends on having a license, a lawyer fears losing the support of his or her professional or trade association. Disbarred, a lawyer cannot present arguments before a judge other than for himself or herself. Like other licensed professionals, lawyers can lose their standing not only for mal-practice but also for failing to bend to the will of the particular organization to which they belong or for becoming an embarrassment to it.[83] This is why, when purchasing an Irrevocable Trust, you should decide what level of security you want, how high a priority you place on it, and how much you are willing and able to manage your own affairs.

Lawyers As Trustees, a Plus

On the other hand, having lawyers as your Trustees has its attractive side. There is the obvious benefit of installing them in the driver's seat while you sit back and enjoy the ride. They can create all the documents you will need, hire a CPA, get any needed licenses from state and local agencies, and open accounts at a local bank while you play golf, fly to Hawaii or tend your roses. Besides, a law firm will probably have more credibility when interfacing with these other corporate entities than your best friend, Howard, or your college room-mate, Grace. The lawyers' familiarity with legal procedures could so make your setup faster and smoother.

> Do not assume that because someone belongs to the Bar, he or she knows how to be a Trustee.

---

[83] As a close parallel, most state dental associations currently have the power to pull the licenses of fully competent dentists whose consciences compel them to warn their patients that so-called "silver" or "amalgam" dental fillings actually consist of more than 50% highly toxic mercury by weight. Such fillings are banned outright in Sweden.

Do not assume that because someone belongs to the Bar, he or she knows how to be a Trustee. There is still a steep learning curve, and in our experience, the average lawyer's attitude prevents humble learning of basic paperwork and other administration skills.

As the assets in a Trust multiply, the professions (if any) in which your Trustees practice may not matter much. If the cash flow produced is enough, they may surrender their licenses to practice law in favor of loyalty to their new slush fund–the assets held for the Beneficiaries.

Howard or Grace, though, might turn out to be far more diligent as Trustees than licensed professionals. These friends are likely to have more personal interest, not just in the revenues which the Trust can create, but also in you and your family.

Speaking of revenues, the fees your Trust can pay the Trustees in its early stages may look like peanuts to lawyers, inadequate to hold their attention. On the other hand, it could be important money to Howard and Grace, further securing their loyalty to you and the growth of the Trust.

Of course, a key reason in your deciding whether to hire a trusted friend or a stranger who happens to be a professional is defining precisely what Trust procedures you want established. Individuals steeped in "the system" will be an advantage mainly if you intend to create a Statutory Trust; usually, their greatest strengths lie in their knowledge of that world.

No matter whom you choose to keep your assets safe, you should directly involve yourself in the administration. There is simply no substitute for keeping your hands on the operations in the early months and years. The downside of this, is your inability to let go. If you cannot delegate and teach others, it may be best that you remain distant from daily operations.

After you place assets in a Trust, you do not own them anymore; the Trustees do. Since, presumably, you are not a Trustee, you have no duty to disclose anything, except under certain limited circumstances. The Trustees are the only ones who know anything of the assets held by the estate. *You graduate to the sublime state of blissful ignorance and overjoyed poverty.*

To help you gain confidence that your privacy can be increased by the proper use of a Trust, consider the implications of the following opinion of the U.S. Supreme Court, handed down in *Hale v. Henkel*:

> "Power to contract is unlimited, and the Citizen may refuse to open his books to the State."[84]

This ruling applies to all contracts, including Trusts. A corporation, on the other hand, is not a contract but rather, a licensing agreement between the citizen and the state. Corporate officers may be powerless to resist demands to open their books from taxing and other government agencies.

Again to quote Mr. Halliday, a Trustee of a Common-Law Trust:

> We live in the information age. Information, that used to be confidential and private, is readily available on almost every aspect of a person's life. Privacy becomes an increasing problem. Trusts traditionally enjoy a protected status around privacy. Often Times (sic), Trust records are difficult, if not impossible, to subpoena.

> In 1995, I followed a court case in Hawaii between the IRS and the owner of a car dealership. The individual's business and family financial holdings had previously been organized into Trust. The Trust was refusing to surrender financial records based on the precedent that Trust records are private and surrendering them could compromise the Trust and risk the interests of the Beneficiaries. The defense attorneys had done notable preparation and presented various court cases that substantiated the privacy of Trust records . . .

> . . . The end result was that the IRS failed to find any fraudulent intent. The judge ruled in favor of the Trust, the Trust's privacy was maintained and the case was dismissed. The case was subsequently appealed to the

---

[84]   *Hale v. Henkel*, 201 U.S. 43, 74 (1905).

Ninth Circuit Court of Appeals and again, the privacy of the Trust was upheld . ."[85]

J. Paul Getty

Further, we can take a good lesson from J. Paul Getty, who knew well the value of privacy. In *The Rich and the Super-Rich*, Frederick Lundberg noted Getty's penchant for privacy:

Getty's entire life has been subdued in pitch. He went to school quietly—first to the University of Southern California, later to the University of California, and, then, to Oxford. He traveled the world quietly, went into business with his father quietly, and later bought large amounts of stock very cheaply—and quietly. He married quietly seven times and as quietly divorced, with no hint of scandal . . .[86]

The Rockefeller Foundation

John D. Rockefeller, arguably the richest man in America at one time, if not in the world, had five sons and one daughter. To this day, exactly how much money his children inherited remains a mystery to the rest of society. The information has been vigilantly guarded since their birth. In fact, none of the terms of the Trusts established for them by their father has ever been revealed, and even the names of the Trustees are known only to the family and a few key advisers.[87]

---

[85]   Halliday, Glen, *AntiShyster News Magazine,* "The Truth About Trusts," Volume 7, No. 1.

[86]   Lundberg, Ferdinand, *The Rich and The Super-Rich*, Lyle Stuart, Inc., New York, NY, p.50

[87]   Lundberg, Ibid., p. 594

Handling Privacy and Challenges To It

Here is a FAQ from a web site: "Who can see the Trust documents?" The answer offered is, "Anyone can see them if you want him to."

In a true Irrevocable Common-Law Trust, though, **no one** may see the documents without the express permission of the Board of Trustees. In fact, before reading them, anyone else should sign a sophisticated nondisclosure agreement or some oath of privacy. After all, is not privacy one reason you want a Trust in the first place?

That sounds good, but remember the important element of training. To handle privacy matters correctly, you and your Trustees must eventually become educated in Trust administration. For example, how should you behave when staring down the barrel of a loaded search warrant? How do Trustees handle inquiries by government or IRS agents? Without a mentor to teach you such basics of Trust privacy, you are likely to make critical blunders. Fending off agents schooled in intimidation techniques is a high art. Without a few basic pointers, the average person will cave in to their stubborn, derogatory attitudes. So, before you plunk down your cash for any Trust, get informed and get smart. With a few ounces of education about what Trusts *are* and the differences between a scam and a real McCoy, you will be amazed at how easily you can bypass the one and pick the other.

Cayman Islands Lifts Veil of Bank Secrecy[88]

Often a favorite place for offshore Trusts and offshore banking, the Cayman Islands once provided a secure place to put money. This was mentioned earlier, but now it is time to provide specific details on how the changes affect individuals. We quote:

---

[88]   *Los Angeles Times*, "Cayman Islands Lifts Veil of Bank Secrecy," August 25, 1999

. . . In a stunning break from tradition, Cayman authorities have turned over records showing that Kenneth H. Taves of Malibu, who is accused of improperly billing up to 900,000 credit card holders, transferred $25.3 million in allegedly illegal profits since mid-1997 to Euro Bank Corp. on Grand Cayman . . .

Although the Cayman government has agreed to release confidential bank information for use in U.S. criminal investigations under a 1990 treaty, it does so only if the offense is a crime as defined by the laws of both countries.

Until three years ago, there were no criminal penalties for Cayman bank officers who covered up money laundering. And because the Cayman Islands has no direct taxation, it doesn't deem tax evasion a crime.

Dead Giveaways

Although we said a great deal about privacy, we also recently discovered the words you choose, and the way you type on a keyboard, gives others a clue to your identity. Despite encryption, you can be tracked and identified to 70% accuracy just by how you express yourself. During Black Hat Briefings in Las Vegas, Dr. Neal Krawetz of Hacker Factor Solutions demonstrated how he and others use nonclassical digital forensics . . . analyzing the words used or the keyboard characters typed . . .[89]

This latest forensic discovery underscores how on top of privacy we must be to prevent unwarranted intrusions into our lives.

---

[89]   Robert Vamosi, *Security Watch*: "The Myth of Online Anonymity," posted on Battlefront.com General Discussion Forum, October 10, 2006, www.battlefront.com

The Silver Spoon Curse

Why is it so necessary to protect the Beneficiaries? Because con artists go through county records to discover them. Now, they can be targeted. For those who come from millions, there is a great effort to obscure any large amounts to which the heirs have access. This ensures the Beneficiaries cannot be readily discovered and the information about their fortune is unavailable.

Chapter 17

Common-Law Trust

R eferred to in previous chapters, but not thoroughly explained, is the Common-Law Trust. Among some groups, organizations and the legal profession, this Trust is the "bad" guy on the block.

No matter how much we tell you a Common-Law Trust is marvelous, there are pitfalls. We address these more in the last chapter of this book.

Our so-called freedom is threatened by bullies. Whoever owns the gold, owns the world. When you think of domination and control, think Common-Law Trust, and like the King of the Mountain children's game, the King will not let you climb to the top. He takes away the ladder. We are here to restore at least some of it. An outline of the Indenture and other agreements are found in Volume II.

What Is a Common-Law Trust?

All Trusts are contractual agreements between three parties: the Grantor and Trustees for the benefit of a third party, the Beneficiary. As mentioned before, a contractual agreement is known as a Declaration of Trust or a Trust Indenture. This carefully detailed agreement establishes the wishes of the Trust creator and his or her instructions to a Trustee or Trustees about the welfare of the Beneficiaries. Without this initial agreement, there is no Trust.

The Common-Law Trust is an Irrevocable Private Trust, and the Beneficiaries hold Certificates representing a portion of their interest in the Trust. A Statutory Trust, though, has no Certificates. The sophisticated nature of Certificates involves skilled administration since they are legal financial instruments. Volume II provides their details of use and application.

An Irrevocable Trust scares many people, who shy away from further investigation. It is necessary to set it up correctly. Otherwise, you may find yourself in trouble with taxing agencies or other people who do not have the Trust Grantor's best interests in mind.

As in all other Trusts, the Indenture sets up the authority. The Trustee gains the power to take assets given to him or her by the Trust Grantor and manage them for the benefit of the Beneficiaries. This means the Trust Grantor transfers assets to the Trustee, and the Trustee then holds them in the name of the Trust.

The Trustees sign the Trust checks. The investment and other financial accounts are opened by the Trustees, and the financial responsibility of the Trust belongs to the Trustees, not the Trust Grantor. Up to this point, the Common-Law Trust is the same as a Statutory Trust.

> The agreement between the Trust Grantor and Trustees forms the Trust and empowers a family through its vested interest, to continue the Trust.

The agreement between the Trust Grantor and Trustees forms the Trust and empowers a family through its vested interest, to continue the Trust. Also, personal expenses, paid with after-tax dollars, may now become pretax business expenses–a writeoff to the Trust that is in the business of managing family assets. This is handled through proper accounting procedures. You can infer from just this tidbit of information there can be many advantages to turning your family into the family business.

Although the Grantor, with the Trustees can take part in running the Common-Law Trust, with this opportunity comes the responsibility of learning the intricacies of Trust administration. The Private Trust is more complex than a Statutory Trust, and is not for everyone

Why This Type of Trust?

So what makes the Irrevocable Common-Law Trust so different? Perhaps, it is the independence of the family, the members of which have taken responsibility for their own destiny, or maybe it is the right to privacy which allows a group to bond. After all, shared secrets, such as how the cash flow is created, can make people more committed. Through Trust Capital Units, each member of the family has a vested interest in achieving family success. This encourages people to want to participate.

Trusts in the Media

Used among the rich and famous, Private Trusts are sometimes addressed in published articles. Because the average person is so unfamiliar with the inner workings of a Trust, the statements about benefits gained are often vague. Here are some of the comments made in various publications:

> "Henry Ford II left the bulk of his fortune, estimated at $250 million, to a Private Trust whose Beneficiaries are unnamed according to his will . . ."

> *The New York Times*, Wednesday, October 7, 1987

> "Upon the death of Mayor Richard Daley of Chicago, Illinois, it was learned that much of his assets were put into Family Trusts after a

1974 stroke. That would put most of his holdings in the hands of his wife or seven children with <u>no public disclosure!</u>"

Combined Wire Services, Chicago Tribune

"Mesabi Iron Company received a ruling from the Commissioner of the IRS allowing it to transfer some of its assets into Trusts so they would <u>not be taxed as corporations.</u> The effect of the ruling is the Trusts themselves were nontaxable."

Wall Street Journal, March 13, 1961

"Rupert Murdoch transferred Boston TV Station WFXT into an independent Trust to <u>avoid cross-ownership laws</u> that would have put the TV station at risk."

Wall Street Journal

<u>Probate Examples Without The Use of Trusts</u>

Mr. A. Deeds, Chairman, NCR, of Dayton, Ohio, gross estate of $13,312,905.00. Total cost and taxes at time of death, $7,902,005, reducing his estate by 58%!

Albert H. Wiggin, retired Chairman, Chase National Bank of New York City, New York, gross estate of $20,493,990.00. Total cost and taxes at time of death, $14,865,310.00, reducing his estate by 72%!

Additional Examples of the Power of Trusts

Ronald Reagan established the "Ronald Reagan Trust" in 1966 enabling him to <u>receive sizable tax advantages.</u> In some years, Mr. Reagan paid no taxes at all while at the same time maintaining a magnificent lifestyle.

H. L. Hunt, the Texas oil billionaire, is reported to have paid $75,000 for the setting up of the first Hunt Family Pure Trust. Today, it is estimated the family uses <u>200 or more Trusts,</u> and we can only guess how many millions this represents.

Joseph Kennedy, father of John F. Kennedy, used many Common-Law Trusts for his family and various businesses still in existence today.

Substance of Transaction

Two important reasons decide whether a Trust deserves classification as a genuine Trust: (a) structure and language of the Trust Indenture and (b) substance of transaction. Again, what counts is not the name, but the operation of the organization; is it being *run* as a Trust—or as a corporation, sole proprietorship, etc.?[90]

Speaking of names, even within Common-Law Trusts, there are dozens of minor variations on the basic pattern, each known by a different name to distinguish it from its near relatives. To keep it simple as you learn your way around, however, just remember: if it looks like a duck and walks like a duck . . ."[91]

Many common Trust elements create a legally set Common-Law Trust Indenture. The private nature of this contract between the Grantor and the Trustees gives the Grantor a broad range of possibilities that are not available through the Statutory Trust.

Before we go too much into the parts and details of a Common-Law Trust, we will give you some of the many and varied types of Trusts within this category.

The Massachusetts Trust

As mentioned before, this Trust originated in the Massachusetts Commonwealth during the colonial era. This is a Business Trust in which a business or (originally) real estate is "vested with" (that is, entrusted to) Trustees who manage it for the owners of the beneficial (equitable) interest (the Beneficiaries). Although Trusts existed for thousands of years when Europeans emi-

---

[90]   Designation of form of trust is not controlling; court will look to substance of circumstances and not labels placed on them by parties, *Johnson v. Hychyk*, 517 P.2d 1079.

[91]   There are, coincidentally, also dozens of types of *ducks*, classified by ornithologists, appropriately enough, into "tribes."

grated to America, the colonists of Massachusetts were the first to provide Certificates of Capital Interest to individuals who placed their assets into the Trust. This practice is used in all Trusts based in Common-Law.

Courts defined the Massachusetts Trust as

> (a) business organization wherein property is conveyed to Trustees and managed for benefit of holders of Certificates like corporate stock Certificates."[92] They defined a "Massachusetts Business Trust" as "an unincorporated association organized under Massachusetts law for purpose of investing in real estate in much the same manner as a mutual fund invests in corporate securities.[93]

Under the heading "Trust estates as business companies," *Black's Law Dictionary* states:

> A practice originating in Massachusetts of vesting a business or certain real estate in a group of Trustees, who manage it for the benefit of the beneficial owners; the ownership of the latter is evidenced by negotiable (or transferable) shares. The Trustees are elected by the shareholders, or, in case of vacancy, by the Board of Trustees. Provision is made in the agreement and Declaration of Trust to the effect that when new Trustees are elected, the Trust estate shall vest in them without further conveyance. The Declaration of Trust specifies the powers of Trustees. They have a common seal; the Board is organized with the usual officers of a Board of Trustees; it is governed by by-laws; the officers have the usual powers like corporate officers; so far as practicable, the Trustees in their collective capacity, are to carry on the business under a specified name. The Trustees may also hold shares as Beneficiaries. Provision may be made for the alteration or amendment of the agreement or declaration in a speci-

---

[92]   *Enochs & Flowers v. Roell*, 170 Miss. 44, 154 So. 299 (cited in *Black's Law Dictionary, Fourth Edition*).

[93]   *Kusner v. First Pa. Corp.*, D.C.Pa., 395 F.Supp. 276, 281 (cited in *Black's Law Dictionary, Sixth Edition*).

fied manner. In *Eliot v. Freeman*,[94] it was held that such a Trust was **not within the corporation tax provision** of the tariff act of Aug. 5, 1909. See also *Zonne v. Minneapolis Syndicate* [citation omitted]. See also Massachusetts Trust."[95] (Emphasis added.)

Other Business Trusts

The definition of a Business Trust has been clarified in the court case of *Berry v. McCourt*.[96] Here it states that if a business is put into a Trust by a Grantor and there are Beneficiaries who did not also contribute to the original corpus, then a Trust has been created. If a business has been put into a Trust by partners, and each contributed his or her own funds, then it is not a Trust, it is a partnership.

As noted earlier, Business Trusts have been defined as "entities which provide a medium for the conduct of business and the sharing of its gains . . . operating under a written instrument or Declaration of Trust . . ."[97] Such a broad definition grants Trusts much leeway, but it also confuses newcomers.

The Massachusetts Trust is so well-known that it has become nearly synonymous with the term "Business Trust". Yet, it is no longer necessarily the Business Trust of choice, and under our definitions it could be an Unincorporated Business Organization more than it is a Business Trust; read further for greater detail.

While all Business Trusts contain one or more business entities which they hold or govern, certain others evolved for different uses. Other major categories of Business Trusts include: Unincorporated Business Organizations (or

---

[94]   220 U.S. 178, 31 S.Ct. 360, 55 L.Ed. 424. (1911)

[95]   *Black's Law Dictionary, 6th Ed.*

[96]   *Berry v. McCourt* (204 N.E.2d 235)

[97]   *Denmark Cheese Association v. Hazard Advertising Co.*, 59 Misc. 2d. 182.

"UBOs"), Management Trusts and just plain old "Business Trusts" of various descriptions.

Management Trusts manage investments held by other Trusts. They hire managers to run the other Trusts or businesses.

Many Trustees of Business Trusts decide to get Employer Identification Numbers (EINs) to ease their movement through commerce. Although this procedure is not mandatory, we recommend it to make operations easier. Without it, it becomes difficult to use a Trust. For instance, it will not be possible to open a U.S. bank account without an EIN.

Unincorporated Business Organization (UBO)[98]

The Trust that is the most misunderstood is the UBO. It is more similar to a partnership than a Trust, as it may or may not involve the family members.

The UBO is set up when Trustees are in place and the Grantor funds it. That is, he or she gives the assets to Trustees, who open bank accounts in the name of the UBO.

A true UBO occurs when the Grantor has funds to invest and requests others to add funds to the UBO; in both cases the Trustees issue Trust Capital Units These are similar to shares in a corporation, but they do not have voting rights. The Grantor shares control with other Trustees.

The remaining investors become the TCU holders, known as the Beneficiaries. In the UBO, it is more likely the Grantor, who has the greatest vested interest, continues to run the organization with other Trustees. If the Grantor is investment savvy, he or she makes investment decisions with the other Trustees.

The percentage of the Trust Capital Units held by the investors determines the percentage of profits at the end of the year. The investors are responsible for any taxes due for funds received. The only difference between a Trust and a

---

[98]   John H. Sears, *Trust Estates as Business Companies*, Vernon Law Book Company, Kansas City, MO, 1921. Reprinted by Lawbook Exchange Ltd., Union, New Jersey, 1999.

partnership is the UBO has no Beneficiaries who did not contribute to its set up. Otherwise, it is the same as a Trust. For example, it is handled through a Board of Trustees which holds the funds in the name of the Trust, and those who put funds into the Trust have only beneficial Interest. This means they have no legal claim on the funds in the Trust, and are subject to the distribution determined by the Board of Trustees. Therefore, any lawsuits against the Trust are only against the Trust, not against the Beneficiaries, who were the original investors. The Beneficiaries are affected adversely should the UBO either lose money through investment complications or by legal challenges, because their distribution will be less.

There have been some advertisements about UBO's that list a notable amount of advantages. Here is a discussion about these claims.

- **There is no yearly fee.**
    - ○ This is mistaken because Trustees must have a vested interest. That is, they are financially affected should the Trust gain or lose. They receive, at the least, payment either based on the number of Trust Capital Units they hold, or on a percentage of distribution.

- **Limited Liability.**
    - ○ This is true for the investors, not necessarily true for the Trustees who are responsible for the funds in the UBO.
    - ○ Although the Trustees are not personally liable if they adhere to the strictures within the Trust Indenture, they are legally responsible as a Trust group for the investments.

- **Privacy: All officers or Members of the Board of Trustees do not have to be revealed.**
    - ○ This is true occasionally. It depends on the investments. For instance, before a Trust can invest with a stock brokerage firm, all Board members involved with the transactions are identified.

- ○ Information needed includes Social Security Numbers. Other types of investments may not need disclosure the Board of Trustees.

- **Your financial records are private under Common-Law and require notification and a court order to be seen.**

  - ○ This is true, but in reality, as you have seen through many television programs, the law enforcement agencies use pressure. Privacy is only as strong as the ability of the Trustees to say "No".

  - ○ If the Trustees cave in, there is no privacy. This is why it is so important that Trustees be trained in legal, accounting and administration procedures.

- **Privacy in personal and business dealings.**

  - ○ How savvy your Trustees are determines how well they can get around many of the challenges where facts about the UBO are requested.

- **Greater control over what you acquired and accomplished.**

  - ○ This is false. Surrendering assets gives control to the Board of Trustees. Only then will the UBO qualify as a legal organization under the current laws. The only control held by the Grantor lies in the power to determine distribution and investments.

  - ○ A couple of the other controls that could be retained by the Grantor are to allocate between corpus and income, and to distribute corpus.[99]

- **Reduced exposure from lawsuits and claims of adverse parties.**

  - ○ This is true.

---

[99]   IRC §674(b)(8) and §674 (b)(5)(A), respectively.

- **Reduced liability when owning and operating a high-risk asset or performing high-risk professional services, thereby saving money on high-priced insurance premiums.**

  - This can be true if the UBO is set up correctly. It is best, though, to put high-risk services or equipment into a separate Trust.

  - Lease large equipment, instead of owning it.

  - Excess funds earned by a high-risk business should be put into a separate legal entity, preferably another Asset Holding Trust.

- **Increased profits by reducing business costs.**

  - This can be true; it depends on the sophistication of the accounting protocols and Board of Trustees.

- **Flexibility and creativity in personal and business planning.**

  - This is dependent on the abilities of people involved in the Board of Trustee as well as the terms of the Indenture.

- **Simplicity of doing business in this increasingly complex society; including buying and selling big-ticket capital assets, businesses and real estate.**

  - We cannot say it is simpler; we can say it is more private.

- **Preserve and distribute assets at your sole discretion.**

  - This is only applicable to the desire and will of the Trustees, who may or may not accede to the will of the Grantor, and to the terms of the Trust Indenture. A well-trained adverse Trustee will not always agree with the Grantor's wishes.

- **Avoid probate and eliminate death taxes.**

  ○ This is only true if the Trust administration handled all legal documents correctly and has investments in the name of the Trust.

- **Reduce or avoid federal and state income or franchise taxes.**

  ○ The Trust does not avoid taxes. It uses passthrough accounting to shift the tax burden to the Beneficiaries.

  ○ This may lessen the overall tax depending on the tax brackets of the Beneficiaries.

- **The Trust may develop its own credit and investment program to provide security and protections for the Beneficiaries at retirement.**

  ○ This is true. The problem, though, is that most financial institutions attach only to a person with a credit rating. They accept a corporation as a person, but most of them do not accept a Trust.

  ○ To set up a credit history, the Trust assets are usually in the millions.

Business Trust Considerations

The IRS has taken a position there is no such thing as a Business Trust. Suspicious of the name, it seeks to destroy this business organization when it can. Their challenges are based on the strategy of proving there is no *Substance of Transaction*.

After a good amount of experience, we agree with the IRS's reasoning. Usually, a Trust is not a good place for sole proprietorships. This is because the engine that drives the business is usually the Grantor. Without this motivated person, the Trust ceases to have a cash flow. Whether or not the Grantor signs his or her name on checks and legal documents, the Grantor holds the Trustees hostage because the Grantor is the sole source of funds. This is the same as a Grantor Trust, as he or she controls the cash flow.

Substance of Transaction applies here, because within a Trust, the Trustees need to be in control of the funds. Trustees cannot be held to the will of the Grantor. We recommend that if a business is exchanged into the Trust, it be changed to a partnership, making the Trust a partner and recipient of a percentage of the cash flow. This allows the business owner to reign over his or her domain, and a cash flow goes directly to those who work for him or her while the Trust reaps a large percentage of the increase. The business pays its taxes accordingly, and the Trust can pass through the profits to Beneficiaries.

Trusts and Partnerships: Business Conduct

Trusts and partnerships need to create a separate stream of income which cannot be attributed to a sole individual.

In a Trust, most of the funds created need to be through income-producing investments. This includes investments in promissory notes, joint ventures, rent collection, and stock portfolios.

The partnership usually produces goods or a service. If only one partner is paid, then it is not a partnership, and if the accounting methods do not support a partnership, then it is a sole proprietorship.

> ***Substance of Transaction*** applies here, because within a Trust, the Trustees need to be in control of the funds. Trustees cannot be held to the will of the Grantor.

For a partnership, the agreement cannot specify that only family members may participate because it can then be judged as a Testamentary substitute— which means funds go into Probate Court to be distributed. If only family members are involved, it should be a Trust, not a partnership.

> For a partnership, the agreement cannot specify that only family members may participate because it can then be judged as a Testamentary substitute—which means funds go into Probate Court to be distributed.

In a partnership, all partners need to receive a distribution. In a Trust, though, while the Grantor is alive, distribution can be at his or her discretion. If most of the distribution, though, is given to the Grantor, the Trust will be treated as a sole proprietorship for tax purposes.

In a partnership, there needs to be a provision for continuation of management. If not named in the agreement, then the partnership can be disqualified. In a Trust, there also need to be provisions for Successor Trustees.[100]

Summary

If setting up a Trust or a partnership, you need to have nontax reasons for forming either organization. In other words, you will need to think of others to make it work. If a Trust, it must be set up for the benefit of the Beneficiaries, and although the tax savings may be the hidden motive, keep it to yourself. You only want what is best for the Beneficiaries, nothing else. The benefits to you will happen without question.

---

[100] Bruce Givner, *Los Angeles Daily Journal* "Court Refines Formula for Family Limited Partnerships," Focus section, May 3, 2005.

Other Trusts

The Holding Trust or Pure Trust

This most basic, bare-bones Trust is established on the format we have already seen. It has an agreement (contract) whereby one party (Trustee) promises to hold assets granted to him or her by a second party (Grantor) for the benefit of a third (Beneficiary). While we have mainly been considering active, dynamic enterprises, in this case the keyword is *hold*. A "Pure" Trust is a static entity, not engaging in business beyond, perhaps, receiving and distributing interest which accrues to it from the assets. It is Irrevocable and should **not** have an EIN. The most common static asset is residential property. If rented, the Management Trust or another business entity so appointed handles transactions through a management agreement. Of course, as with any other distribution, taxes may be due on any funds distributed as profit.

> A "Pure" Trust is a static entity, not engaging in business beyond, perhaps, receiving and distributing interest which accrues to it from the assets.

The Asset Holding Trust also is based on Trust Capital Units and issues certificates to the Beneficiaries and Officers of the Trust. For Trusts to remain separate, the Beneficiaries or combinations of Beneficiaries must be different in each Trust.

Statutory and Common-Law Trust Differences

The process through which Beneficiaries are served by one of these is different from the other. When there are conflicts and confusion within a Statutory Trust, we are sometimes consulted to provide choices. As a result, we get to see how various "Brand X" Trusts work. So, here are some of the differences and what they mean to both the Trust Grantor and the Beneficiaries.

Trustee Motivation

Of the Irrevocable Statutory Trusts that we have come across, few have an adverse Trustee who had "substantial adverse interest"[101]. They have a Trustee getting a percentage of distributable income or an annual fee. This fails to motivate the Trustee to take particular interest in aggressively increasing the Trust assets for the welfare of the Beneficiaries'. Instead, the Trustee takes a percentage of the distribution, year after year, enough to be satisfied. For example, corporate bankers who become Trustees are not considered Trustees with "substantial adverse interest."[102] They have their set percentage and do make some investment moves to increase the assets, but they do not take advantage of reasonable ventures where the earnings could be substantial.

Grantor's Control

Also, we have seen where the Grantor of a Statutory Trust has not preserved his or her involvement in the Trust administration, as allowed by the Internal Revenue Code.[103] What we see, instead, is that many professionals have taken over investing funds for the Beneficiaries, and, fearing to lose money, or lacking any particular interest in multiplying the funds, have been too cautious. If the Grantor remained as an adviser, or kept the power to control where the money

---

[101]   The Trustee holds a large percentage of the corpus of the Trust.

[102]   *Morton vs. Commissioner of Internal Revenue*, 109 F2nd 47, Jan. 9, 1940.

[103]   IRC §674(b)(3)

would be invested, the fiduciary would be relieved of that risk-taking responsibility. To the one who sets up the Trust, this risk-taking is a necessary part of multiplying the assets, and the Grantor might be skilled in this aspect of asset accumulation.

Trustee's Personal Interest

The Statutory Trustee, who might be a stranger to the Beneficiaries and, sometimes, to the Grantor, ensures accounting and legalities are in order, and is not involved with the personal interests of the Beneficiaries. Usually, little or no communication exists between the provider and the receiver of funds, so the Beneficiaries do not have the advantage of a mentor. Wisdom passed on to the Beneficiaries from the Grantor is lost, as is the family history, which can be well kept in the Private Trust.

High Taxes and Distribution

Sometimes Trustees are unaware of the advantages the Trust has in giving out income to the Beneficiaries. We have had telephone calls about the excessively high taxes a Trust must pay. The callers fail to understand the lawmakers do not expect a Trust to keep all the money it earns, but to share it. Further, the callers or Trustees have little concern about how much tax the Beneficiary must pay, only that the Trust should not pay the tax. While there are many ways to make a distribution without overburdening the Beneficiary with taxes, this is sometimes not the Trustees' focus.

Alternatively, the Beneficiary can pay taxes on funds not received so the Trustees may reinvest the funds for long-term greater gain. This is legal and addressed in the IRS Publication 17:[104]

> **Estate and trust income**. An estate or trust, unlike a partnership, may have to pay federal income tax. If you are a beneficiary of an estate or

---

[104] *Your Federal Income Tax for Individuals,* Publication 17, Catalog Number 10311G, Part Two, Income, Other Income.

trust, you may be taxed on your share of the income shared or required to be shared to you. However, there is never a double tax. . . .

Current income required to be distributed. If you are the beneficiary of a trust that must distribute all of its current income, you must report your share of the distributable net income, whether or not you have actually received it.

Current income not required to be distributed. If you are the beneficiary of an estate or trust and the fiduciary has the choice of whether to distribute all or part of the current income, you must report:

1) All income that is required to be distributed to you, whether or not it is actually distributed, plus

2) All other amounts actually paid or credited to you

up to the amount of your share of distributable net income.

Conversion of Assets

The statutory system usually provides for only an income account, and possibly some property that yields a monthly or quarterly cash flow. Other assets which the Beneficiaries could use, such as a family home, are often quickly converted to cash and invested, either on the death of the Grantor or when the Trust is set up. This scenario could apply to a private Common-Law Trust, but it is not needed as it is with a Statutory Trust. Statutory Trusts cannot hold a private business, and, if one is left by the death of a Grantor, it is immediately sold to reinvest the funds or make a cash distribution. In a Common-Law Trust, though, the business can be carried on by the children of the Grantor, or converted to cash—but why convert a profitable business into cash?

Provided the original Grantor left it in Trust to the children, or is not primarily involved, the Common-Law Trust can keep a business

The Grantor's Share

In the Common-Law Trust, the Grantor holds Trust Capital Units, which represent a percentage of the corpus of the Trust, and receives a pro rata share of the profits. In a Statutory Trust, the Grantor surrenders ownership, and may be unable to get extra funds if needed. In a Common-Law Trust, the Trustees may allow the Grantor to cash in some Trust Capital Units or may give him more funds through a loan, or a quarterly distribution of the cash flow, if the Trust Indenture allows. This entire area has been grayed out by current IRS policies, and CPAs have few to no guidelines.

Why A Common-Law Trust? Personal Advantages

Asset Protection

If thieves and other types of con artists do not know where and what the assets are, then they are not inclined to scheme to get them. One of the many reasons to put assets in a Trust is to be invisible on paper. Should the government or others want to take what they think you have, they cannot find it because it is not in your name, and not yours anymore. A Common-Law Trust is designed to allow the Grantor to live any life style he or she wants, and to take the necessary risks in life without the worry of having assets seized.

Inheritance

We have all heard the stories of how someone's relative passed on and the lawyers and taxes devoured almost all the estate before the inheritors got their portion. If any Irrevocable Trust is managed correctly, then death does not cause a change of ownership. The ownership of the assets is in the name of the Trust, and in the Common-Law Trust they can effectively be perpetual through the renewal of the contract.[105] Therefore, if mother dies and her assets are in

---

[105]   The "Remoteness of Vesting," or the Rule Against Perpetuities used in Statutory Trusts does not apply, as the Common-Law Trust is a viable contract with an end date of 25 years or less. A detailed discussion regarding this point is given in Volume II; also see Mega Trust or Dynasty Trust which has gotten around the Rule Against Perpetuities, Appendix E.

Trust, the assets remain in Trust and can be used by the Beneficiaries, or sold to convert them into a steady cash flow for the Beneficiaries.

Reasons for an Irrevocable Statutory or Common-Law Trust

Would you rather pay the IRS or give the money to people who support you?

With a Trust, the people who support you are paid first, and this is treated as a business deduction of the Trust. The IRS receives taxes on the money paid to the Beneficiaries.

For example, if your income puts you in the 40% tax bracket, then you are most likely seriously looking for a way to reduce income tax. After setting up an Irrevocable Trust, the 35% to 40% of the money slated for the IRS is now deductible as fiduciary fees, payments to Beneficiaries and business expenses. You not only reduced your personal tax burden, but your Trust now supports an army of people to help in building a solid asset basis to last for generations.

Here are some of the common legal and tax advantages of **any** Irrevocable Trust:

◊ Reduce gross estate for estate tax purposes —Everyone has an estate. An estate refers to the sum total of what you own. If you have a life insurance policy, investment accounts, and three homes, you get interested in reducing your gross estate so you fall into a lower tax bracket.

◊ Shift the income tax burden to those in a lower tax bracket. What if, instead of paying for your child's education, you placed money in a Trust, and the Trust paid for the education? Suddenly, you land in a lower tax bracket!

◊ Eliminate probate and other estate costs. With a Trust, there is no probate or inheritance tax because when assets are placed in a Trust, they can be perpetuated generation after generation. Not attached to a person who dies, all issues of probate and inheritances taxes end.

◊ Solutions to liquidity problems. You bought your house for $50,000. Now, it is worth $250,000. If you sell it, you owe capital gains; if you exchange it into an Irrevocable Trust, the tax basis of the home changes. Fair Market value at the time the Trust receives the home, is the value of the asset, thus lowering the capital gains if the Trust sells the home later. Of course, the reverse is also true. If the value of the real estate decreases, then the Trust suffers.

Some counties are now changing their rules about a change of ownership into a Trust without reassessment of the property value which results in paying more taxes. Some of them insist they will only allow the transfer into a Trust if at least one Beneficiary is a family member. This presents a conflict of privacy, for if Beneficiaries need to be named, then this information becomes public record. In the chapter on Privacy, we went into detail about why no Beneficiary's name should be made public.

◇ Provide independence and security for the Beneficiaries. Perhaps you have a second spouse who does not get along with your children. If you die first, your children may lose everything. If you create an Irrevocable Trust, you prevent anyone from interfering with the inheritance status of the children or any other recognized Beneficiaries.

◇ Provide significant tax savings to the Trust Grantor. You can continue living in a comfortable life style, while drastically reducing your tax liability.

◇ Provide financial protection for a relative who cannot take care of himself or herself. The Irrevocable Trust is an excellent way to set up competent care, at a notable tax advantage to the Grantor of the Trust.

◇ Maximize long-range estate planning for the benefit of future generations. The Irrevocable Trust gives incredible flexibility and opportunity to increase assets without significant tax increases.

◇ Offers protection against personal lawsuits. How can you be sued for what you do not own? Legal title belongs to the Board of Trustees.

Characteristics of the Common-Law Trust

- Offers protection against personal lawsuits. How can you be sued for what you do not own? Legal title belongs to the Board of Trustees.

- A properly trained Board of Trustees provides strong privacy under the laws of the United States.

- A Common-Law Trust is a lawful entity and lives on after the death of the Grantor.

- Assets properly put into the Trust are safe from probate.

- Offers large personal tax advantages.

- Through restructuring of assets, cash flow can substantially increase.

- Because of gifts that can be given from a Trust, recipients of these gifts, that is, Beneficiaries, do not pay tax until the gift is more than $12,000.00[106] a year for each Beneficiary.

- Trust Capital Unit Holders have no voting rights; otherwise, the Trust can be judged a corporation.

- Trust management is in the hands of the Trustees.

- No document recording requirements. "The Trust Contract is carried out by private parties for personal purposes, and is not registered with the corporation Commission."[107] Contracts are not registered at the County Recorder's Office.

- Issues at least 100 nonvoting Trust Capital Units in the form of Certificates.

- Not dependent on state or federal governments for its existence.

- Providing proper procedures are followed, may engage in lawful business enterprises anywhere in the world.

- If its Indenture so specifies, the Board of Trustees may speculate in any venture, including buying commodities, municipal bonds, racehorses or even gaming.

---

[106] This amount is subject to change. Check with a tax professional for the current amount allowed.

[107] *Hodgkiss v. Northland Petroleum Consolidated*, 104 Mont 328, 67 p 2nd 811.

- Not limited to conducting business in any one state.[108]

- Not subject to probate.

Personal Liberty

The Common-Law is rooted in the belief that people have fundamental rights under the law.

> It has survived, moreover through several periods of political crisis which seriously disturbed the balance between (sic) three elements fundamental to the English constitution–the prerogative of the Crown, the privileges of Parliament, and the individual liberties of personal security, personal liberty, and private property.[109]

The Irrevocable Common-Law Trust, based in ancient tradition, survived hundreds of years of political turmoil. The rules are basic to human nature. People use the Common-Law Trust to unite family, increase bonding and camaraderie, and to unite in a common cause—the increase of assets for the benefit of the Beneficiaries.

You are probably getting a sense of how this Trust game operates. There is much more to know, before you are ready to make any serious decisions.

---

[108]   *Shirk v. City of Lafayette*, 52 F. 857 (1892).

[109]   Arthur R. Hogue, *Origins of the Common-Law*, Liberty Press, p. 241.

Chapter 18

Offshore and Foreign Trusts

T he Statutory Trust is no longer applicable in this discussion. We suddenly step off the map into a new reality. The subject of jurisdiction now becomes one of our major concerns. That is, who has the power to settle disputes about Trusts? The answer to this question involves situs. Situs means where the Trust physically does business.

The Difference

Contrary to popular opinion, the definition of the United States is not what most people think. The federal government, identified as the United States of America, is under contract by the 50 states, administers among them and between them. The 50 states are superior to the federal government, except where political pressures blurred the lines.

IRS is Not an Agency of the United States

Also, the Internal Revenue Service (IRS) is NOT authorized by the federal government, nor is the Internal Revenue Code (IRC) federal law. There are no records of its being codified, as the IRS is not part of the United States.[110] The following is a quote from Dan Meador, a well-known researcher of the tax laws. In his summary[111] of the Diversified Metal Products case referenced in the footnote he reports:

> Diversified Metal was served a notice of levy for money owed to the T-Bow Trust. To discover rightful ownership, Ohman filed the inter-pleader action for Diversified Metal. In his complaint, he stipulated facts. His fact #4 is as follows: "Defendant Internal Revenue Service (IRS) is an agency of the United States government.

> In her January 24, 2000 response, U.S. Attorney Betty H. Richardson made the following correction to Ohman's averment: **"Denies that the Internal Revenue Service is an agency of the United States Government** but admits that the *United States of America* would be a proper party to this action." (Emphasis added)

The key point here is there is a distinction between the United States Government and the United States of America. They are, clearly, two different jurisdictions. The United States of America, a corporation, manages the several states. The united states form "We the People" of the U.S. Constitution.

We realize these statements will probably add to a growing confusion about the issues of authority and jurisdiction. The knowledge needed to understand properly what is going on is not part of this book. For you to track the intricate web of the Federal Reserve Bank, its collection agency the IRS and the federal government, takes times and patience. Later in this chapter we refer you to a book written by Eustace Mullens about the Federal Reserve. That is a good

---

[110]   *Diversified Metals Products v. T-Bow* Civil No. 93-405-E-EJL, United States Answer and Claim, United States District Court of Idaho.

[111]   Dan Meador, *Income Tax Dissension.* "Who & What is the Internal Revenue Service? History & New Evidence." April 1, 2000.

place to start. The curious will need to put the pieces of an intricate puzzle together from there.

This basic understanding is not only a motive for forming a Domestic Foreign Trust, but is critical knowledge when you form any other nonstatutory entity. You need to know the limits and liabilities. You can be ignorant and get by with any Statutory Trust, but you cannot be ignorant of both laws and tax consequences when you get involved with Domestic Trusts, Foreign Trusts and Offshore Trusts. No, they are not the same.

Many have gotten "caught" in the subgame of Offshore Trusts, and few know what a Foreign Trust is. Because it appears you do not need to pay taxes if funds are in a foreign country, the entire issue of Offshore Trusts becomes a temptation. Although we will mostly avoid the major and deeper issues of taxes within this book, we will address the issue of taxes in reference to Offshore Trusts.

Venue

For those who are unaware of jurisdictional issues and why they are important, it works like this: the place (venue) where you operate your life has certain rules and procedures. What rules you break, determines what judge you go before. Some offenses, for example, are against a city or county, some ordinances against state laws, and some against federal laws. The same is true with a Trust. The place of venue, the situs of the Trust, is stated in the Trust Indenture. For example, the place can be the State of California, or it can be California state. These are two different venues. The first one is where a Statutory Trust operates; the second is where a Domestic Foreign Trust operates. Domestic means within the 50 states of the United States, not the United States of America, a corporation. Foreign means "foreign to the federal government," also referred to as the U.S. Government. All 50 states are foreign to the U.S. government–and no, we are not hallucinating—"The United States government is a foreign corporation with respect to the state."[112]

---

[112]　　*Corpus Juris Secundum* 20 §1785.

Evolving over the past 200 plus years, the federal government developed an intricate, confusing web of lies and deceit to hide the truth from the American people.

United States Courts

We have not lost our mind. The IRS, though, recognizes the difference, and here are the legal cites so you can see we did not make this up. 26 U.S.C. 7701a (30)(E)(I) defines a United States person as "(E) any Trust if a **court** within the United States is able to exercise primary supervision of the administration of the Trust." At (B) in that same section it states "the term 'foreign Trust' means any Trust other than a Trust described in subparagraph (E) of paragraph (30)."

This means Trusts that do not have court-appointed Trustees are not United States persons.

States are Separate Countries

You may be frowning in wonder at what just happened. Let us fill in the gap. The 50 states are separate countries from the federal government; the United States of America is a corporation that manages the 50 states. The Trust can be under the jurisdiction of the United States of America if it is managed by a court-appointed Trustee. It can be under the jurisdiction of the states if it is not administered by a court-appointed Trustee, thus making it foreign to the U.S. Government.

Under this definition, if the rules and regulations—the law of the Trust—establish clearly the Trust operates in a Common-Law venue, then it is a Foreign Trust in reference to the corporate United States. We think you are now beginning to get the picture of why many lawyers have not been trained in this particular realm of Trust law.

We will be using the word foreign to indicate outside of both the corporate United States and in another country. If we capitalize Foreign Trust, we will be talking about a Common-Law Trust, or any other Trust that is Domestic in the United States.

Do not confuse the issue of Foreign Trust with offshore entities. These are two separate issues. Not only is a California Trust set up under Common-Law classified as Foreign, so is a Trust set up in another country if it is not controlled by a U.S. Court. An Offshore Trust could be a Foreign Trust.

Unless the assets of your Domestic (Foreign) Trust grow large or you own foreign property or investments, you do not need to "go offshore" to set up more Trusts or other businesses. The Common-Law Trust can invest offshore and manage offshore investments.

Many people who choose Offshore Trusts do so merely to avoid taxes (sometimes without examining the downside). If taxes form your motivation, the Offshore Trust you consider may not be set up properly and may be what the IRS terms "abusive." We will go into much greater depth on this issue in Volume II. At this point, though, we simply want you to get the idea.

The Offshore Trust is essentially the same as a Domestic Common-Law Trust but established outside the fifty states. The Offshore Trust uses a foreign Trustee and may have a bank account either in the country of its situs or in the United States. It does not need a U.S. EIN. This may erroneously lead some to believe they will not have to pay federal income tax from such a Trust.

The proper method for setting up an Offshore Trust is the same as for Domestic Trusts, except the corpus is located in a foreign jurisdiction and the rules of the foreign country need to be considered.

Distance of Trustee = Disinterest

Offshore Trusts have distinct disadvantages. You must deal with offshore Trustees who may be unfamiliar with your particular enterprise and its stateside business environment. If problems arise, you may have to travel to the country where the Trust is set up and contend with the applicable laws in that jurisdiction. These may be unfamiliar and written in a foreign language. Usually, the Trustees will not come to the United States to appear in court for you if your problems are in the United States.

Money Laundering

The Money Laundering Act of 1998[113] targets offshore entities (including Trusts) as well as many offshore investment schemes. If you have an offshore bank account and are merely _accused_ of money laundering, your offshore funds may be confiscated. This act increases the government's power to force forfeitures by creating a _rebuttable presumption_[114] the source of the accused's U.S. funds (Offshore investments) is illegal. It singles out "shell" corporations ("international business corporations" or IBCs) and bank accounts held in nations with financial secrecy laws, on the premise the funds in them are tainted and should be seized.

> If accused of money laundering, with your assets confiscated, you will be able to contest the seizure in a U.S. court only if you waive the privacy protection granted by the host country.

If accused of money laundering, with your assets confiscated, you will be able to contest the seizure in a U.S. court[115] only if you waive the privacy protection granted by the host country. If you agree to open your books to prove your innocence, you might spend much unrecoverable time and money in the effort with no guarantee of exonera-

---

[113]   H.R. 4005—Money Laundering Deterrence Act of 1998 and H.R. 1756—Money Laundering and Financial Crime Strategy Act of 1997 found at: http://commdocs.house.gov/committees/bank/hba49305.000/hba49305_0f.htm

[114]   The burden of proof is shifted from the government to you. You are guilty until you prove yourself innocent, which may take more time and money than you realize.

[115]   Robert E. Bauman, _Forbidden Knowledge_, Agora International, Inc. 1998, p. 55

tion. Even an eventual win in such cases is often a Pyrrhic victory (see Glossary) which leaves the business and its principals exhausted and wondering what they have won. How strenuously this law is enforced is a direct reflection of the great reward for the IRS, SEC, etc. Motive is enough to make Offshore Trusts targets.

As we know, communications and international treaties continue to shrink the world, and the result is that Offshore havens are becoming fewer and less secure. Rather than counting on obvious distance and the kindness of strangers, both of which may prove illusory, most people who make fully informed decisions choose to buy a properly designed Domestic Foreign Trust Indenture which can withstand any legal challenge. Then, they take a hands-on approach to both learning about and running their Trusts and stay in touch with Trustees with whom they are familiar. Further, Trustees who understand jurisdiction are worth a million dollars right there, because they can defend against any onslaught from the IRS or other agencies looking for a quick trip to the bank.

> Trustees who understand jurisdiction are worth a million dollars right there, because they can defend against any onslaught from the IRS or other agencies looking for a quick trip to the bank.

Many people have questions about the differences between an Offshore and Foreign Domestic Trust. Since the IRS is fond of breaking Offshore Trusts for the same reasons it finds Domestic Trusts faulty, there is not any difference between the two types of Trusts. Both need a Grantor, Trustee, Beneficiaries, and to prove *Substance of Transaction*.

There is a difference, though, between each of the Trusts regarding which one is suitable for what types of assets.

If the assets are physically found in a foreign country, you may need an Off-shore Trust and will need an Offshore Trustee located in the same country. Taxable funds created here in the United States of America, though, if taken offshore to scam the tax agencies, can bring many complications and grief, including allegations there has been money laundering.

The Offshore Trust must be created under the laws of the country in which the Trust is set up. Many countries do not allow Trusts, but instead use International Business Corporations (IBCs).

Grantor/Trustee Relationship

We recommend the Grantor should always know the Trustee and establish trust between them. Too many people have lost money by thinking they avoid taxes through placing money Offshore, and then the Trustee takes off with the money, or the IRS breaks the Trust.

The same rule applies to a Foreign Domestic Trust. Why place money into the hands of stranger? A Trust is about trust.

If, for some reason, you have assets placed in an Offshore Trust, but the assets are physically located in the USA, you can be challenged, audited or involved in legal technicalities. If you have an offshore Trustee, the odds are, the Trustee will not come "onshore" to rescue you. The purpose of a Trustee is to protect the assets for the Beneficiaries. Some Offshore Trusts are holding companies for people's money, and are not genuine Trusts holding assets for Beneficiaries. Therefore, the Trustee has no interest in showing up in court to support anyone.

If you are thinking of buying an Offshore Trust, understand the issue is always substance of transaction. You cannot hide behind the paper of a Trust Indenture or Declaration of Trust when the actions taken by those managing the Trust do not support the Trust's purpose to benefit of the Beneficiaries.

U.S. Citizens

Taxation works this way: if you are a U.S. Citizen, no matter where in the world you go, you owe taxes to the IRS on your taxable income. It does not matter if you have a job in Mexico, Uganda or Russia. You earned it, you owe it.[116]

If your Trust is in Belize, and the money going into it was earned in the United States, the Trust may owe taxes. If the money going into the Trust in Belize was

> **If your Trust is in Belize, and the money going into it was earned in the United States, the Trust may owe taxes.**

earned in another country, that country probably wants its taxes paid too. If any money in the Trust in Belize is paid to a U.S. Citizen, that person must pay taxes on the money received.

DO NOT set up a Trust to avoid taxes. Set up a Trust for the Beneficiaries, who pay the taxes. Few people know the inner workings of the IRS. If you understand the Beneficiaries pay the taxes, you will find the best Trust.

"But, Judge, I Wasn't Money-Laundering!"

Because of certain RICO[117] laws, some Grantors of Offshore Trusts discovered they may face federal criminal charges if they try to bring their funds back onshore. This traps them in a Catch-22: declare the income and pay taxes on it, or leave it unreported and run the risk of having it seized—or worse, going to jail themselves. At this point, many become frustrated and disenchanted with

---

[116]   There are exceptions and other details concerning overseas earned income. The issue is it is tied to your Social Security Number whether or not you declare it, or use it with the foreign entity. Check with your CPA.

[117]   Racketeer Influenced and Corrupt Organizations (RICO) was enacted by Section 901(a) of the Organized Crime Control Act of 1970, Pub. L. No. 91-452, 84 Stat. 922 (15 October 1970).

the Offshore solution. "After all," they say, "what good is an Offshore Trust if it doesn't help me avoid taxation legally?"

Only a properly set up Irrevocable, *Domestic* Common-Law Trust can move Offshore money back home without risk. That sounds strange, but it is true. The reason is simple: a well-designed Domestic Foreign Trust can use tax savings built right into the Internal Revenue Code (IRC) itself, including the technique of passing profits straight through to the Beneficiaries as a distribution. The Trust claims the "income."

The Only Need For Offshore Trustees

Much confusion and misinformation exist about the entire subject of Trusts. This begins in sections of the IRC which should be ruled void for vagueness, to Irrevocable Statutory Trusts designed only to exploit specific tax loopholes. Add to this Common-Law Trusts, which are no more than paper scams, and Offshore Trust companies which promise the world. Sadly, many well-intentioned people, to protect their assets from taxation, move them Offshore, only to learn they have been misinformed or misled.

Here is a hint. If you understand that you are a slave of the rich, then you need to find out what the rich legally do to reduce and even avoid taxes. If you follow along in their footsteps, you are more likely to be mistaken for one of them.

The only ones who *may* need an Offshore Trust are those who own physical property in another country. In such cases, they should have at least a Trustee who is a resident or citizen of the foreign country. He or she represents the Domestic Trust in the country where the assets are found, or a Trust structured under the laws of that country, managed by people in that country. For example, if you have a Domestic Trust which holds property placed in France, one of the Trustees should be a French citizen or resident. In every other circumstance, a Domestic Trust can handle all transactions easily and efficiently, well within the guidelines of U.S. tax laws, gaining maximum tax benefits and running no risk of violating the RICO statutes.

Investments and Taxation

When making offshore investments, many people hire Offshore Trustees because investment programs require that they use an Offshore Trust or an IBC. This is acceptable provided they do not count on it to protect them from the U.S. income tax. Remember, investment income and your wages are taxable no matter where it is earned if it is paid out to a U.S. Citizen.[118] Your Offshore Trust with a bank account in a U.S. Bank can receive the funds, but once it gets into the hands of a U.S. Citizen, it is taxable. If a distribution or cash is sent to you, you owe the tax. Your Social Security Number makes you liable for it regardless of where you live or where the payment originates, or whether or not you use your Social Security Number. The best way to handle this is to channel the funds into a Domestic Trust whose trained Trustees manage the distribution, reinvestment, tax reporting, etc.

Internet Traps

Perusing the Internet, we found some strange ideas about Offshore Trusts. Here is our own take on them for your benefit.

Asset Ownership

As a Frequently Asked Question (FAQ) one web site asks, "Who owns the assets?"And then answers correctly: "The assets are owned by the Trust." In other words, the offshore Trustees (usually strangers to the Grantor) have control *and ownership* of the assets. You hope yours will prove honorable, but some Offshore Trust Indentures we reviewed are poorly written. The rights of the Grantor use hazy terms. We are doubtful of the legality of the Trust or its real intent.

Do not assume all Offshore investments or Trusts are questionable, though. We do not claim any expertise in this arena. Our experience with the Offshore Trustee who would not come to the United States, though, is real and firsthand.

---

[118]   Cook v. Tait, 265 U.S. 47, 44 Sup. Ct. 444 (1924)

No-Interest Loan Strategy

One web site promises prospective clients that, once their Offshore Trusts are set up, they can draw all of their funds out of them in no-interest loans. When we asked one veteran CPA[119] about this tactic, his response startled us.

> The rules are vicious and very demanding. The loan proceeds need to be reported to Uncle (Sam), and default on loan payments triggers distribution of income. It is possible to be taxed on the same money twice if anything goes wrong. It is a tangled web!

Further, before the Trustees can give loans to anyone, the Trust Indenture must give the power to the Trustees, and must describe under what circumstances loans can be given. No-interest loans are no longer tolerated since too many "scam" Trusts tried this scheme. A loan to or from a Trust must be at a reasonable lending rate.

Risks v. Guarantees

An FAQ on another web site asks, "Can I lose money by putting it into a Trust?" The company posting that site guarantees that its customers' funds will be safe. This hopeful assertion leaves us asking how it can guarantee the stability of the local government (especially in a small country), let alone the future of the entire financial world? So far as we know, money is not safe anywhere, life itself is a risk, and anyone who guarantees the security of your money—even the FDIC has a limit— should be viewed with the utmost skepticism. Besides, we know of some Offshore programs which simply cannot pay anyone back. Of course, some others pay wonderful returns, but a *guarantee*? Well, really!

---

[119] Per a CPA who is also a specialist in Trust accounting.

Domestic Trusts: *What* Confusion?

If you ever hear the oddball complaint that Domestic Trusts should be avoided because U.S. tax and legal rules are unclear, know that you are listening to a poor student, an Offshore Trust salesperson or both. To us the rules boil down to just two points: 1) **get real**. That means get a real adverse Trustee, real Beneficiaries and a real Grantor. 2) Use **passthrough** accounting, so the Beneficiaries pay the tax (at lower rates and after expenses are subtracted). Simple enough for you?

Oh, there is one other small point which even most Offshore Trusts omit: **training**. To operate a Trust correctly, the Trustees and officers must know exactly what they can and cannot do—and how to do it. Funny how often that little "detail" gets overlooked.

So, the basics are simple, but the Trust case law is extensive, and you would be smart to read some of it before creating your Trust. We have a set of three key cases which we named "When Is The Grantor Taxable?" This set is in Volume II.

Not only is the Common-Law area mostly lacking suitable training for both Grantors and Trustees, but even lawyers create intricate Trusts, giving two inches of paper to their client without instructions on how to do all the transfers and other paperwork. Just how many people do you think can do it correctly without help and training? Few indeed.

Cayman Islands

Back in August of 1999, the *Los Angeles Times*[120] reported that investigators of an international credit card fraud traced advances to the Cayman Islands. On this pretense the secrecy laws of the Cayman Islands, long known as "the Switzerland of the Caribbean," were breached.

---

[120]   *Los Angeles Times*, "Cayman Islands Lift Veil of Bank Secrecy," August 25, 1999.

In November of 2001, the Cayman Islands Governor Peter J. Smith, Treasury Secretary Paul O'Neill of the U.S.A. and Christopher Meyer, the British ambassador to the U.S. were involved in a signing agreement to share tax information and to track down violators.[121]

This paves the way for audits to uncover tax evasion, drugs, money-laundering and other misdeeds.

The article states the U.S. has lost $70 billion in tax revenue each year because of Offshore tax havens, but we need to correct this statement. The Federal Reserve lost $70 billion in tax revenue, since none of it goes to the U.S. government anyway.[122]

We would like to remind our readers the powers that rule this world can bribe anyone, anywhere, any time, and if bribery does not work, blackmail, extortion and worse do the job. Tax havens are all subject to corruption and disappear as those who wish to control and dominate the lives of everyone, keep us all stirred up in a nonstop battle for our freedom. This is also known as distraction.

To get the details of how the IRS works, you need only search the Internet. This book does not focus on the IRS but only on some of the issues of the Federal Reserve Bank. If you want more information, we recommend the book, *The Secrets of the Federal\l Reserve.*[123] The Internet provides a reliable source of information about both the Federal Reserve Bank[124] and the Internal Revenue Service.

---

[121]   *Los Angeles Times*, "Cayman Islands Will Share Tax Information", November 28, 2001

[122]   *Grace Commission Report*, "President's Private Sector Survey on Cost Control, Volume I, January 15, 1984.

[123]   Eustace Mullins, *The Secrets of the Federal Reserve*, Bankers Research Institute, Staunton, Virginia, 1991.

[124]   Appendix C introduces you to one article regarding this subject on the Internet.

Because the issue of Trusts is so strongly tied to the financial system, it is wise for those who are considering putting assets into any Trust to have a grasp of the realities of this world's finances.

Chapter 19

Religious Trusts

Since there are so many previous court rulings regarding Religious Trusts, the limits of what can and cannot be done are clear. A Religious Trust Indenture for members and leaders of a church can be created. This entity does not depend on a state-created privilege such as IRC § 501(c)(3) for its tax-exempt status. Furthermore, the tax-free status does not stop with the place of worship itself but extends to each of its individual members.

Legal research regarding the Corporation Sole and the Ecclesiastic Trust gives evidence that Religious Trusts are recognized by many states in the union. It has recently come to light that the control the IRS has over religion is startling.[125] To keep a tax-exempt status, a cleric of any sort cannot make what are defined

---

[125]   Briefly, IRS section 501(c)(3) states "organizations, including churches and religious organizations, must abide by certain rules: Their net earnings may not inure to any private shareholder or individual, they must not provide a substantial benefit to private interests, they must not devote a substantial part of their activities to attempting to influence legislation, they must not participate in, or intervene in, any political campaign on behalf of or in opposition to any candidate for public office, and the organization's purposes and activities may not be illegal or violate fundamental public policy."

as "political statements" from the pulpit. If a Corporation Sole or an Ecclesiastic Trust is properly set up, the IRS issue can be avoided. Like all other entities the IRS does not like, though, the leadership may be challenged to prove the legality of the tax-exempt status, and both the Church and its members harassed.

We have the experience of one religious leader in his quest to discover the appropriate ways to establish a Corporation Sole. We share his interview with you. The interview has been edited for clarity and slightly redacted to preserve privacy.

Per others, though, the Corporation Sole is not limited to the method this Reverend used. We make no recommendation or judgment, as we feel it is up to the reader's further investigation.

The Mysterious Corporation Sole

An interview with the Reverend, High Priest of the Nation of Leviticus:[126]

AC: We often get inquiries about a Corporation Sole because it is a form of a Religious Trust. We also have conflicting information regarding whether or not it is purely religious, or if it can also be an educational institution. Could you please clarify?

Rev: There is no such thing as a Corporation Sole without its also being an Ecclesiastic Corporation Sole. It is automatically null and void if the leader is not a member of an old religious organization and cannot prove his or her lineage back at least 500 years.

AC: When you say it is "null and void," what exactly do you mean?

Rev: A Corporation Sole needs to be recognized by the state and/or federal government. If it is not recognized (as a religious entity), it cannot enjoy its unique nonprofit status.

---

[126] Name has been changed for reasons of privacy.

AC: How old is the term Corporation Sole?

Rev: We know that a Corporation Sole is a rollover from British law. The current Queen of England is the leader of the Church of England, which is a recognized Corporation Sole.

AC: Are there any references in law or history books where the information can be found?

Rev: There are several legal cases that have been recorded in California and other states.

AC: I understand that you kept submitting the Corporation Sole papers for your religion to the Secretary of State in California, and they were rejected. Could you tell me what happened and why?

Rev: We followed the basic format of many of the political groups who are writing Corporation Sole paperwork and selling them to people. The legal assumption was that if a person declared himself or herself a Corporation Sole, he or she was tax exempt. At the time, I believed the research that had been done was valid, so I used much of their work and created 16 pages declaring the Nation of Leviticus a Corporation Sole. I submitted a Declaration of Status to the California Secretary of State. The paperwork was rejected. I resubmitted it, and it was rejected again without an explanation. I submitted it three more times, and was again rejected without an explanation. I called the Office of the Secretary of State on several occasions and was not able to get any further information, until one day, I was quite fortunate, as one of the staff members was a Christian. This person questioned me extensively to determine whether I was truly ordained, and to determine my religious understanding. When she was satisfied that I was qualified to know the correct procedure, she took the time to explain to me what was wrong with the paperwork. I was astounded when this person told me the correct paperwork must contain a specific type of information, and it was to be no longer than one page!

AC: One page? Is this true in just California?

Rev: No. We contacted several other states. We found the requirement to be the same. However, last year,[127] the State of Arizona did not recognize a Corporate Sole. It claimed there was no such thing. We recently established the Levitican Empire of the Nation of Leviticus in Arizona, and the papers have been filed there.

AC: Is the Corporation Sole only recognized at the state level?

Rev: No, it can be recognized on a federal level, but it becomes a contradiction of terms, or a "Catch 22."

AC: What do you mean?

Rev: On the federal level, a Corporation Sole must be a continuation of a religious order; the Corporation Sole also must have a board of directors. Here's the trick. To set up a Corporation Sole at the state level, the person must be the highest-ranking official of a two-part church. There is no board of directors, and it's an individual that operates and controls the entire religious order.

AC: What is a two-part church?

Rev: There is a mother church that provides the religious direction of the offspring churches. For example, the Catholic Church is a two-part church. The pope is the leader of the mother church, and then each church established by the Roman Catholic Church is an offspring church. There are many of the older religions that are established in this format.

AC: Since you used that example, I'm under the impression that a Corporation Sole is like a benevolent dictatorship?

Rev: Yes, and there is no board of directors. However, the Bible is the Dictate.

AC: Why do you believe there is a conflict?

---

[127]   The Reverend refers to 1998.

Rev: Those who are misinformed may want to get a 501(c)(3) tax-exempt status. The federal government is always willing to be part of anyone's church. The true Corporation Sole excludes the federal government and state government as well. A Corporation Sole does not ask permission of the government to exist; it simply notifies the government that it does exist.

AC: Explain this more. The federal government is willing to be part of any one's church? How does that work?

Rev: When a church asks permission of the IRS to have a tax-exempt status, a church opens its books to the IRS and then must adhere to certain procedures or it loses its tax status. This means the IRS has the potential to control religious direction and dogma.

AC: Do you think this happened?

Rev: I know this happened, because churches are silent on several issues, where they should be quite outspoken.

AC: I can see this could go off into many different fascinating religious discourses. I will leave that for another interview. I need to focus on clarifying the Corporation Sole's status. Have you heard of a Corporation Sole's filing for a 501A status?

Rev: That is a nonprofit religious organization tax-exempt status, but again, the IRS can now audit the church's books, and again control the direction of the religion. This is what is meant by the term "state religion."

AC: Since you have gone to the effort to establish the Nation of Leviticus as a Corporation Sole, what are some of the advantages?

Rev: For members who are truly part of a Corporation Sole, they are personally tax-exempt; they also are not eligible for federal or state benefits. To some, this may be frightening. The members must take a religious position regarding matters of taxation. A Corporation Sole is for those who have a strong ethical belief system, and who are willing to take a religious stand.

Because the membership is not eligible for any state or federal benefits, the Corporation Sole is financially responsible for its members. There is the potential in this situation, that if the tax status of the member is questioned, or some other situation arises, the member may need to go to a court of law. Should this occur, the mother church assists in the defense of the member, who is under the authority of the leader of the Corporation Sole.

AC: Does that mean you personally have to appear in court?

Rev: No, I can send a representative, but if it is local, I'm likely to appear in court.

AC: Has this happened?

Rev: Yes, a couple of times.

AC: For the Corporation Sole to qualify in the eyes of the state, are there certain rituals that must be included in the religion?

Rev: Ministers have to be trained in ecclesiastic procedures, and ordained by the high priest who has a lineage back to the founder of the religion. Baptismal rituals are required for Christian organizations and other types of rituals for other religious sects.

AC: It sounds quite different from most other religions.

Rev: Yes, it is more of a proactive approach to actualize one's belief.

AC: Thank you for your time.

The Corporation Sole is a controversial matter. There are those who oppose the point of view given in this chapter, and who claim the structure is not limited to a two-part church. This type of Religious Trust is not our expertise, and we merely report the recorded conversation here.

The following definition comes from Wikipedia, the free encyclopedia.

A corporation sole in English law is a legal entity consisting of a single person ("sole"). This allows the corporation to pass vertically from one holder of a position to the next, giving the position legal continuity.

Most corporations sole are church-related; for example the Archbishop of Canterbury and most mayors are corporations sole. In contrast to a corporation sole, a corporation aggregate consists of two or more persons, typically comprising a board of directors.

The corporation sole is inherently compatible with certain churches, and in particular the Roman Catholic Church, because of its top-down governance by bishops. A single bishop governs an entire geographic region of churches, known as a "diocese." Church property is titled to the bishop who serves in the office of the "corporation sole." It is largely because of the need in certain churches for a corporation which is governed by a single person the corporation sole came into existence.

While most corporations sole are used for legitimate and legal church purposes, there has been a widespread abuse in recent years of the formation of many new corporations sole which are being used for tax evasion purposes. As a direct result, the US Internal Revenue Service issued Revenue Ruling 2004-27, warning of abuse of corporations sole under United States of America tax law.

Most U.S. states which still provide for corporations sole only permit them for religious purposes. However, historically they have been legitimately used for other purposes as well. For example, mayors of certain English towns have traditionally been corporations sole.

Likewise the monarch of the UK is a corporation sole – she or he may possess property as monarch which is distinct from the property she possesses personally, and may do acts as monarch distinguished from their (sic) personal acts. In fact, the British monarch is one natural person but several corporations sole -- Her Majesty in right of the United Kingdom is a distinct legal person from Her Majesty in right of Australia, which is in turn distinct from Her Majesty in right of Canada, and Her Majesty in right of New Zealand, and so on. Likewise, she has a distinct corporation sole for each of the Australian states and Canadian provinces.

There is ample reading available on the subject of the Corporate Sole on the Internet, along with an IRS warning.[128]

---

[128]   http://en.wikipedia.org/wiki/Corporation_sole

Chapter 20

What Trust is Right For You?

O kay, you are still with us after getting past Chapter 8, where we listed all the reasons not to have a Trust. Armed with at least a working knowledge of Trusts, how they came to be, their subsequent history, and their uses and abuses, you are nearly ready to make a choice.

You may not believe it, but at this point you now know more about Trusts than do most of the people in this country. For you to achieve the real benefits a Trust makes possible, though, it is necessary to delve further.

As we noted earlier, *any* properly completed Trust provides better asset protection, more efficient and easier asset access for the Beneficiaries, and a better tax posture than does a Will. From hereon, we will refer to Statutory Trusts and Private Trusts only.

Rating the Trust Types

Before going into a detailed discussion of the Trust types and the purposes for which you might wish to use them, it is important to remind you that Statutory Trusts are more easily understood. Because they are commonly accepted by the legal and financial professions, using one is likely to be a more comfortable experience. This, in turn, provides not one, but a series of resources on which you can draw in creating your own Trust or Trusts.

Like everything else in life, though, just because people set themselves up as authorities, does not necessarily mean they have all the answers and, therefore, they could guide you down the wrong path. Even though you should be able to rely on sound legal advice, there are many cases where a Trust has not worked out the way it was planned, and other cases where Statutory Trusts proved to be deceptive. This will be handled in more detail later in this chapter.

When selecting and funding a Statutory Trust, much still depends on your knowledge, research and what you learn through consulting with proper professionals.

The combined experience in the Common-Law Trust of all the contributors to this book is more than 50 years. We claim no similar familiarity with other Trust types.

> If you are not the adventurous or risk-tolerant type, but wish to do better for your Beneficiaries than you could with a Will, then the Statutory Trust is preferable.

If you are not the adventurous or risk-tolerant type, but wish to do better for your Beneficiaries than you could with a Will, the Statutory Trust is preferable. Either the Living Trust or the Irrevocable Trust may be the way for you to go. Also, if you are more of a maverick than a herd follower, more of a calculated risk taker than a risk avoider, have the time and are willing to study and learn, the Private Trust is better. You are likely to be more comfortable with the power, flexibility, financial and tax leverage for you and your Beneficiaries inherent in a Private Trust. Here, you not only can define a broader portfolio and assets the Trust will accept, but your wishes can be more precisely spelled out without some of the limits of the Statutory Trust.

Why is there such a difference between a Statutory Trust and a Private Trust? Creativity and flexibility are maximized in a Private Trust, precisely because it is not statutory. Under the U.S. Constitution, Article I, Section 10, you may make a private contract to do just about anything, as long as it does not harm others. Statutory Trusts may limit some of your investment choices. This is because of legislation passed based on experience, or by those who have influence over the political arena. Please remember, though, that no matter what we tell you about a Private Trust, the Statutory Trust comes automatically with the backing of both the legal and financial communities. Any Private Trust needs trained Trustees, or Trustees who are willing to be trained.

Thanks to decades of prior experience, though, many of the sound rules long found in the Statutory Trusts are usually incorporated into the Private Trust. For example, the instructions in the Trust Indenture need to include whether the Trustees have the right to lend or borrow money to or from the Beneficiaries. If the instructions do not exist, then the funds cannot be used in that manner. Further along this line, lending money to the Grantor cannot be without interest. As it happened in the past, the Grantor funds the Trust, then the Trustees give him or her the money back without interest! This is not a Trust used for the Beneficiaries.

Renewable Contract

Through a Private Trust or any Irrevocable Trust, you can lay the foundations for multigenerational success and prosperity more easily than you can with a Statutory Trust. This is because the contract between the Trustees and the Beneficiaries can be renewed every 25 years, thus making it enduring, depending on the will of each generation. For example, the Pennsylvania Land Trust was set up by one of our Founding Fathers and lasted past 1900. It disbanded because it became nearly impossible to manage the assets–too many Beneficiaries!

A Statutory Trust has a definite end time, which is usually the third or fourth generation. Further, in this Trust, the idea of privacy may be minimal or nonexistent. In speaking to many lawyers on this subject, they cannot fathom the need for such privacy. Some lawyers find alien the idea that if others do not know the assets in the Trust, then they cannot take them. Those lawyers involved directly in asset protection, though, are more keenly aware of the need for privacy.

Set Up a Life Change—Why?

Operating through a Private Trust provides a new way of seeing the world. Setting up a Trust shifts ownership from you as an individual, to the Board of Trustees. Now, your checking account reflects only your personal expenses, and any funds coming from the Trust become a K-1 taxable distribution to you. If you no longer own a car, but the Trust owns a car and you can use it from time-to-time for Trust business, all those expenses you once bore for your personal car disappear. Therefore, how you handle your own money, separate from the Trust, becomes an interesting journey.

This is why we do not recommend putting all of your assets into a Trust, since you would surely like to have your own pile of cash. As you can see, though, there is a good possibility you can substantially lessen your income tax bite at the end of the year.

Trusts are often associated with the names of J. Paul Getty, John D. Rockefeller or the Kennedy family. In this setting, a Trust represents power and secrecy. These elements are not part of an average person's life. By not using Irrevocable Trusts, though, you automatically exclude yourself from some astonishing possibilities.

As we try to lift the veil obscuring Trusts, we hope to broaden your scope and vision. This can make your world a little more intriguing.

Motive

A Trust should be designed for your unique view on life. This includes spiritual values, as well as educational priorities. Sometimes, a Trust will be applicable to what you need to accomplish. So, before a discussion about Trusts and setting up a life change can occur, you need to consider motivations and out of these motivations, what business or Trust vehicle may be best for you.

Some people want to pass their assets to their children or to charity. These are usually older people who now grapple with the emotional issues of death. They talked to lawyers and CPAs. They investigated Trusts.

> A Trust should be designed for your unique point of view. This includes spiritual values, as well as educational priorities.

There are other people who have businesses and want to protect assets from lawsuits. These are people who understand that if they put their home into a Trust under the names of Trustees, and they lose a lawsuit in their business, their home will not be taken to pay the debt. These people have probably seen their friends lose their assets in a divorce or because of other unfortunate financial circumstances.

There are people who realize that an Irrevocable Trust removes the assets from all the family members and puts the assets into the hands of third parties who can professionally manage them. This keeps the more morbid family members from waiting for the Trust Grantor to die. Further, it limits the possibility the Beneficiaries will mishandle or squander their money, or be duped out of their assets. It takes money to learn how to handle money, and most people have no such training.

Share Now, Not Later

Trustees can manage assets so a cash flow is given to the members of the family during the lifetime of the Grantor. This has the magical effect of removing anxiety from those family members who have a difficult time making money, and it relieves those creatively inclined so they have some cash flow to manifest their dreams. This newfound shared wealth usually causes a heartwarming effect on the entire family as people realize that they are recognized. Of course, there can be other complications which may arise, but in general, sharing assets works wonders for a myriad of family problems.

Depending on who the Trustees are and how the Trust is set up, the family members can get involved in the financial planning and administration of the Trust estate.

Taxes

There are also those who want to avoid extreme tax liability. Moving assets that bring in a large cash flow, such as a stock portfolio, into the hands of third parties, that is, Trustees, takes away the tax load from the Grantor. Irrevocable Trusts have a different way of handling taxes through passthrough accounting. It may interest you to know that each Beneficiary of your Trust can receive up to $12,000.00[129] per year as a gift. This reduces the taxable basis of the Trust, and can be an incentive for people to put assets into a Trust. We believe that most parents would rather give the money to the Beneficiaries than they would to the tax agencies.

Structure Choices

There are several options of how to set up a business to reduce taxes and take care of family members. Use a corporation when dealing with a high-volume business. Tax consultants can advise you about the advantages. Limited liability companies also have certain advantages.

Because the one who knows how to run the business is the greatest asset, loss of him or her may end the business. The Board Of Trustees becomes subject to his or her whims, for the "owner" is the financial engine of the Trust. Therefore, we usually suggest a partnership, and the Trust becomes a partner. Leaving a

---

[129]   This amount is subject to change; check with your accountant.

business in a Trust can work, though, as long as after the sole owner exchanges it he or she then allows the Trustees to run it.

In a Statutory Trust, it is assumed that any business left to the Trustees will be sold. After it is sold, the Trustees invest the cash for the Beneficiaries or pay out the earnings of the sale to them. It is common to sell a business listed as part of the assets of a Living Trust. If the business is successful, and the management competent, this decision to sell the business can be a loss to the Beneficiaries.

Statutory and Irrevocable Trusts

In a statutory Trust, usually CPAs and lawyers are involved with whomever the Grantor chooses as the Trustee. The Trustee can be an aunt or uncle or other member of the family and consults with lawyers and CPAs about the tax liabilities and other decisions of the Trust after the Trust Grantor passes. These personally selected Trustees have little to no training about Trusteeship.

While a Private Trust is likely to be set up without CPAs and lawyers as Trustees, the Board of Trustees consults with them in matters about taxes and law. The Trust documents are not filed at the county, and Beneficiary names are not available to those who may inquire. The Board of Trustees of a Private Trust has more power than a Trustee of a Statutory Trust and therefore has more discretion about investments and distribution to Beneficiaries. These types of Trustees must either have Trust experience, have mentors, or receive Trustee training.

A Statutory Trust must be recorded at the County, thus making the Beneficiary names public. It is not uncommon for them to be directly contacted about assets. Then, there is the possibility the unscrupulous can take advantage to woo them away from their inheritance.

Staying Power

Any organization that allows others to have a vested interest in it usually has more staying power than one which does not. Contrary to a Living Trust which often ends when the Grantor passes, or the Sole Proprietorship which may not survive the owner, a corporation that sells shares has a body of people who are interested in its success. The more of the shares owned by a person or a group of people, the more interest and influence with the Board of Directors. Like an Irrevocable Trust, the Board of Directors perpetuates the life of the Corporation.

Vested interest in a Common-Law Trust comes in the form of Trust Certificates. These Trust Certificates are nonvoting, but they represent a percentage of the corpus and can allow the person who holds them to receive a percentage of distribution of the profits of the Trust. A corporation is a business, and it is not necessarily a business for the family. A Private Trust, though, is more likely to be structured around the needs of the family, for the family. This provides the family with a motive for staying together and working as a single unit. From here, this can evolve into a dynastic power. Here lies the secret of the "plutocracy" families, that is, the Rockefellers, Kennedys, Du Ponts, etc. Whether or not they have this Trust type is unknown, but we do know that they have a powerful vested interest in staying together.

> A corporation is a business, and it is not necessarily a business for the family. A Private Trust, though, is more likely to be structured around the needs of the family, for the family.

Set Up a Life Change—How?

As stated before, a corporation is created by permission of the state. This gives the state and taxing agents carte blanche to examine the books and to get into the business of the corporation. A corporation is set up by filling out an application and sending money to the state. In return, it sends a book of instructions and the Minutes to set up the corporation.

There are several ways to set up a Trust, depending on the Trust type. A Grantor Trust can even be established by buying forms at a stationery store—not something we recommend. It is, obviously, better to consult with a lawyer. Also, Internet sites exist where the format for a Living Trust can be accessed.

The Irrevocable Statutory Trust is complicated. This complexity requires attention to details by the Grantor, who usually cannot set it up without the help of a lawyer.

The Common-Law Trust is even more complex and is based on different principles. People who want to establish this Trust should consult with professionals in the Common-Law Trust area. The Grantor must be knowledgeable and dedicated, as well as have support of people who have experience in the complexities.

Because of lack of knowledge, some lawyers may scoff at any attempt to create a Private Trust, and especially mock the reference to "Common-Law Trust" because all they heard about Nonstatutory Trusts is that these Trusts are scams. The IRS makes sure there is plenty of publicity about such scams, and provides no information about how to properly set up the Common-Law Trust.

In Volume II we present several IRS Revenue Rulings for study.

Gray Area

Here is a caution about any Trust. It is no casual matter. Even if you buy the stationery forms and fill them out, you need to at least do some research and ask questions of professionals before completing the forms. The entire world of Trusts is a murky, gray world where definitions and protocols are not well-defined.

We have been asked to review Trusts and found that not only have the "uninitiated" in the law created some extraordinarily doubtful Trusts, but lawyers are also guilty. They should have access to good legal documents. Some have set up bizarre Trusts. Some unscrupulous lawyers even use standard "back doors" to Trusts so they can financially bleed them. These standard back doors are more common than you might suspect in Irrevocable Statutory Trusts. So, buyer beware![130] When we discussed this revelation with a lawyer we met casually, she laughed and said it was common.

Declaration of Trust

As we mentioned before, a document to set up any Trust is known as an Indenture.[131] A good Trust Indenture is complex and has twenty pages or more. The rule is, "Every little detail helps the future of the Trust." The Trustees look to the Indenture to provide clarity about decisions they make about Beneficiaries and investments. Anything the Trust Grantor can do to avoid confusion by the Trustees about decisions they may need to make for the Beneficiaries should be put into the Trust Indenture.

> One of the most important features of an Indenture is determining the order of inheritance and how inheritance is to take place. This is where many "what if" clauses are explored.

One of the most important features of an Indenture is determining the order of inheritance and how inheritance is to take place. This is where many "what if" clauses are explored. For example, what if the first Beneficiary dies without children, or what if the Indenture was created when a child was fifteen years old and suddenly another child is born? What if the main Beneficiary becomes involved in drugs and alcohol?

---

[130] Found in an Irrevocable Statutory Trust created by an attorney is the following under section titled "To Make Payments and Distributions" (4) By making expenditures directly for the benefit of the Beneficiary, *the Trustee shall not be required to supervise or inquire* into the application of any funds so paid or applied, and the receipt by the payee shall be full acquittance of the Trustee. (*Emphasis added*).

[131] Also as a reminder, a Trust Indenture is known as a Declaration of Trust or any combination of the two terms.

How is that to be handled? Who inherits and in what order due to various circumstances?

The answers to these questions must be in a real Indenture, whether Statutory or Private, that is designed to handle distribution over at least two generations.

The Indenture also lists the powers of the Trustees. One of the powers to spell out is the right to mortgage property. There is a standard list of the powers of the Trustees included in most Indentures that should be edited by the Grantor, or at least understood. For example, do you know what an "undivided interest" is? If not, then you need to ask questions.

Suggested points to include in an Indenture are provided in Volume II.

Funding

Once the initial Trust document is set and the rules and regulations of the Trust established and signed into being, the Trust needs to be funded. A bank account is set up by the Trustees, and the initial funds and assets to set up the Trust, known as initial corpus, are either transferred or exchanged to Trust accounts. After the Trust is set up, other people can usually add to the funds or the Grantor can put in more money. Any beginning money added to the Trust sets up a "floor" from which the accounting evolves. When the Trust investments are less than the initial corpus, the funds received are then applied, first to principal until the initial corpus is recovered, and then to income. This is in accordance with certain accounting rules and regulations.

Before even initial funds can be put into the Trust, though, Trustees have to be named, and in a Common-Law Irrevocable Trust you may also want to name an Executive Secretary or a General Manager.

Administration

The difference between a Private Trust and a Statutory Trust lies in the administration. Irrevocable Statutory Trust administration is usually less involved and more distant from the Beneficiaries than an Irrevocable Private Trust. The focus of a Statutory Trust is on accounting, not necessarily on the personal needs or evolution of the Beneficiaries. An Irrevocable Private Trust usually has Trustees who can be more interactive with the family, and the family members have an opportunity to participate. This also needs sophisticated administration, and more frequent meetings of the Board of Trustees. In a Statutory Trust, meetings are probably not required unless mentioned by the Trust Grantor, as Minutes may not be needed. Minutes are vital to managing a Private Trust.

Goals

The trick to having a Trust be successful lies in the Grantor's having fixed specific goals for the group of people for whom he or she set up the organization. If the goal is only to pass on assets, that can be simple. But if the goal is to see the family members are educated in a specific way, taken care of in a certain manner, or any other wish the Grantor has, then the Trustees must take a more active role. For example, some Trusts are set up to take care of a handicapped member of the family. If a bank takes care of managing this Trust type, it will hire a caretaker. A Private Trust may also hire a caretaker, but it is likely the Trustees will be more involved and see the other family members are active in making sure this person is well cared for.

We do not mean to imply that Statutory Trustees are not likely to take this extra step, only that, in a Private Trust, this is more likely.

Involvement and Details

Those interested in setting up an Irrevocable Common-Law Trust must first realize it takes more time than a Statutory Trust and more attention.

If you pay for documents to create a Trust, whether through a lawyer or through a private company, you need to realize that you must be involved. As pointed out before and in accordance with guidelines, and the Internal Revenue Code, the Grantor of an Irrevocable Trust can hold some powers even though the Trustees hold legal title.[132] One of these powers is deciding beneficial distribution, and the other is to keep control over investment decisions. If these two powers are kept, it means that you, the Grantor, will be included in the Board of

---

[132] Morton Freilicher, *Estate Planning Handbook with Forms*, Prentice-Hall, Inc., Englewood Cliffs, N.J. (1970) p. 157-158 and IRC §674(b) and (d).

Trustees to review the cash flow of the Trust and to aid with investment research.

Many Grantors are surprised to learn after starting their Common-Law Trusts that they have to take part in training the Trustees how to take care of the assets. This is because the Grantor has the reasoning behind the investment decisions and asset locations all in his or her head. He or she also has a specific set of views that can only be experienced in response to circumstances during meetings of the Board of Trustees. To ensure effective administration and long-term survival of the Trust, these details must be communicated.

In a Irrevocable Statutory Trust or a Statutory Living Trust, this link between the Trustee and Grantor may or may not happen. For example, in a Charitable Remainder Trust, the Grantor died and his brother became the Trustee. The Grantor never took the time to tell him where all the assets were and how he was administering them before he died.

In a Common-Law Irrevocable Trust, the Grantor must be involved with the Trustees in training them to manage to the family and teaching the Trustees where the assets are and how they need to be handled. Going back to the Charitable Remainder Trust Grantor, he had been involved in several different types of investments. Real estate was one of them. When he died, it took the Trustee over a year to gather all the information and papers to establish himself as the Trustee to take over the accounts,.

Those who should not get an Irrevocable Common-Law Trust are those people who delegate the administration of their assets to others and who do not want to be involved with the details. We have spoken to a couple of CPAs about Common-Law Trusts, and discovered that most of their clients are expecting the CPAs to manage their assets–and do not care whether the assets are in a Trust or not. The clients are not of the mind-set to become involved in the intricacies of setting up a Common-Law Trust or any other Trust system.

Impact

Because of the impact setting up a Trust has on other family members, and the attention needed to set up an Irrevocable Common-Law Trust, it causes a life change; the advantages are wonderful, and the adventure astonishing. Some members of the family will be unhappy with the decision, while others will be elated. Broken lines of communication among family members may need to be reestablished to prevent too much upset.

Chapter 21

Resistance

B eneficiaries are the essence of life, those to whom we pass on our legacy
and who benefit from our contributions to society. They are the reason
for living. Even if you do not have children, the future of our world
depends on the next generation.

Heirs: The Favored and the Flawed

Of course, there are times where someone does not want to pass on a legacy to
the children, and there are those situations where people are just plain greedy
and mean.

Bloodline

Beneficiaries are usually your children or grandchildren who represent the
family genetic line, also known as the "bloodline." In a Statutory Trust, that is
a Living Trust, or an Irrevocable Statutory Trust, to be eligible, the Trust recipients must be of the bloodline[133] or adopted. In a Common-Law Trust, though,
Heirs Beneficiary can be anyone chosen by the one who set up the Trust. For

---

[133]   Also known as 'issue of the body.'

example, in the original Rockefeller Trust which held the Standard Oil Empire, the Beneficiaries are allegedly the people of Earth.

If you do not have Beneficiaries to whom you can pass on your worldly goods, then those in need, close friends or people who helped you through life might be suitable. The major benefit to naming friends to receive the legacy is that they can become closer to the Grantor of a Common-Law Trust–at least, one would think the honor of being named might be appreciated.

I cannot, I will not

Naming Beneficiaries, though, is sometimes not so simple. Many times the first resistance to passing possessions to the next-in-line often comes from the Trust Grantor. An Irrevocable Common-Law Trust sets up a cash flow to Beneficiaries while the Grantor is still alive (Inter Vivos Trust). Sometimes we hear the strangest reactions, and often the saddest excuses, to avoid passing assets.

When counseling people that sharing their wealth is the purpose of the Trust, we find it difficult for some to grasp the following two points:

- They will have enough to share when assets are restructured.

- It is a great benefit to the Trust to pass on the wealth.

The initial wall of resistance stems from, "I never had anyone ever support me, so why should I give money to people before I die?" This leads us to realize that when a generous pattern has not been fixed by previous generations, it takes an effort to break poverty thinking and, perhaps, even innate selfishness. While the overall need for survival keeps people in a limited focus on self, in reality, sharing assets assures survival.

Tax Breaks

Passing on wealth gets the Trust a tax break. For example, you can decrease your gross income by giving up to $12,000.00[134] a year away to each Beneficiary, thus you have less money of your own on which to pay taxes. In fact, the

---

[134]   Check with appropriate accounting personnel to get current amount of deduction.

Trust does not pay any income taxes if all profits are distributed and then Beneficiaries pay taxes on them. The Grantor cannot keep the funds anyway. Either give money to the IRS, or to the Grantor's offspring. For some reason, many Grantors would rather pay the income tax than give away the money.

The Devil

Oddly enough, though, one of the greatest challenges in teaching people how to set up and use a Common-Law Trust is to get them to understand the value of Beneficiaries. The Beneficiaries automatically protect assets by their vested interest in the future of the Trust. It is being created for them. This resistance from the Grantor about selecting Beneficiaries also often stems from the complete lack of support by the Grantor's family during the formative years. Either poverty was a big issue in the early childhood, or the parents believed hard work was such a divine virtue, that financial support to follow one's dreams became akin to supporting the devil.

The Last Penny

Some people panic because they feel they might need all that money in their old age. Gripped by fear, they will not give up a dime, even if putting their money in a Trust allows assets to multiply. The assumption here is they will be sick, and medical bills will soar. The Grantor wants the best care, even if his or her last penny is given to the doctors. Of course, the Grantor remains a TCU holder in a Common-Law Trust. No Board of Trustees can ignore this fact.

Control and Domination

There is also the need some people have to keep children on a leash. They can do this by doling out their money to them on a whim, keep children begging for more, and even competing with siblings. This type of parent thrives on being able to manipulate those dependent with dollars, and thus keep them subject. Once the Trust is settled, and has a strong cash flow, that particular issue no longer applies, as the Trust can issue a predictable check, whether it be a mere $100 a month, or a whopping $20,000.00 a month. Either way, the Beneficiary is freed from the controlling needs of the parent.

Manifest Dreams

Another common belief among the average person is that Beneficiaries should work for the money, lest they become corrupt. Perhaps they will be lazy, expecting a handout, or turn to drugs because they have no purpose. It is always astonishing to us that people think so little of their offspring. What people would these errant children be if they were financially supported? What would happen if the children could manifest their dreams instead of working 9 to 5 in a dreary job, slaving for others who know how to build wealth? Where do you want your children to be in the next ten years? Locked into a slave status, compromising their ideals to make a buck? Just where did that idea come from? Is this known as the Christian Work Ethic? Maybe if children had enough money, or extra money, you would discover that they had some great ideas to contribute to both the family and the world.

Easy Money

As we have previously shown, the wealthy do not expect their children to work, and they do not think of them as useless and lazy. We can suppose that they even silently mock the rest of us because we are so foolish in our thinking, and that we have set our minds to toil in their fields while they reap their fortune. By the way, the rich make money out of money–an investment here, an investment there, a gamble on the right business and they have an overnight success. A slave to no one, they choose to work doing what they love to do, whatever that is. Yes, some even use their cleverly earned cash to go sailing, or to compete in some awesome sports event, such as circumnavigating the globe in a balloon.

Caged Bird

The hardheaded position that people need to work to build character does have merit, and we are not against the idea. We want people to realize, though, that long-term enslavement is damaging. If people want their children to learn about hard work, five to ten years are enough, otherwise the deeply ingrained slave mentality makes even retirement a fear. It is also a fact that when a person has been 9 to 5 patterned, it takes a long time to get out of this social programming. Developing a new view about life, and grasping the ideas to increase personal worth, can be overwhelming. Not having ever having freedom to explore his or her own talents, such a person might behave like a caged bird. Though you may open the door, the bird never flies out. The wealthy who use our toil for their gain count on that, by the way.

The Dream Home

Of course, some children have enough wits, pluck and skills to find their ideal jobs. They do not need parental support or help from a Trust, but who would not want some extra backing, and an opportunity to explore greater possibilities? For those lucky children, would you want them to get a loan from a bank for that dream home, or would you rather have a cash-rich Trust loan them the funds? A friendly Trust family banker is always helpful, and the Trust earns money on the interest. This earning by the Trust passes on to the Beneficiaries through periodic distributions.

The Rich And The Poor

Then, there is always, "I do not have enough money." Some people, no matter how much money they have, never have enough. Oodles of money seep into every crevice of some people's lives, and still they are "poor." This is a poverty complex that knows no end, and takes much internal processing by the Grantor to overcome so the Grantor may learn how to share wealth. John D. Rockefeller was like this; everyone hated him. He became friends with a preacher, who convinced him to start a Charitable Trust. Nearly overnight, and with the help of the heavily reported, high profile handing out of dimes, suggested by a publicist, John D. became a great benefactor, and the resulting goodwill brought about even greater wealth.

Shock

Surprised reactions by those named as Beneficiaries range from the astounded, "Why me?" to the angered, "You cannot do this, you are being scammed, and I will have nothing to do with this Trust!" Why such reactions, and what do they mean?

When assets are properly restructured, though, people who have always carefully kept track of their pennies may suddenly realize they have far more than they ever expected. Their prior money attitude deeply affected their children, who now believe their parents have gone mad, thinking that the restructuring of their funds has given them more than the parents could possible ever have. Hysterically, they deride and degrade their parents for their foolish behavior of putting their assets into a Trust. The good news? With careful Trust management, those same Beneficiaries become believers in about five years, and see their own potential for wealth.

Some children believe that when their parents die the children will get the house, the bank account, and the cars in the garage. When funds are put into any Irrevocable Trust, they are out of reach of the children. They will no longer inherit them. The Beneficiaries can use the goods, and get a cash flow from them, but do not own them. There is an initial shock as Beneficiaries have to rearrange their thinking, and the backlash can be astounding. The unbelievable greed that sometimes surfaces may even be frightening. All the issues of lack of trust, betrayal, favoritism and downright rage come to the foreground. The Beneficiaries may fear their inheritance has been ripped from them, and that everyone around their parents conned them. If there is more than one child involved, this can throw the entire family into crisis. Again, it takes about five years for the children to figure out they got the deal of the century, and they are loved and supported, but in the meantime, there are no secrets left in this family.

> When funds are put into any Irrevocable Trust, they are out of reach of the children. They will no longer inherit them.

Beneficiaries can initially be liabilities. The "dark" children surface. It is more often the rebellious children who eventually become part of the Trusts's administration team. This is because they have an interest in control, and want to know the details of the finances. With proper training, their interest turns into an asset.

Special Cases

Beneficiaries with addictions or who may display criminal behavior need special treatment, and the Grantor must counsel with the Trustees to give them specific instructions. Since the assets are never in the names of the Beneficiaries, the Trust can be spared many of the more distressing problems caused by Beneficiary irresponsibility.

Financial Ignorance

Criticizing Beneficiaries because they do not know how to handle money may be inappropriate. Did anyone ever give them a large enough amount of money so they could learn how to handle it? Living from paycheck to paycheck is not the schoolroom atmosphere needed to teach people how to create or even manage a fortune. As reported on the radio in Philadelphia in the 1960s, Lamar Hunt, H. L. Hunt's son, lost a million dollars on a new business venture. When reporters asked what Mr. Hunt what he thought of this, he replied (paraphrased), "My son has nine million more to practice on."

It takes money to make money, and it takes practice and experience. If Beneficiaries are unfamiliar with the terms of wealth, such as interest income, margin accounts, dividends, selling short, bear market, and the like why does anyone expect them to know how to handle money? Give them a few thousand to experiment with, and some proper mentoring, and they just might learn something. This is how the wealthy do it. They pass on their knowledge to their children, maybe even at the dinner table where they share their business venture stories and introduce their children to the ideas that movers and shakers of the world hold to be true.

Disruptive Children

What if a Grantor just plain does not like his or her children? There are all sorts of reasons for this. One might be the Grantor was not so kind or available when the children were in the formative years. If the Grantor did not take the time to make friends with his or her offspring, then why should the children care about their parents? Sometimes, though, children are just downright mean, selfish and abusive.

Control and Domination

There is also the classic situation where one parent pits the children against one another, and this dissension and manipulation includes turning children against the spouse. That is a thorny one to resolve, and sometimes the communication channels necessary to clear the emotional wounds never happen. The reasons for the dysfunctional relationship may be many, but the result is the same. Children simply dislike one or both of their parents and display this in myriad ways. We recommend that something be left to them anyway. Simply because of their blood relationship, they can claim some of the inheritance. Why throw the entire Trust fortune into a legal battle? There are many ways this can be handled to satisfy the Grantor.

The Payoff

Probably the most shocking statement we ever heard was from a third party who knew about a beneficial distribution, but had no idea of how a Trust works. He exclaimed, "Why would you just give money to people?" The Trustee, startled at the reaction, replied, "All the needs of the Trust are satisfied, and the extra funds are passed on to the Beneficiaries." The reaction of the Beneficiaries was even more startling. They never received a beneficial distribution before this, and the Board of Trustees gave them no warning. The surprise paid off, and the overwhelming gratitude satisfied the Board of Trustees and the Grantor. After all, that is why we do Trusts. There is a special perk in helping others.

Who Are the Heirs or Beneficiaries?

Once past the resistance, choosing Beneficiaries becomes the issue. One would think that this is simple if the Grantor has children, or adopted children, but not so. It depends on the relationship with the children. From a disabled child, to a child with criminal behavior, to the irresponsible, to the divine and favored child, the Grantor has to decide how to manage each. In a Irrevocable Statutory Trust, these factors are more defined in the Trust Indenture, leaving less judgment for the Trustees to make about each child. In the Common-Law Trust, individual needs can also be defined, even though the Grantor continues to take part in and advise the Board of Trustees, so this becomes an ongoing process.

The law states that each Trust must have different Beneficiaries, so when forming more than one Trust to ensure asset separation, it becomes a problem if the Grantor has only one child. The next eligible set of Beneficiaries can come from the Grantor's siblings. By law, the blood relationship takes precedence over other Beneficiaries.

Adding nieces and nephews automatically involves the parents of the chosen Beneficiaries. This gives them a vested interest in the Trust being formed. This increased support adds to the safety of the assets. After all, if your children become the Beneficiaries of your brother, you are much more likely to support your brother's endeavors. This often proves to deepen the sibling relationship, or even heals old wounds. Since the overall intent of the Common-Law Trust is to bring the family together, this tactic has proven to be worth its weight in gold for the long-term survival of the family.

Bereft Of Friends

If you do not have children, friends can become the Beneficiaries of your Common-Law Trust. We have even seen the situation where a person claims to have no friends for potential Beneficiaries. With the poverty and despair in this world, how can people fail to choose even one person as a Beneficiary? We know people who spent their entire life making money, yet have no one to leave it to. If you are one of these people, all we can say is, "Open your eyes, look around, join a club, get to know people."

Financial Leverage

As a Common-Law Trust evolves, it builds financial leverage. The objective is for the Trust to perform like a family bank, and to provide private mortgages and loans for family members. Solid family leadership gives generations to come the advantage, and provides financial stability instead of the hand-to-mouth survival that many of us experience. With this added support, we just might be able to develop some leaders to take our world into a better place.

The Risk Factor

The initial group of people to start the Trust are usually those who have taken risks to collect the assets. These are financially savvy individuals who discovered other ways of making wealth. They stepped out of the norm to discover a broader spectrum of reality in which they can create the rules to their own games. To continue the build-up of assets, train the next generation. We recommend that at least one child who displays a talent or an interest in the finance/accounting arena be trained. This child should get an education in accounting or law. Preferably, there will be two Beneficiaries worthy of this task. As mentioned before, the adverse Trustee will likely remain as Trustee after the Grantor dies, and should be a strong mentor so the qualified progeny become skilled Trustees to carry on the legacy.

Before this transition happens, though, the favored son or daughter learns at his or her parent's knee the lucky gambler techniques and holds a management position in the Trust to take those calculated risks. These risks will continue to augment that golden goose to forever shower good fortune on the rest of the family.

Chapter 22

Protection and Support

Few would turn down the opportunity to join a group offering protection and support. To create that environment, though, takes dedication to the greater good.

Shelter from the Storm

W hen the skyline of New York lost a measure of its height and grandeur on 9/11, the emotional tone of the world downshifted a few notches. Many people now live under greater stress in one or more aspects of their lives. This circumstance offers an excellent background to examine the calming and stabilizing effects of the ancient, proven wisdom built into an Irrevocable Trust and especially the Common-Law Trust.

A Better Future

Because many feel uncertain now and more than usually challenged, we share with you our vision. These are the deeper reasons we have for striving to bring this time-honored information about the Common-Law Trust out of obscurity and make it available beyond the privileged classes. Recent world event make this revival and popularizing of Common-Law Trusts timely; they have been tested in many earlier periods of unrest (Roman wars, the Crusades, the American Revolution, etc.) and proven reliable. As repeatedly demonstrated throughout history, without trustworthy relationships, nothing is certain. **The true values in life lie not in money or political power, but in competent and caring people committed to helping one another.**

Trust Builds Wealth

Human relationships based on trust create wealth, not the other way around. While life holds no guarantees, trained people dedicated to common goals offer the strongest chance for group comfort and security. As people get involved in various forms of Trustee administration training, we strongly encourage them to build trusted relationships among Grantor, Trustees and Beneficiaries, and to nurture and improve their communication. Then, if difficulties arise, they can count on one another. If one of them has special needs, the others provide for him or her. Money is not necessarily a major part of the solution—sometimes not an element at all. Maybe what is needed is the loan of some piece of equipment, a place to live or just plain wisdom from Trustees. Through this support, Trust members can get the guidance needed to avoid many of life's pitfalls.

Assistance To The Beneficiaries

When a well-managed Trust exists for several years, the Trustees become familiar with the other Trust Officers and the Beneficiaries, and the assets multiply. Then, if a crisis arises—in the family or in the broader community—members of the Trust can pull together to respond effectively. When Trust Beneficiaries or other family members need work, they may be able to contribute their skill to help manage the family assets.

Extra or unused equipment may help those out of work to pick up odd jobs. A computer, desk, truck, automobile or other useful item may be the missing ingredient which turns an otherwise idle Trust member into a thriving entrepreneur who contributes to the Trust's expanding wealth. Because Trustees interact with bankers, corporate executives, brokers and other professionals, a friendly recommendation in the right ear may prove to be exactly what an out-of-work Beneficiary needs to get a job.

A Beneficiary of one Trust recently found himself caught in the chaos of New York following the World Trade Center disaster and unable to find an apartment. Friends allowed him to sleep on their couch, but jobs were in such short supply he could not find work to support himself. Enrolled in school there, he could not leave the city, either. To relieve his predicament, the Trustees sent a laptop computer in a rolling case from their inventory, plus some extra funds.

Reason For Being

Such timely, real-life support is what Trusts are all about. By helping people get on with their lives in tough times through removing as much undue stress as possible, Trustees fulfill the faith placed in them by the Grantor. This is what each Board of Trustees is charged to provide, first by building the assets year by year, and then by responding properly when the need arises. With this support, a Grantor's Beneficiaries may follow their God-given talents to aid our beautiful, but troubled, world. Moments like these refresh the Trustees' awareness of their purpose and why they work so hard to create and preserve Trust assets.

Speaking of working hard to keep assets for the family, here is the story of a valiant man, who had so much to give, that he shared his wealth. We include this now because this foreshadows some of the information in our second book which focuses more on the technical nature of an Irrevocable Common-Law Trust. Although this is based on a court case, we "upgraded" the legal details to be more user friendly, as we have with other court cases in Volume II.

The following article, "Beneficiaries and the Battle of Betts," specifically displays how a Trust campaigns for the Beneficiaries, and protects them:

Beneficiaries and the Battle of Betts

This case brings out many aspects of an Irrevocable Trust, as well as its complexities. For those of us who work with Trusts every day, it is wonderful to know that Mr. Betts outfoxed, them all.

Commissioner of IRS vs. Betts[135]

Mr. Betts, obviously a generous man, created an Irrevocable Trust in the early 1930s for his family, which received a bounteous steady income. In those years the Board of Trustees paid the income tax for the Trust by dutifully filing the needed paperwork (Form 1041 and related schedules). The IRS, for various and seemingly baffling reasons, decided that Mr. Betts should pay taxes on the income even though the Trust had already done so. The amount assessed for back taxes was substantial.

To appreciate the depth of this particular matter, we need to understand some of the Trust details. When the Indenture was written[136], Mr. Betts, a stockbroker, kept the power[137] to make the investment decisions.[138] Further, the income collected each year was paid to his mother and his wife. On the death of either of them, the survivor received 100% of the Trust income. If both Beneficiaries died during his lifetime, for the balance of his life the income was added to the principal. After he, his mother and his wife passed on, the Trust estate was to be divided equally among his children or their lawful descendants. If Mr. Betts's mother and any of his known descendants survived him, or if he should survive both his mother and his wife but leave no descendants, the Trust would transfer to his Heirs Beneficiary as outlined in the Trust agreement. This also included his sister and brother.

---

[135]   123 F.2d 534, 41-2 U.S. Tax Case (Nov. 26, 1941)

[136]   The contract where the Trust Grantor and Trustees agree how the Trust should be administered, who the Beneficiaries are, and any long-range strategies for building the corpus of the Trust.

[137]   I.R.C. §675(4)B "A power to control the investment of the Trust funds either by directing investments or reinvestments . . ."

In other words, all parties named gained from the Trust, while the Grantor, Mr. Betts, received none of the funds from its investments.

Directing Investments

Ignoring the great benefits offered the Beneficiaries, the relentless IRS agents on the case claimed that by directing the investments, this provident family man kept control of the Trust. This rationale allowed the agency to hold him liable for the tax. Fortunately for Mr. Betts, his ironclad Trust had no a chink through which to attack him as Grantor. To decide whether our humane stockbroker was in control of the Trust administration and had the power to revoke or alter the Trust agreement, a federal judge examined the Trust Indenture. He discovered that Mr. Betts waived all power to revoke or alter the Trust agreement except with the approval of his wife, mother, sister, or brother.

For whatever personal or professional reasons, the IRS agents refused to stop there. The U.S. attorney continued to complain the Beneficiaries did not have "substantial adverse interest" and would bow to the will of the Grantor. Thus, the attorney argued, the Grantor still had the power to revoke the Trust and revest the estate in himself. He based his position on the premise that Betts's mother, brother, sister and wife, whose consent he needed to revoke the Trust, did not have substantial adverse interest.

The court needed to discover whether the wife, mother, sister, and brother were under the control of Mr. Betts. In other words, would they qualify as "adverse parties"? An adverse party is one who is so substantially vested in the Trust that he or she has much to gain if the Trust assets increase and loses if they decrease [139].

---

[139]   I.R.C. §672(a) The term "adverse party" means any person having a substantial beneficial interest in the Trust which would be adversely affected by the exercise or nonexercise of the power he possesses respecting a Trust. A person having a general power of appointment over the Trust property should be deemed to have a beneficial interest in the Trust.

As an adjunct to this, note that Mr. Betts was not legally obligated to support his mother, sister or brother, nor required to be as generous with his wife as he was. Therefore, if the Trust dissolves, all of them were adversely affected because their Trust income ends and all funds would revert to Mr. Betts. Therefore, the court determined that these Beneficiaries qualified as adverse parties. Its ruling reads:

It may be that because of family affection they might consent to a revocation but that fact does not of itself destroy their quality of adverse holding protected by the statute. What Congress had in mind obviously was such a person as has a vested right under a Trust agreement to insist on its performance and cannot be compelled to surrender the same. Such persons are both the mother and the wife. We find no justification for reversal of the finding of the triers of the facts the Beneficiaries were adversely interested.

Control and Disillusionment

This showed that Mr. Betts neither controlled the Trust nor could he easily dissolve it. As the court stated, "his power of revocation was an exceedingly remote possibility and contingent on the decision of others . . ," At this point in the case, the thoughtful reader may wonder whether the government had an ulterior motive. It seems this can be used to set up a legal precedent defining Trust guidelines. Is the IRS blind to the obvious or does greed rule the agency and its superiors? Clearly, this generous family man neither controlled nor benefitted from this Trust he created.

In any event, although the IRS's first two arguments failed, it tried still another tactic. Failing to persuade either the trial court or the appeals court that Citizen Betts was fair game for its money hunters, it nevertheless rolled right on to submit his Trust to its next legal test, "the fruits of the ownership." It did not matter the agency cited many (but inappropriate) court cases to support its claim; Mr. Betts did not enjoy any of the Trust income (fruits of ownership) and received no other benefit from the Trust.

Still undaunted, the insistent IRS attorney argued that if Mr. Betts survived the Beneficiaries, he had the power to revoke the Trust. The court rejected this idea, too; it ruled the power to revoke was not vested in him but "was a remote possibility, contingent and uncertain with no insurance of ever coming into existence." The IRS's argument collapsed because there was no way to control who would die in what order. After all, Mr. Betts might die before his mother or wife.

Substance of Transaction

Today, the issue of adverse interest has an added dimension. Because the Beneficiaries enjoyed the Betts Trust income consistently for three years, the Trust was well established by a legal principle called substance of transaction. In other words, since it conducted its routine business as an Irrevocable Trust, its day-to-day transactions confirmed the intent and tax status of the Grantor.

Even today, some might claim that a mother and a wife can be adverse parties under the circumstances described here. The last 50 years, though, of court cases reveal that using that argument alone is inadequate to prove a Trust as Irrevocable[140]. Too many people misused this aspect of Trust

> Scam Trusts have no beneficial distribution going to anyone other than the Grantor, who, usually, compromises the Trust by making him or herself a Trustee.

---

[140] For convenience, we repeat this information: IRC §672© **Related or subordinate party.** . . (1) The Grantor's spouse if living with the Grantor; (2) any of the following: The grantor's father, mother, issue brother, or sister; an employee of the grantor; a corporation or any employee of a corporation in which the stock holders of the grantor and the trust are significant from the point of view of voting control; and

procedure. Further, too many fail to understand that beneficial distributions must be given to others named in the Trust instrument. In today's all-too-popular "scam Trusts," wives and mothers are often named as Trustees without enough structure in place to give them substantial adverse interest. At the same time the Grantors fail to surrender control of the assets. Scam Trusts have no beneficial distribution going to anyone other than the Grantor, who, usually, further compromises the Trust by making himself or herself a Trustee.

By comparison, a closing statement in the battle of the Betts Trust shows the Trust he set up was managed properly. As the judge said, "There is no question but that income payable to the mother is in excess of any amount which there is legal obligation upon respondent [Mr. Betts] to pay under the Illinois Statute." That is, the cash flow Betts provided for his mother through his Trust far exceeded what he was obliged to give her.

Beneficiaries First

Despite the challenges an Irrevocable Trust may face as it multiplies its assets, its final goal is the welfare of its Beneficiaries. It may be slow gathering enough financial momentum to share as described here, but its Trustees will do well to remember Mr. Betts's skill and generosity as a financial manager and patiently follow his example.

---

subordinate employee of a corporation in which the Grantor is an executive.

Chapter 23

Cash Flow

A Trust is much like any other vehicle; the driver-manager or Trustee decides where it goes and what it does. This fundamental reality needs serious study by anyone setting up a Trust.

Initially supplied by the Grantor, cash flow, the fuel of any Trust, may continue to be pumped by him or her. In a Common-Law Trust, the General Manager, who is sometimes the Grantor, often handles the day-to-day activities, with then Trustees playing a guiding but less active role until they become more familiar with the assets. They oversee the accounting and legalities, ensure the Beneficiaries get their distributions and pay the taxes, but, in general, are less assertive and may be hesitant and shy away from risk. To the world they appear as the movers, while sometimes they are "fronts." Ideally, the steering position is inherited by the child most qualified to climb into the driver's seat left vacant by his father or mother.

Any Trust group must first acquire enough cash to make a significant investment yielding a steady dependable payout. The most immediate and sometimes the easiest way to achieve this is to invest in a business or sell residential property through a Trust. The most suitable way to become involved in a business is through forming a partnership. Direct the profits from the partnership to the

Trust where the Board of Trustees can place it where "money can more than multiply itself."

Once a strong cash flow is established, it funds charities, educational institutions, and, of course, the Beneficiaries' own projects and businesses. Support for any of these recipients further benefits the local community by creating jobs and other businesses.

What future would you choose: one where your children must work two jobs or one in which they raise the standard of society and invest in their dreams for a better world?

Making It!

There are a great many pitfalls when starting a business, from owner ignorance of marketing and accounting, to the financial games played by lenders. During this learning curve, if possible, find financial support outside the usual channels.

Because it is statistically proven that most businesses fail in the first five years, the leasing game becomes profitable. This applies to the restaurant business, where equipment is partially paid for, and when the buyer defaults, the equipment is sold or leased afresh to another startup company. Default usually comes at that critical time in the company's development where a change of direction would save the business, except the clock runs out.

If only the cash distribution from a Trust could just set up that lucky someone blessed with a bright idea—or do you suppose that is how the rich would set up a lucky Beneficiary?

Because you may not grasp how the rich think, we present the following to "rewire" your belief. After all, continuous wealth is founded on having the right connections, and realizing how the game is played.

Cash Flows In . . .

Sometimes, it seems just like magic: all that lovely money washing into a Trust's bank accounts. Unfortunately, it takes more than magic to get the cash pump primed and flowing for the Beneficiaries. It takes planning and strategy. Generation after generation pays close attention, and the pump handle must never be idle. For a Trust to be well funded and productive, its gathered assets must be large.

Understanding Cash Flow

If you do not have a basic understanding of accounting, what is likely to happen to the cash flow? Even if you depend on accountants to advise you about the "bottom line," the accountants are not usually the ones responsible to develop the next scheme to make a business work. The accountant is not the one to close the business deals and make split-second decisions about the various matters concerning productivity. Without an understanding of the accounting, those decisions may not be as accurate as they could be.

The marketing budget in any company is likely to be one of the largest expenses, but the ratio of marketing to cash flow needs careful balance. Without getting the word out the product is unique and the best, it is not likely people will buy. The early cash to get the marketing rolling to bring in the business, though, can be a major drain on the budget. This is where most businesses decide to get a start-up loan, which adds pressure to the performance of the business, and often cuts the product's quality.

Employee expenses can be the largest item in the expense column, especially when combined with payroll tax commitments, matching funds, and other benefits. What if, though, the owner's salary–often in the long-run the largest single payroll item–were not even a factor? What if the owner of this business received a personal cash flow from the Trust? This gives the fledgling business a great benefit, as the first expenses are not so great, and may add notable time to that five-year clock.

Of course, having a cash flow to support you allows you to manifest your dreams and have the time to both gain the business experience you need, and to dabble in what has meaning to you.

That Bright Idea!

If you had enough funds, you could probably make almost any business succeed simply by lasting longer than the competition, by being able to use the wisdom gained in the long run and through sheer tenacity.

For those who start a business, the first five years are usually grueling. The learning curve is steep, especially if the business you start is based on a new idea and mentors are rare or nonexistent. Unfortunately, manifesting the dream, whatever it may be, can bring you into the light of harsh reality. We must remember, though, "If you want something you have never had, you must do something you have never done before."

Nurturing Beneficiaries

Most people have never had the experience of receiving from a Trust fund a check in the mail regularly, either monthly or quarterly. Whether the check is large or small, it offers support to the Beneficiary's life style. The larger the check, the less the need for the Beneficiary to compromise himself or herself by working for others.

Here is a myth: "If you give too much to your children, they become spoiled." Children should work for a living so they can recognize what they have." These are thought patterns laid into our society that have nothing to do with reality. In truth, nature has plenty of food, and infinite possibilities, but our financial system is used to restrict the people to keep them busy, and to keep them working.

Born Millionaires

The rich, who have no such constraints, support their children. The parents are willing to ensure their children receive the best educations and experience the finest of material goods. A child may be born into a Trust worth millions! Trustees support the child from the first breath and ensure the child's well-being. As mentioned before, when a child grows and marries the funds stay with the Trust for the benefit of the child, subject neither to nuptial agreements nor divorce settlements. It is a different way of living, a way most of us never experience.

Money Destroys Character?

As previously stated, there is no case on record in which the children of the wealthy have been left penniless for their own benefit. Further, if drawing benefits from a huge Trust fund does not destroy character, it stands to reason that drawing benefits from Social Security does not destroy character, either. The entire idea is false.

The rich manipulate the people into believing money erodes morals by making sure that some specific cases come to light.

In reality, if people do not have to work for a living, they are drawn to what they do best, and what they enjoy the most. People can manifest their talents, nurture the world we live in, and, above all, be happy.

Money is Happiness?

Happiness is not based on money. In fact, we might even go so far as to state that happiness has nothing to do with money, except that in our society, where money is used to manifest our dreams, the two are tied together.

If the family has the foresight to plan for the Beneficiaries, then the future of that family has endless possibilities. One way to do this is through an Irrevocable Common-Law Trust. Are you just a little bit curious about how it all works?

Rather than having your children work for a living, might it be more beneficial to have them work in a creative environment or even better yet, create jobs for others through entrepreneurial opportunities?

Chapter 24

Family Empowerment

W orld history is filled with the rise and fall of economies, governments, and even civilizations. To reach the top (or remain there) when a new order rises, families need organization. To be strong enough to get through hard times, a stash of assets large enough to help them climb, hold on or buy their way back in is necessary. National governments are short-lived, and the family which governs itself has the best chance of surviving calamity. No culture shows this fact better than the Chinese, whose rock-solid extended-family village withstood thousands of years of tyrants, some calling themselves "emperor," others "chairman."

Flexibility and Survival

One of the greatest assets which survives and grows with the proper use of the Common-Law Trust is the family history. Through it, each succeeding generation builds on the lessons of the past. Suppose your skilled parents and grand-parents bought land and passed on to you several choice pieces of real estate in prime locations. With it, they passed on the knowledge of preserving and developing holdings? How much further ahead would you be in developing a real estate business or taking over the management?

The more people working toward a common goal, the more receptor points a group has to receive valuable data. When their efforts serve not only the group's interests but their own and their family's, their focus sharpens, lessening distractions and multiplying their effectiveness. When the Board of Trustees meets, it brings to the table more choices offered by many minds. This broader base of interested partici-

> Also, the shared talents and pooled tangible assets give the Board greater leverage to perpetuate the Trust and, thus, to survive.

pants identifies multiple resources. This gives the Trustees and manager or managers of the business greater power to act wisely and timely for the good of all.

Thanks to this assortment of choices, the Common-Law Trust offers flexibility. Also, the shared talents and pooled tangible assets give the Board greater leverage to perpetuate the Trust and, thus, to survive. All participants in the Trust have personal stakes in its success. They are likely to pull their own weight and seek ways to increase cash flow and to reduce waste.

Setting up any Trust is complex, as will be shown in Volume II. Not only will we provide the basic points, but through a story told about the Trust Certificate Register of one Trust, we dramatize a scenario of how "it" is done. As a much simpler beginning point, we offer the fictitious story titled, "Romance and Trust" found later in this chapter. This explains a Trust consultation and the various preliminary decisions to be made.

Although this example of Romance and Trust is about a man who has notable wealth, in reality, people with far fewer complexities set up Trusts–the secret being how willing everyone is to pull together. You may be qualified to have a Trust even if your financial circumstances are far less than in this example.

The overall idea, though, is to empower the family and significant groups through sharing. So let us ask the question one more time:

Why should you place some of your assets into the hands of another person?

Family Trials and Tribulations

Family Dissension

Having Trustees handle the estate minimizes bickering and fighting among the heirs. Because title is divided, the Beneficiaries get the use of the goods and a share of the profits, but without the headaches of ownership and competition for parental affection.

Intrigue

Sometimes intrigue and darker motives exist in large inheritance matters. In an extreme case, someone may plot to get the assets. This might be one of the greatest reasons many wealthy people place their goods into an Irrevocable Trust. The Trustees are the only ones who know what the assets are in an estate. Those who scheme to get assets through stealth may not even be able to discover what assets are part of the Trust, where they are and who holds the legal title.

Keep the Assets in the Family

The third reason is many people who have large assets fear their children may marry a person who is after the family estate. The following shows this wonderful advantage of an Irrevocable Trust.

Romance and Trust

Imagine a gentleman in love with a lady. Not just any gentleman, this man has had a successful business career and amassed a substantial net worth. Unfortunately, his personal life has yet to match the success of his career, as attested to by child support and alimony payments to two ex-wives. The lady with whom he is enamored has never married, provides well enough for herself but has not achieved anywhere near the success the gentleman has. They have discussed marriage, at least in the abstract.

Prenuptial

Given his history, and the financial disparity between the couple, his friends (and his attorney) strongly advised a prenuptial contract. The memory of two divorces inclined him to agree.

When he raised the idea (once again, only in the abstract) the woman gave him a different perspective. She said that she saw a prenuptial agreement as a way to sabotage the relationship by agreeing in advance what to do when it failed.

Reflecting on what had gone wrong in his previous marriages, and why, he could see a certain wisdom to her argument. Besides, he knew that if she married him it would not be for his money. Of course, a friend reminded him he had "known" the same about wife number two, right up to the bitter battle in divorce court.

As talk of marriage became less and less abstract, the issue of a prenuptial agreement loomed larger and larger as a potential showstopper. It finally reached a point where the couple decided to seek counsel from a third party and scheduled time to talk with a common friend, a minister.

During the conversation with the minister, they got to the real issue behind their feelings about the prenuptial agreement. It came down to trust. Did he trust her and her motives? Did she trust him to do right by her?

A Matter of Trust

As they discussed the trust issue, the minister realized that he might have a solution to the problem. He reported his congregation had recently received a large gift from a Trust set up by one of the members. Could a Trust possibly provide an alternative to the prenuptial agreement which they could both live with?

When they both agreed to explore the possibility, the minister found the phone number of the member whose Trust had made the gift to the church. After the minister called the member and explained the situation, the member agreed that a Trust offered an excellent solution to the problem and gave the minister the name and phone number of his Trust specialist.

Before they left the minister's office, the couple talked with the Trust specialist on the phone. She agreed that a Trust could provide an answer to each of their needs in this situation, and then told them of the costs in both time and money necessary to set up a Trust. They readily agreed it would be a worthwhile investment and set an appointment to meet with her. She also got their e-mail addresses so she could send them information to study and suggest books they should read before their meeting.

At their meeting the Trust specialist explained that a Trust works by having a person transfer his or her property or possessions to a Board of Trustees. It then holds same in Trust for named Beneficiaries. Sometimes, if the couple wants to be involved in Trust administration, it can use some of the assets. Therefore, the gentleman would have nothing his potential wife could take in case of a divorce, and he could use some of the property and possessions. His wife-to-be would still have what she had brought to the marriage and, under the community property laws, a claim to half of what the couple made during their marriage, but nothing more. Both readily agreed that this was fair and made at least as much sense as a prenuptial agreement.

Goals and Ambitions

So, they got down to business with the specialist inquiring about what the gentleman wanted to do with his money, as well as what obligations he had. While listening carefully and asking questions that could have only come from years of experience, the specialist made pages of notes. She then asked the woman what she wanted and some questions about her finances, and took more notes.

When they finished the interviews the specialist said that she could see the couple loved each other and she looked forward to helping them achieve their goals. Explaining she needed time to digest the information and draw up a plan, she offered the suggestion that they get back together the following week, and they agreed.

Trusts, Alimony Payments and Ex-wives

During the second meeting the Trust specialist laid out a plan that proposed a Management Trust and under it five different Business Trusts:

- The gentleman would set up two Trusts, one for each of his two ex-wives, to make the alimony payments.

- He would set up a third Trust to provide for the child support payments and college expenses for his children.

- He would set up a fourth Trust to hold his premarriage assets.

- The potential wife would also set up a Trust to hold her premarriage assets.

After many questions, answers and extensive discussion, the couple requested two weeks to think about the proposal and decide exactly how it wanted to continue. The Trust specialist agreed that would probably be wise and set an appointment. Before the couple left she told each to consider whom to have as Trustees and as the Trust Protector for each of the Trusts.

The following week, the gentleman had his divorce attorney contact both of his ex-wives' lawyers and explain what he proposed to do about the alimony payments, child support and college expenses. Once the ex-wives' lawyers understood that having the money in a Trust guaranteed the alimony payments would continue no matter what happened to the gentleman, they had no problem getting approval from their clients. Of course, the same applied to the idea of a Trust to provide child support and college expenses.

After the third meeting, the couple agreed that it would follow the Trust specialist's proposal. It wanted a few minor changes, though.

Instead of a single Trust for all three of the gentleman's children, he wanted to set up a Business Trust for each of them. The Business Trust format gives the most financial flexible management. Once his first ex-wife understood what he wanted to do, she asked if she could also put something into the Trust for her children. When ex-wife number two heard this, she insisted that she also wanted to put something in the Trust for her child. To simplify matters, they all agreed to set up a Trust for each child. The Trust specialist recommended that they set these Trusts up as Asset Trusts under the ex-wives' Business Trusts.

Child Support and College Expenses

These Trusts not only provided child support and college expenses; they assured each child had a proper financial foundation for his or her life. Besides giving the gentleman a certain peace of mind on the subject, his fiancé felt that by encouraging him to be generous in doing this she could reassure the children that she was not after their inheritance.

Equalizing the Marriage

They also wanted another Trust set up as their Family Trust; the gentleman offered to fund the Trust with $250,000 as one of his wedding presents to his wife-to-be. They told the Trust specialist that working together on how he would give away his money had drawn the two of them closer together as she saw more of his generosity and he saw more of her support.

Having heard their ideas, the Trust Specialist agreed they made a lot of sense. She then explained what it would take in the way of time and effort to put each of the Trusts together. Given the work involved, she estimated six to nine months before they would complete the documents, especially given the extent of the gentleman's holdings. He promised to have his staff make it a priority to help on the matter. After all, the couple already scheduled their friend, the minister, and his church's chapel for a day in just under eight months for the wedding.

Multiple Needs

As the owner of three businesses, the gentleman did not believe in putting all of his eggs in one basket. Also, his study of the materials given him by the Trust specialist convinced him of the value of having more than one or two Trusts, given that he could afford to set them up properly, which he could. Therefore, he decided to set up seven Trusts, one for each of his three children, one for each of his two ex-wives, one for his premarriage assets and one as a Family Trust with his new wife. She would also set up one for her premarriage assets.

After spending a few hours filling out a questionnaire for each Trust, the gentleman met with the Trust specialist. They discussed the answers he provided and determined the purpose of each Trust. That information would come in handy in choosing the people involved in the Trust. Obviously, the gentleman would be the Grantor, and the Beneficiaries would vary by Trust. This left the key positions of Trustees and Protector for each Trust to be filled.

Adverse Trustee

The Trust specialist explained the need to have at least one adverse Trustee on each Trust to make it a legitimate Trust. She also explained that she had a handful of people working with her, serving as Trustees on Family Trusts, and that they would be available to work as Trustees on any Trusts she helped the woman and gentleman set up. Not related to the Grantor, they qualified as adverse Trustees. Since he would probably also want people he knew working as Trustees on the Trusts, she would train them to properly handle Trust administration. They agreed each Trust would have at least one experienced Trustee. The other Trustees being recommended by the gentleman.

One of the Trustees working with the Trust specialist happened to stop by the office just as the meeting ended. The young man started working as Trustee on a Trust set up by a friend of his, and impressed the Trust specialist who invited him to work on one other Trust. He explained that he was working on an MBA and enjoyed the Trust work, as it gave him an education into building wealth that surpassed what he could get in the classroom. His personality clicked with that of the gentleman and, after a discussion with the Trust specialist, they all agreed the young man would work as the adverse Trustee on some of the Trusts set up by the gentleman.

After further conversation, the gentleman realized he might not want the young man as the adverse Trustee on the Trust for his premarriage assets or his new Family Trust. He felt that could create a conflict of interest should he want to hire the young man to help run one or more of his businesses. The specialist assured him she could provide another qualified adverse Trustee for each of those two Trusts.

Over the next two weeks the gentleman managed to find the people to serve as Trustees on each of the Trusts. He filled the Trustee positions on his children's Trusts by approaching their godparents. The older son's godfather, an insurance agent, the daughter's godmother, a realtor, and the younger son's godfather, a small business owner, each agreed to serve on his or her respective godchild's Trust. He let each of the ex-wives pick her own Trustee. These were Trustees without experience, so the Trust consulting firm supplied the second Trustee on these Trusts.

Board of Trustees

For his own Trusts the gentleman decided he needed three Trustees. As first Trustee he would use the young man he had met at the Trust specialist's office. A friend of his from college, whom he had done business with over the years, would also serve as a Trustee. Finally, a young lady, who also worked with the Trust specialist, would serve as the adverse Trustee.

Having the Trustees in place, he was ready to find Protectors for the Trusts. His first wife suggested that he use her attorney as the Protector on her Trust and the Trusts for each of her children. Knowing the attorney to be both competent and a worthy opponent of anyone who would challenge the Trust, the gentleman readily agreed. On hearing about this, his second wife suggested her attorney for her Trust and her son's Trust. Once again, the gentleman agreed. As Protector on his own Trusts he chose an attorney who served him well as corporate counsel over the years.

Meanwhile, his potential wife had also met with the Trust specialist about the Trust for her premarriage assets. She agreed it made sense to have the same young person as adverse Trustee on her Trust as would serve on the Family Trust that she and her husband-to-be were setting up. She selected an uncle to serve as the second Trustee. An old friend of hers who worked in arbitration agreed to serve as Protector on her Trust.

Rules and Regulations

With the cast assembled, it was time to draft the Indentures for the Trusts. While this could have come first, the woman and gentleman agreed with the Trust specialist that it would be worth letting the Trustees and the Protectors join on this exercise. This would give everyone a fuller understanding of what the Trust they served on was about and why it existed. It also helped them better understand their particular roles.

Obviously, the couple hoped the Trust would grow over time, but of all the Trusts, the new Family Trust proved the simplest to set up. The entire res, also known as the corpus, consisted of $250,000 cash to start the Trust. The Beneficiaries were the husband and wife-to-be, his children and the state park. He and his children had spent many happy hours camping in some of the state parks. By naming the state parks as a Beneficiary, it becomes impossible for a court to challenge the Trust without the presence of the state's attorney general representing the people.[141]

Funding and Cash Flow

Since the Trust set up for the woman's Trust involved so few assets and so few people, it took next to the least amount of time to set up. She deeded her equity in her condo to the Trust. According to the Indenture, after expenses any money from renting the condo would go first to her to pay the mortgage. Any profits from the rent would go to pay the expenses of the Trust and to the Beneficiaries. As Grantor, the fiancée named as Beneficiaries her husband-to-be, herself, a favorite charity, and a group of public libraries. (By naming the public libraries, people of the state become a Beneficiary and it never hurts to have the attorney general on your side if someone challenges your Trust in court.) Her car went into an Asset Trust, with Trust Capital Units from the main Trust; these provided income for the Asset Holding Trust to pay for the maintenance, insurance and eventual replacement of the car. Jewelry, artwork and other valuables went into a second Asset Trust with enough Trust Capital Units to cover the insurance.

---

[141]   California Government Code 12591

While each of the gentleman's ex-wives had kept the house after the divorce, his attorney (he could afford the best) had made sure he kept a 50% financial interest in each house. Each ex-wife got to place her house in her Trust in exchange for Trust Capital Units, which were divided among the children's Trusts. The gentleman also put plenty of stocks and bonds into each of the ex-wives' Trusts to ensure payments at least equal to their alimony payments. Each of these specific Trusts had an end date to coincide with the end of his obligation for alimony payments.

Child Support Payments

Each child's Trust received enough in the way of stocks and bonds to ensure the beneficial payments to the child (via the mother as the adult guardian) met or exceeded the gentleman's child support payments. Also, there were enough funds to cover the expenses of running the Trust. Although a term requirement for child support was included, this set up surpassed these legal duties.

As part of his financial planning for putting his children through college, the gentleman bought a condo near a college on each child's first birthday. His thinking was that, by buying the condo with a 15-year mortgage, it would be paid off when the child graduated from high school. It could be used to get a loan to help pay for the child's education or provide the child a place to live while in college. Each child's Trust had an Asset Trust to hold the condo the gentleman bought for that child. A stipulation in the Indenture stated that money from the condo (each of which had positive cash flow) would go the child's main Trust, to be held for educational expenses.

To ensure a close working relationship between his children (who got along, even when their mothers did not), the gentleman had each of the children's Trusts issue 15% of its Trust Capital Units to each of the other siblings' Trusts. This would give the children a vested interest in the success of their siblings.

Since the gentleman put a fair of amount of his personal stock from his corporations into the various Trusts, he did so with the stipulation the Trusts assign the chairman of the board of each respective corporation their proxies. This allowed him to share some of his wealth with his children and ex-wives without giving them control of his companies. (Had the proxies been assigned to himself, he would have been seen as the owner of the stock for tax purposes under Internal Revenue Code 675(4)(A)).

By moving his premarriage assets into a Trust, and setting up all the other Trusts, the gentleman got ideas how to use his own Trust to help his businesses.

While setting up the Trust he and his lady agreed to use instead of a prenuptial agreement, the gentleman realized the value of using Trusts in estate planning and assuring his children's futures. He had also realized he could use Trusts to improve the bottom line for his businesses.

The most obvious example involved the company cars. His companies provided company cars for over a dozen field reps and top executives. While the companies had the money to buy the cars outright, they realized far greater tax breaks by leasing the cars and writing off the lease payments. In fact, it was enough of an advantage that his accountant promised to shoot the gentleman if he ever bought a car again.

Leases

After a conversation among the gentleman, his accountant and the Trust specialist, he had the Trustees draw up the paperwork for the Trusts to buy the cars and then lease them back to his companies. They agreed to not have more than two or three cars in each Trust to limit the exposure to liability in case of an accident.

It turned out the best way for him to do this was for the Trusts to be Business Trusts under the three Holding Trusts he had set up for his children. This meant that through the lease payments for the equipment, a portion of the money from his companies would go to help pay for his children's educations. He also arranged for major office equipment (for example, expensive copiers), as well as other equipment for his businesses to become assets in the Asset Holding Trusts, generating more lease opportunities. None of this redirection of funds went to him.

While doing this, he realized he stumbled on the solution to a problem he had with one of his businesses. He and one of his top engineers had come up with a new way to make one of their products. It involved a unique way of using three different pieces of equipment together. This resulted in cutting the time of manufacturing almost in half and cutting the expense by a third. Obviously, this would give his company a real edge in a competitive market. The problem was that he knew at least one of the three sellers he would buy the equipment from would let his competitors know what he had bought. Eventually a smart competitor would put the pieces together and figure out what he was doing (or, to use the technical term, reverse engineer the process).

The epiphany that helped solve his problem came when he realized that each of his three children's Trusts could buy one of the three pieces of equipment and then lease it to his company. By having the equipment bought by three separate "companies" (that is, the Trusts, each using a fictitious name) and delivered to three separate addresses, he could keep confidentiality. After all, no Trustee could tell anyone to whom the Trust leased the equipment.

Given his faster turnaround on orders and his competitive pricing using the new process, his company got enough new business that it needed to expand into a new facility. During a discussion with the accountant, they talked about the advantages of buying versus leasing. The accountant then asked "Why not do both? Put together a Trust to buy the building, and then have the company lease it from the Trust." By doing this, the business got the tax advantages of the lease, while the Trust realized the appreciation of the property and profits from the lease payments.

Research and Development

Meanwhile, another of the gentleman's businesses had a slightly different problem. It owned all of its equipment, but needed to spend more money on research and development. The company was asset rich but cash poor, and he felt that this could harm its capacity to stay innovative and competitive. The accountant stated that from an accounting point of view, it would be helpful for the gentleman to let the Trusts buy the equipment and lease it back to the company. This would give the company the cash it needed and a set of tax write-offs, while the profit from the leases would once again go to his children's Trusts.

Obviously, all this depends on the Trustees of his children's Trusts working with the gentleman to make this happen. Fortunately, they knew him to be an exceptional business leader and agreed that any venture he undertook would be a good investment.

On a more personal business matter, the couple decided to buy a new home. While his businesses were doing well enough he could afford to pay cash for the house the two of them wanted, you can imagine the accountant's reaction to that idea.

Looping Profits

The gentleman talked with the Trustees on the Trust he had set up before the wedding and explained that he wanted to borrow money from the Trust to buy the house. They agreed to loan him the money at a rate equal to the average of the best rates he could get from any other three established lenders. This removed questions about the legitimacy of the loan. He and the wife would get the interest write-off on their taxes, and the Trust realized the profit from the loan.

Chapter 25

Anomalies, Black Holes and Dreams

I rrevocable Trusts offer fantastic possibilities and opportunities to you and your family. That said, we want to be sure you recognize and understand the following key factors:

- Getting a Common-Law Trust is not be the easiest path to choose

- The possibility of opposition along the way

- If you have a particular ambition, it may be the best financial system available

- If well managed, it is the safest vehicle for protecting both assets and Beneficiaries

- Requires dedication and time.

We have not written this book to convince you to set up a Trust. After comparing and distilling our collective experience, we want to be sure you know what you are getting into before you get involved in Trusts. The greater message is the need to take responsibility for you and your family the best way possible amid a strange political era where your assets can be the target of the greedy.

Before we get into the anomalies and black holes of reality, we want to share with you our dream.

Redistribution of Wealth—The Right Way

The International Bankers thrive on war. By selling weapons and ammunition to both sides of any conflict, they continue to dominate the planet with their never-ending build-up of wealth. Destitute lives churned up into desperation and distress through poverty become fodder that breeds armies. Outrageous beliefs give all religions and patriots a reason to die. By keeping people riled up so they cannot think and do not have time to properly educate themselves, those in power stay in power. Isolated in their towers, these controllers separate themselves from humanity and thrive on the chaos and destruction they create.

Redistribution of wealth is anathema to the dominant players of this world. Therefore, putting ideas into the minds of the people that perhaps the status quo is not permanent and that better nondominating ways are possible, will not gain support from the well-*oiled* wealth.

> Starting with our particular social reality, the education needed to get people to share and trust is a monumental task.

A properly structured and managed Trust is good for the family—if morals and ethics are instilled with business savvy. Yet, what if one after another, these functional family groups hooked into each other? As one group thrives, it fuels another. If one group fails, support comes from the network. A simple idea, illustrated in Appendix D, shows how surplus is shared with Beneficiaries and with other Trust groups.

Appendix D displays the Callis Family Trust, which has both Beneficiaries and Exchangers. One of the Exchangers is the Xenter Family Trust. The amount of Trust Capital Units is not shown on this chart; we can assume the Xenter Family Trust became an Exchanger in the Callis Family Trust for at least 25 Trust Capital Units and, thus, became eligible to receive distribution.

While the Xenter Family Trust is a Beneficiary of Callis Family Trust, the P. L. Family Trust became an Exchanger in the Xenter Family Trust for 25 Trust Capital Units. It is eligible to receive a payout when Xenter Family Trust has a surplus, or has a profit.

Wealth redistributes as it continues to pass from one Trust to another.

Managing this wealth requires educated Trust members. Thus, training and mentoring are essential to the organization.

Some of the Trust Officers appear on more than one Trust, and on the Abagail Sorrenson Family Trust. Janet Foulson, Grantor, appears as the General Manager working with the Board of Trustees.

About the birds-eye view of the collective Family Trust group found in Appendix D, the second illustration shows that some Trusts overlap, while others do not. It is best to avoid too much overlap. The idea is to share the wealth, not keep it in one pile. We saw in Chapter 6, where we discuss tactics of the rich, how the right hand's washing the left hand is not going to help the overall situation–since there is no sharing of resources.

There is a story told that one of the large family organizations has a Business Trust that shares its profits with a Charitable Trust. Then the Charitable Trust gets services from the Business Trust. For example, when the Charitable Trust needs a new building, it hires the Business Trust to build it. The new building's funding is the beneficial distribution just received from the Business Trust and so is given back to the Business Trust to construct the building. What is wrong with this picture? Charity? Does not sound like it to us. This is much like a dog chasing its tail. The money goes from one Trust to another and back.

To stop the attitude of hoarding, we need to restructure our consciousness. To improve the other is to strengthen ourselves and secure our future, but the way this Business Trust/Charitable Trust operates, the profits are not shared. Kept within the same two pockets, they continually passed back and forth. We wonder how many other games were played this way.

Starting with our particular social reality, the education needed to get people to share and trust is a monumental task. The mountain of pain picked up by simply being a child and enduring the average family and social strictures that now exist, needs resolution. The grief and anger each person carries goes back to birth, and many times even back to those controversial past lives. We already come in fully loaded and charged, then deal with the standard dysfunctional lives found in this wounded world.

> By adapting a policy of shared wealth, paper money eventually disappears or changes its characteristics to something different.

This ideal of sharing is simply a dream, but one to be mulled over and considered. Where are you on the sliding scale of getting along with others? How would you rate yourself? Are you too angry to trust? Too fearful or confused to tell the truth? Do you want to hurt others, or do you notice that you do not necessarily want to hurt others, but you do anyway?

One of the worst problems is selfishness. Can you give to others? Does it make you happy to know you help them?

You are just as guilty if you are on the other end of the scale. Do you avoid arguments and sacrifice yourself to please others? This makes you a liar, for you pretend to agree when you do not agree at all. Eventually, you will do damage. All of these unresolved issues which drive you are in the way of simply sharing a harmonious life with others.

It has been so long since "normal" occurred, that we can hardly remember a time when it was not this way. If you search yourself, you will realize that you innately know, deep inside, that at one time you did live at peace with others.

These wheels (Trust groups) connecting to other wheels, in overlapping circles are the ideal: a human family continuously sharing wealth and knowledge while bringing up the "bottom." The bottom consists of those lacking support. This ranges from the homeless to the criminals.

By adapting a policy of shared wealth, paper money eventually disappears or changes its characteristics to something different. It might be replaced by other values. Shared wealth does not stop at the bank, nor begin there.

Spread through a Trust circle of ten or fifteen families there may be four farms, eight businesses and twenty vehicles, while another Trust group has other goods and services to share. We suggest a different way to view government, communication and education.

Chinese children share. No one is special or a hero. In the West, we shun such ideas, yet a cohesive and bonded group is far superior to any other system. Taught from childhood to share and join in, the idea of working for a living becomes obsolete, replaced by the idea that serving others is an honor. What? Yes, it is natural for healthy people to want to support one another. It is human. What would the world look like then?

Let us try a few ideas. Free energy becomes the norm, the deserts cultivated, the forests well cared for, wild animals watched over and the children safe.

> Free energy becomes the norm, the deserts cultivated, the forests well cared for, wild animals watched over and the children safe.

This may be too gentle for you, especially the rugged individuals, but we daresay the task of reclaiming the beauty of this world offers many challenges. This will not be an overnight success. We need many generations to achieve this vision.

What about cities? There would probably not be so many of them. Transportation would be swift, smooth and focused on rapid public transit, with "cars" being for local running about.

Now to the more specific and troubling matters of the Trust world.

Muddled Messes

If the Trust has enough cash flow to hire the finest administrative staff, and the Trustees have become well trained over the years, this does not, in and of itself, assure a smooth ride. The idea of an adverse Trustee assumes that at some point the Grantor and the Trustees will come to a disagreement. Whatever the disagreement is, the Trustees are on the side of the Beneficiaries, while the Grantor has other plans in mind. For example, the Grantor may want to earmark funds to buy an apartment building, but the Trustees feel this is too risky because their duty is to ensure the distribution to the Beneficiaries. Here, a Board of Trustees can come to shouting matches. This, though, is not the worst disaster because it is, ultimately, a healthy argument.

Where the real problems occur is in lack of attention to detail and endless distraction. Trustees who do not care to review financials, but simply sign documents in response to the request of either the Grantor or the administrative staff, are usually dangerously unqualified for the job. This is more likely to occur with Trusts that do not have a large cash flow. A sure sign of lack of interest in new Trustees is when they come aboard, then show no willingness to invest time or energy into learning to be good stewards of the assets entrusted to them. Another sign is when they do not charge for their time because they do not take the Trust seriously, and thus, are not hands-on and focused. Such inattention can destroy your Trust.

Another problem is the Grantor keeps too much control, thus failing to train Trustees by giving them assignments to sort out details and come up with solutions.

Trustees need to be involved. Common behavior and signs of Trustees who are not competent and thus not an asset to the Trust, Beneficiaries or the Grantor are:

- Fail to ask questions.
- Appear only to sign checks
- Not available to the Beneficiaries for advice.

- Do not know the current financial trends.

- Not aware of the cash flow.

- Pay no attention to helpful information given to them, such as Policies and Procedures, current news reports and books relating to Trust matters.

- Fail to set or attend Board of Trustees Meetings, or add to or edit a Board of Trustees agenda.

The same can apply to a Protector[142] in name only. He or she is never updated and does not inquire about the status of the Trust. A Protector should insist on attending at least one Trust meeting a year.

An Executive Secretary who has no skills can be the downfall of a Trust group. Without computer talents, communication experience and the ability to write a letter, the Executive Secretary can be more of a liability than an asset. Someone in the Trust group must be able to write Minutes, and Minutes must be properly written.

When teaching Trustees how to write Minutes, we are often shocked at the results. From poor spelling and bad grammar to outrageous statements and name-calling, we have seen it all. Remember that these documents may be read by others and should reflect the values of the Trust. One of the greatest problems lies in decisions made without a Board of Trustees meeting with Minutes to give the Trustees authority to act accordingly. Often, several months pass before anyone in the Trust group thinks that perhaps there should be some documentation and authorization for activities. Minutes save many Trusts. They record the history of decisions, as well as who became ultimately responsible for the activity in question. The more detailed the Minutes, the clearer the communication.

---

[142] The person appointed by the Grantor to oversee the functions of the Trustees. We devote a chapter to the functions of the Trust Protector in Volume II.

Poor or nonexistent communication is one of the biggest downfalls of a Trust group. Untrained, uncaring and plain sloppy administration will get an Irrevocable Common-Law Trust into more trouble than you can believe. Any attack on a poorly managed Trust can bring it down.

The issues of Minutes and the abilities of the Executive Secretary may not apply to the Irrevocable Statutory Trust.

If you care about the Beneficiaries, you will care about significant administration protocols.

By the way, careless management in any organization eventually ruins the business.

Disruptive Beneficiaries, Jealous Siblings

An entire Trust can be brought down by Beneficiaries who feel cheated, and siblings who cannot tolerate a brother's or sister's success. The hateful can drag a Trust into court many times, exhausting resources.

We previously covered dissatisfied Beneficiaries. Remember, it is not money they lack but love and enough attention. The sibling problem is more difficult because it is our parents, or the parents of our spouse, where the issues remain unresolved, with whatever childhood matters have yet to be settled.

One of the solutions of a disrupted Trust is for the Board of Trustees to turn all assets over to charity, after which none of the Beneficiaries gets an inheritance. This can be done if there is a provision in the Trust Indenture giving the Board of Trustees this alternative.

Ph.D. in Trust Talent Needed

Another big downfall with a Common-Law Trust or an organization with shares, units or other types of ownership division, is administration of the Certificate Register. In the Common-Law Trust, the matter is even more complex when applying reasonable distribution methods and procedures. In training administrative personnel, it seems difficult for the mind to initially sort out how to properly assign what are active and earned Trust Capital Units and what remains inactive unless corpus is sold. We only touch on this subject here. We will go into much greater detail in Volume II.

When a Trust is set up with distribution clearly expected, all else falls into place, including competent Trustees and the administrative staff to support them. From this flow the obvious protocols to set up the Trust Certificate Register.

In scam Trusts, it is the Certificate Register that is misapplied. Instead of properly assigning Trust Capital Units on Certificates to Beneficiaries, Trustees, and Officers of the Trust group, all the Certificates go to the Grantor. This immediately moves the Irrevocable Trust to the Grantor Trust status, and thus the Grantor becomes taxable and liable.

Not So Rich

The big anomaly about the Common-Law Trust is that it does not take oodles of money to create or keep. This applies only IF there is a cohesive family unit that has taken the time to learn how to do it properly. A Common-Law Trust can be run on as little as $20,000.00 profit a year when the incentive includes the large potential to be gained. Few families, though, can handle the administration needed to run a Trust this tightly, on so few dollars.

With their different personalities and needs, including diverse goals, it may feel impossible to train children to think about accounting, legal applications and administration. This educational strategy takes planning and strong leadership with everyone pitching in both knowledge and time. Where there is a will, there is a way. We have known Trusts that during some years had such scant cash flow that it seemed like the Trust lived on fumes instead of money and in other years cash just dumped into the checking account.

Cash Flow

For smaller Trusts, cash flow is often the issue. Volatile markets, and lack of enough connections to strong and consistent investments, can prove to be tremendous problems. So far, the most viable investments are businesses and partnerships. Bear in mind, though, the current aggressive activities of both the IRS and the SEC.[143] Yet, if the long-range goals remain intact, with the family and Board of Trustees cohesive, even these troubles resolve.

Although diversification of investments helps to relieve the greater difficulties, through experience we find that even placing funds in over 20 investments may not lessen the troubles. This is the test, where the issues of common goals and an encouraging group will make a Trust outlast the bad times and the opposition.

Target

Some fear the Common-Law Trust may become a target for the IRS. This has some small merit. Historically, such trouble came from two causes: The first was inappropriately handling the 1041 tax return, and the second was when a web site advertised the availability of Common-Law Trust services.

The results of the former have not been settled, other than to say the Common-Law Trust we describe herein is fully acknowledged by the IRS as Irrevocable

---

[143]   *Wall St. Roundup*, "SEC Going Too Far on Crackdowns, Chamber of Commerce Says," from Bloomberg News, Associated Press, early 2006.

and not "abusive."[144] The results of the latter contributed to the content of this book and more so to Volume II. Having tested what works and what does not work has given us many revelations about how both the IRS and the courts handle Trust complexities.

There was a third incident, but the IRS dropped the pursuit. Although the Employer Identification Number can tag a Trust, it cannot indicate whether it is Common-Law or not.

The issue of handling challenges goes back to know-how, administration skill and Trustee training.

Even if the IRS looks into a Trust, knowing the proper way to cope with it quickly resolves the issue. As we said before, a Trustee who can go to an IRS interview, fully informed of rights and jurisdiction, is worth his or her weight in gold. We have seen this happen, and are pleased to report the pivotal issue here is knowledge. Often, the IRS paperwork is in error and can be corrected with a communication from a properly trained Trustee and paperwork from the Trust.

This same knowledge applies to inquiries from the FBI and other agencies. The Trustee needs to know what he or she can and cannot say. The main strength here is that when the Trustee knows he or she is to protect the Beneficiaries. The answers, carefully worded, are not the babbling of a fool, where all spills out–as shown so often on television.

> Even if the IRS looks into a Trust, knowing the proper way to respond has often been a great bonus. A Trustee who can go to an IRS interview, fully informed of rights and jurisdiction, is worth his or her weight in gold.

---

[144] In addition, all exchanges of assets for Trust Capital Units were not questioned.

Once asked by a lawyer if we were involved in illegal activities, one of our Trust members was astounded. The answer came, "What? You think we would do that? No, we know one of these Trusts will land in court someday. We do everything according to the letter of the law. We manage them tightly."

So, will you be a target of enforcement agencies? Assume that you will be and run the Trust as though you need to argue your case before a judge. Here lies the secret of knowing what to put into Minutes. If you think they might someday become public, take care and be clear. Although at the moment the odds are against your Trust's getting tangled up with agencies and courts, you still need to be vigilant.

If we frightened you, that is good. Now, you need to decide whether you want to step forward, or remain in the safety of the cozy world of "the system."

Old Age

One of the most common problems with any inheritance issue is the mental condition of the elderly. One reason for an Irrevocable Trust—they cannot change their mind and give all their assets to strangers. Even with an Irrevocable Trust, the elderly may try to change their minds, and here is where the real conflicts arise with the adverse Trustee who works for the Beneficiaries. Handled correctly, there will be no fear that mom or dad can change his or her mind if unable to remember earlier decisions or, in the event of remarriage, forget you are the Beneficiary.

The Mystery

We have revealed much, yet left a great deal unsaid, particularly the vital details. What are the rules for creating Minutes? How is a Trust Certificate Register set up? How is a Trust's bank account opened? What are the protocols for transferring or exchanging properly into a Trust? What do you say to agents of the government? How do you keep the paperwork? How do you keep your Trust current with recent laws?

You will find many answers in Volume II, and some of the answers come only through connections, finding a magical mentor and study. Those learning to become Trustees will gain much from sitting in on interviews with government agents. This mentorship is what gives Trustees confidence.

We found all the answers to make a Trust work correctly by piecing them together from court cases and snips of experience here and there. Oddly enough, the Internal Revenue Code holds much of the information, for it was written when these Trust types were more often used.

The secrets to setting up a Common-Law Trust are out there, but you must be well enough informed to recognize them when you see them.

The Journey Continues . . .

Volume I is but the primer. We invite you to get Volume II, designed for those serious about having a Private Trust, for professionals and those who want to know more.

Glossary

Acceptance: An agreeing, either expressly or by conduct, to an act or offer by another party. Conclusion of a contract, and the parties become bound by that contract.

Active Trust: A Trust where the Trustees actively participate to preserve and increase the Trust estate, as opposed to a Passive Trust, where the Trustees merely hold title.

Administrator: A person the court appoints to manage the probate of the estate of a person without a valid Will.

Adversary: Any individual who has a substantial economic interest in the body or income of the Trust (or business), which gives him or her reasons to act for personal best interests.

Adverse Trustee: An opponent to the Grantor. A Trustee who can disagree with the Grantor and who has authority over him or her, otherwise the Grantor is taxable.

Allodial: Free from the tenurial rights of a feudal overlord. The property owner "owns" the property as opposed to Fee Simple, where the property passes on to heirs, and is not owned. Allodial property is yours to do with as you please. You own land from the center of the Earth to the center of the sky, including all mineral rights.

Arm's Length: When the Trustees has "independent interests" from the Grantor. They are "unrelated parties each acting in his or her own best interest" (see below), the Grantor has an arm's length distance from the Trust. This satisfies the legal requirements the Trust is for the Beneficiaries and it is genuine. Compare the following from *Black's Law Dictionary Sixth Edition:*

Arm's length transaction: Said of a transaction negotiated by unrelated parties, each acting in his or her own self-interest; the basis for a fair market value determination. A transaction in good faith in the ordinary course of business by parties with independent interests. Commonly applied in areas of taxation when there are dealings between related corporations, *for example,* parent and subsidiary. *Inecto, Inc. v. Higgins,* D.C.N.Y., 21 F.Supp. 418. The standard under which unrelated parties, each acting in his or her own best interest, would carry out a particular transaction. For example, a corporation sells property to its sole shareholder for $10,000. To test whether $10,000 is an "arm's length" price, how much would the corporation sell the property to a disinterested third party in a bargained transaction.

Artificial: "Created by art, or by law; existing only by force of or in contemplation of law. Humanly contrived. 'Artificially' drawn is a Will or contract using apt and technical phrases and presents a scientific arrangement." (*Black's Law Dictionary, Fourth Edition*).

Bank Trust: This refers to either a Trust held and governed by a bank, or in a Common-Law Trust, a Management Trust that handles the money for other Trusts in a bank account.

Beneficiary: A person named to have and hold the equitable interest in a Trust estate; holders of the Certificates of Capital Units, who will receive payments when the Trust so dictates.

Bequest: A gift of property made through a Will.

Capital Units: Stated on a Certificate is the amount of Units representing a portion of the Trust corpus. The percentage of Units held allow the holder to receive a percentage of corpus if it is distributed, and a percentage of profit when allocated.

Certificates of Capital Units: Given in exchanged for property. The number of Units representing a percentage of the Corpus is stated on the Certificate. If the Trust ends, the CU holder receives that unit share of the capital investment in the body of the Trust.

Certificates of Beneficial Interest: The Units held represent a percentage of income distribution.

Chancery: Originally, kings heard cases personally but later delegated this duty to the chancellor (secretary) whose power grew accordingly. The Lord High Chancellor (or Lord Chancellor) is now "the highest judicial functionary in England" (*Black's Law Dictionary 6th*). Therefore, "chancery" (a contraction of "chancellery") originally meant simply the office of a chancellor, but its own status changed into a court system as the power and prestige of the chancellor increased. Now also known as a "court of equity . . . which administers justice and decides controversies in accordance with the rules, principles, and precedents of equity, and which follows the forms and procedure of chancery; as distinguished from a court having the jurisdiction, rules, principles, and practice of the Common-Law." In America, Common-Law and equity courts were merged by the Field Code. For its guiding, the central principle of the code is that "distinctions between actions at law and suits in equity and the forms of all such actions and suits, heretofore existing, are abolished." It substituted the "one form of action for the enforcement or protection of private rights." *The Field Code II Common-Law procedure in a Nutshell*;

http://www.drbilllong.com/Jurisprudence/FieldII.html

Chattel: Every species (type) of property, movable or immovable, which is less than freehold (freely held and owned).

Common Law: The part of law developed over time through court decisions and court opinions, rather than by decree of statues or other legislative acts, including those laws inherited from English old-time law.

Common-Law Trust: A Trust organization which is express, active, inter vivos, irrevocable, and simple or complex; in which the Trustees hold full fee simple title to the Trust assets in joint tenancy. The Beneficiaries of which are the holders of Trust Certificate Units. A contract in the form of a Trust.

Community Property: Undivided interest in real or personal assets owned and gained during marriage by spouses; owned by the two of them. By agreement between the spouses, community property can be nullified by transfer from one spouse to another.

Complex Trust: A Trust that may pay out both principal and the Trust corpus. The opposite of a *Simple Trust* which needs a specific amount to be paid to one Beneficiary each year. The Complex Trust allows the Trustees to decide what, if, and how much is disbursed or kept by the Trust and taxed to the Beneficiaries.

Conservator: A protector and guardian whose business it is to enforce certain statutes and legal agreements. Not a Trustee, but someone appointed from the outside to arbitrate an estate.

Consideration: Regarded as the equivalent return given or suffered by one party for the act or promise of another. Essential to the force of a contract. Something offered, something accepted, that is consideration.

Contract: An agreement in which a party undertakes to do or not do a particular act. Elements of a written contract are: 1) parties competent to contract, whose names appear in the writing, 2) the subject matter of the contract, or a clear statement of what is to be done or not done, 3) lawful and valid consideration; and, if made of mutual promises, then a clear and explicit statement of what each party promises to do or not to do, 4) assent of the parties, which is evidenced by signatures.

Conveyance: The instrument by which an act of property transference happens, usually in writing. Bill of Sale, Deed, etc.

Corpus: The body and capital assets. The *property* in the Trust. The Trust principal.

Corpus Juris Secundum, Literally, "second body of laws," following the Corpus Juris of Roman law. This borrowing further underscores the tendency of the current courts to refer to Rome for guiding principles.

Creator: The One who creates a Trust, settles the initial funding to the Trust, and invites the Trustees, same as *Settlor, Grantor,* and *Trustor.*

Decedent: The person who has died.

Declaration of Trust: An agreement outlining the duties and bonds of the Trustees to serve the Beneficiaries per the wishes of the Grantor. A contract in Trust form. Also known as a Trust Indenture. See Indenture. The acknowledgment in which the Creator and the Trustees declare the Trust to exist, taking title to property for holding and sign agreements to do so; what a bank would see for opening accounts. It declares the fiduciary set up of assets, and what is filed with the county. See **Trust Document** and **Trust Indenture.**

Deed: Documented proof of ownership of property. Usually filed with the county.

Disclaimer Deed: Used in community property states to deny a spousal claim to property. Similar to a Quit Claim Deed.

Devisee: The person who receives a gift or real property by a last Will and Testament.

Enfeoffs: To invest with a feudal estate or fee.

Estate: All property owned by a person at death. This includes both real and personal property.

Express Trust: A Trust expressly set up by a Grantor, as opposed to a Trust settled by a Will or implied, and thus, created by a court.

Equity: "That part of the law which, having power to enforce discovery. It "Administers Trusts, mortgages, and other fiduciary obligations." It also manages and adjusts Common-Law rights where the courts of Common-Law have no machinery and "supplies a specific and preventive cure for Common-Law wrongs where courts of Common-Law only give subsequent damages . . .As old rules become too narrow, or are felt to be out of harmony with advancing civilization, a format is needed to gradually enlarge and adapt to new views of society. To carry out this on a large scale, without ignoring existing law, is to introduce, by the prerogative of some high functionary, of a more perfect body of rules, discoverable in judicial conscience. It stands side by side with the law of the land, yes overriding it in cases of conflict, as on some title of inherent superiority, but not claiming to repeal it. Equity is such a body of rules." (*Black's Law Dictionary, Fourth Edition*)

Equity, courts of: Administers justice according to the system of equity and according to a specific course of procedure or practice.

Equity Trust: A Living Trust that holds property for a family or individual who is a Beneficiary.

Executor: A person named by the Testator in a Will to manage the estate.

Fair market value (F.M.V.): The agreed value of the item when placed in Trust (or received by a taxpayer). The price when the transfer or exchange happens. This can be the appraised value or the agreed value, as there are some items that have no fair market by their nature. This dollar value sets the basis for whether the property increases or decreases in value from the date of the transfer or exchange. (See *Commissioner vs. Marshman*, C.A. 6 7279 F 2d 27 (1960)

Family Trust: A Living Trust or Grantor Trust used to pass ownership of property and avoid probate. It may not avoid estate taxes. After Grantor dies the Trust becomes a **Testamentary Trust**.

Fee: In law, an estate of inheritance in land, either absolute and without limit to any particular class of heirs (fee simple). It can also be limited to a particular class of heirs (fee tail); an inheritable estate in land held of a feudal lord on condition of performing certain services; a territory held in fee.

Fee Simple: Absolute title and authority to use and dispose of property in whatever way one may wish. It is without limits to use and who may receive the estate: Trustees of Common-Law Trusts have this title to the assets of the Trust.

Feoffor: One who enfeoffs or grants a fee.

Fiduciary: From the Latin meaning to "Trust." I Trust you. A person in a position of trust, responsibility, and confidence. Usually applying to matters of money and property and is based on trust.

Fiefdom: The domain controlled by a feudal lord or organization controlled by a dominant the person or group.

Foundation: An organization (corporation or Trust) holds assets for a purpose, instead of for others (Beneficiaries). The income and assets are for charitable and gifting purposes for undetermined specific uses.

Guardian: A person with legal control and responsibility for a minor child or an incompetent adult.

Grantor: The person who grants and gives over the initial funding to set up the Trust. Same as Creator, Settlor or Trustor.

Grantor Trust: Any Trust set up by a Grantor for his benefit. He or she controls the funds and assets during his or her lifetime. The funds and assets of this Trust pass to others named in the Trust at death of the Grantor. Because of the benefit and control, the Grantor or Settlor is taxed on the income, per the Internal Revenue Code (IRC).

Heir: 1) A person who is legally entitled to inherit, through the natural action of the law, another's property or title on the other's death. 2) Anyone who receives property of a deceased person either by Will or by law. 3) A person who appears to get some trait from a predecessor or seems to carry on in his tradition. *Webster's New World Dictionary, Second College Edition* (1974)

Heir Beneficiary: In the civil law, one who has accepted the succession under the benefit of an inventory regularly made. *Black's Law Dictionary, Revised Fourth Edition* (1968)

Heir, Legal In civil law, a legal heir is the one who takes the succession by relationship to the decedent and by force of law. *Black's Law Dictionary, Revised Fourth Edition* (1968)

Indenture: A written contract binding a person to work for another for a given time. An obligation to perform a duty.

Inter Vivos Trust: A Trust created during the lifetime of the Grantor. They are "alive" together, as opposed to a Trust created from a Will at death.

International Business Corporation (IBC): A corporation incorporated (formed) in an offshore jurisdiction.

Intestate: A person who dies without leaving a valid Will. The status of having died without a valid Will.

Irrevocable Trust: Any Trust in which the Grantor keeps no power to revoke or cancel the Trust agreement, and no power to have the assets returned to him or her, as opposed to a Revocable Trust.

Joint Property: All property owned jointly with another party or parties.

Joint Tenancy: An undivided interest in property held by two or more people, who all hold the same title and rights of possession, at the same time, jointly, and under which the survivors take the entire interest. In a Common-Law Trust arrangement, the Board of Trustees holds title in joint tenancy to all Trust assets.

Joint-Tenancy Deed: The deed which stipulates that both husband and wife (any two parties) own all the property together, not in halves.

Jurisdiction: A court's right to hear and decide a case based on the following: place, action and parties. All three factors must be met before an action can advance.

Living Trust: A revocable Trust created and controlled by a person, whose assets transfer at death, thus avoiding probate, but not taxes. Family Trusts, Grantor Trusts, Estate Trusts, Reversionary Trusts, Preservation Trusts, etc. A Trust set up while the Creator is alive.

Nonadverse party: Grantor's father, mother, issue, brother or sister; an employee; a corporation in which the Grantor has most stockholdings, and, thus, voting control; a subordinate employee of a corporation in which the Grantor is the executive. IRC §672©.

Offshore Jurisdiction: Some examples of well-known offshore jurisdictions are: The Bahamas, British Virgin Islands, Isle of Man, Belize, Antigua, The Turks and Caicos, Nevis and St. Kitts, Luxembourg, etc.

Offshore Trust: A Trust formed in an offshore jurisdiction.

Privilege: Benefits granted or allowed by a governing body. Exemption for certain burdens, or preferred treatment. All privileges come with limits and requirements. An IRA continues tax-free until a person reaches age seventy when funds are removed and then taxed.

Probate: Procedures under court direction and supervision deciding ownership to allocate estate and property either bequeathed by a Will, or cases without a Will.

Pure Equity Family Trust: A Trust for holding, maintaining and preserving assets.

Pyrrhic victory: "A victory won with staggering losses, such as that of Pyrrhus (319-272 BC.), King of Epirus, over the Romans at Asculum in 279 BC." (*American Heritage Dictionary*)

Quitclaim Deed: A legal instrument by which one transfers all of his or her right, title and interest in real estate to another party without guarantees as to what the right, title, or interest in the property is. A deed stating, "I quit my claim to the property."

Rebuttable presumption: "A presumption which may be rebutted by evidence...it shifts the burden of proof." *Black's Law Dictionary*, *Fourth Edition*. For our purposes, the term means the burden is on you to prove you did not carry out some crime the government asserts you did.

Res: That which is held and reserved; the body, or the capital of a Trust as opposed to the income or interest.

Reversionary Trust: Any Trust where the ownership of the Trust assets goes back to the Grantor when the Trust ends.

Revocable Trust: Any Trust in which the Creator-Trustor may withdraw personal property assets from the Trust and by it dissolve the Trust. A Trust that performs under an individual's control and discretion for this person's benefit with a right to cancel.

Rule against perpetuities: A rule in property law which restricts a contingent grant or Will from vesting outside a certain period of time. If there is a possibility of the estate's vesting outside the period, regardless of how remote, the whole interest is void, and is stricken from a grant. The rule prevents people from holding assets indefinitely—a concept often referred to as control by the "dead hand" or "mortmain." That is, the purpose is to "limit the Testator's power to earmark gifts for remote descendants."[1] Some argue the rule also prevents the concentration of wealth in society. When a part of a grant or Will violates the Rule, only that portion of the grant or devise is removed; all other parts that do not violate the Rule are still valid conveyances of property.

Settlor: The one who settles the assets to the Trust. Same as Creator or Grantor.

Simple Trust: Required to pay out a specific amount to Beneficiaries each year; all income, not part of the body.

Situs: "...the place where a matter is considered, for example, for jurisdiction over it, or the right or power to tax it. Situs of a Trust means the place of performance of active duties of a Trustee." *Black's Law Dictionary, Fourth Edition.*

State: A separate country, foreign, for the federal government, the United States of America is a separate corporation that allegedly manages the 50 states.

Tenants in Common: An undivided interest in property held by two or more people in common. There is no right of survivorship; an individual's interests passes to heirs, not to survivors.

Testamentary Trust: Any Trust set up by a Will, Grantor or Living Trust which does not take effect until the death of the Grantor.

Testator: A person who sets up a Will.

Transfer: An act by which the property of one person vests in another, whether by sale, gift, exchange, or otherwise.

Statutory Trust: Granted into creation by the laws of a state or government and subject to all laws and stipulations of that granting body. It is, therefore, open to scrutiny and invasion of rights and property by the granting body.

Trust Document: The full written contract of the Trust, complete with names, terms, Minutes, letters of acceptance, schedules of assets, Certificate Units, etc.

Trust Indenture: Also known as a Declaration of Trust or Grant of Trust. The fundamental document to codify the Grantor's purpose for settling the Trust. It defines its internal procedures, sets the limits about what it may and may not do, and forms permanent instructions to, and the sworn duty of, the Trustees.

Trustee: The person or entity appointed or elected to conserve, protect, and manage the assets or properties transferred to a Trust.

Trustee Fees: A Trust must have Trustees who will govern the assets in the Trust for the Beneficiaries. The fees are paid yearly.

Trustor: Same as Grantor, Donor, Settlor, or Creator.

Undivided Interest: Synonymous with Undivided Right. "An undivided right or title, or a title to an undivided portion of an estate. Owned by one or more tenants in common or joint tenants before partition. Held by the same title by two or more people, whether their rights are equal as to value or quantity, or unequal." This applies to those married, groups and a Board of Trustees. *See Black's Law Dictionary, Fourth Edition.*

United States: ...includes the Commonwealth of Puerto Rico, the Virgin Islands, Guam and American Samoa. 26 CFR 170.59 Meaning of Terms.121(e)(2).

United States of America: A corporation managing the several (50) states and separate from the United States. *Diversified Metals Products v. T-Bow*, Civil No. 93-405. E-EJL, United States Answer and Claim, United States District Court of Idaho.

Venue: The area (usually defined as a county or parish) in which an action occurs which results in legal proceedings; the area from which a jury is drawn and where the trial is held.

Void: Canceled, of no legal force or effect, useless. A voided contract or Trust means it is no longer in effect or valid.

Warranty Deed: A legal instrument to transfer all right, title and interest in real estate to another. At the same time, it makes certain legally enforceable guarantees, including the fact of said person's full title to the property, and said person's right to convey the property.

Yellow journalists/journalism: "Journalism that exploits, distorts, or exaggerates the news to create sensations and attract readers. [Said to be short for *Yellow Kid Journalism,* an allusion to the 'Yellow Kid' cartoons in the *New York World,* noted for sensationalism and vulgarity.]" *The American Heritage Dictionary of the English Language,* Houghton Mifflin Company, Boston, 1976.

Appendix A

Understanding Jurisdiction

by: Anonymous

The Apprentice and the Quakers

An Oath

In all of history there has been but one successful protest against an income tax. It is little understood in that light, primarily because the remnants of protest groups still exist, but no longer wish to appear to be "antigovernment." They do not talk much about these roots. Few even know them. We need to go back in time about 400 years to find this success. It succeeded only because the term "jurisdiction" was still well understood at that time as meaning "oath spoken." "Juris," in the original Latin meaning, is "oath." "Diction" as everyone knows, means "spoken." The protest obviously did not happen here. It occurred in England. Given the origins of our law are traced there, most of the relevant facts in this matter are still applicable in this nation. Here is what happened.

Printing Presses

The Bible had just recently been put into print. To that time, only the churches owned copies, due to the extremely high cost of paper. Contrary to what you have been taught, it was not the invention of movable type that led to printing this and other books. That concept had been around for a very long time. It just had no application. Printing wastes some paper. Until paper prices fell, it was cheaper to write books by hand than to print them with movable type. The handwritten versions were outrageously costly, procurable only by those with extreme wealth: churches, crowns and the nobility. The wealth of the nobility was attributable to feudalism. "Feud" is Old English for "oath" The nobility held the land under the crown. But unimproved land itself, save to hunter/gatherers, is rather useless. Land is useful for farming. So that is how the nobility obtained wealth. No, they did not push a plow. They had servants to do it. The nobility would not sell their land, nor would they lease it. They rented it. Ever pay rent without a lease? Then you know that if the landlord raised the rent, you had no legal recourse. You could move out or pay. But what if you had no way to move out? Then you'd have a feel for what feudalism was all about.

Servitude and the Oath

A tenant was not a freeman. He was a servant to the (land)lord, the noble. In order to have access to the land to farm it, the noble required the tenant kneel before him, hat in hand, swear an oath of fealty and allegiance and kiss his ring (extending that oath in that last act to the heirs of his estate). That oath established a servitude. The tenant then put his plow to the fields. The rent was a variable. In good growing years it was very high, in bad years it fell. The tenant was a subsistence farmer, keeping only enough of the produce of his labors to just sustain him and his family. Rent was actually an "income tax." The nobleman could have demanded 100% of the productivity of his servant except . . . under the Common-Law, a servant was akin to livestock. He had to be fed. Not well fed, just fed, same as a horse or cow. And, like a horse or cow, one usually finds it to his benefit to keep it fed, that so the critter is productive. Thus, the tenant was allowed to keep some of his own productivity. Liken it to "personal and dependent deductions."

Journeymen

The freemen of the realm, primarily the tradesmen, swore no such oaths nor owed such fealty. They knew it. They taught their sons the trade so they had also be free when grown. Occasionally, they took on an apprentice under a sworn contract of indenture from his father. His parents made a few coins. But the kid was the biggest beneficiary; he would learn a trade. He would never need to become a tenant farmer. He would keep what he earned. He was only apprenticed for a term of years, most typically about seven. The tradesmen did not need adolescents; they needed young men strong enough to pull their own weight. They did not take on anyone under 13. By age 21 an apprentice would have learned enough to practice the craft. That is when the contract expired. He was then called a "journeyman." Had he made a journey? No. But, if you pronounce that word, it is "Jur-nee-man." He was a "man," formerly ("nee"), bound by oath ("jur"). He would then go to work for a "master" (craftsman). The pay was established, but he could ask for more if he felt he was worth more. And he was free to quit. Pretty normal, eh? Yes, in our society that is the norm. But some 400 years ago these men were the exceptions, not the rule. At some point, if the journeyman was good at the trade, he would be recognized by the market as a "master" (craftsman) and people would be begging him to take their children as apprentices, so they might learn from him, become journeymen, and keep what they earned when manumitted[145] at age 21! The oath of the tenant ran for life. The oath of the apprentice's father ran only for a term of years. Still, oaths were important on both sides. In fact, the tradesmen at one point established guilds (means "gold") as a protection against the potential of the government's attempting to bind them into servitude by compelled oaths.

> When an apprentice became a journeyman, he was allowed a membership in the guild only by swearing a secret oath to the guild. He literally swore to "serve gold," and only gold.

When an apprentice became a journeyman, he was allowed a membership in the guild only by swearing a secret oath to the guild. He literally swore to "serve gold," and only gold. He swore he would work only for pay! Once so sworn,

---

[145] "... releasing or delivering one person from the power or control of another." (*Black's Law Dictionary, Fourth Edition*)

any other oath of servitude would be a perjury of that oath. He bound himself for life to never be a servant, save to the very benevolent master: gold! (Incidentally, the Order of Free and Accepted Masons is a remnant of one of these guilds. The Masonic oath is a secret. The Masons would love to have you think the "G" in the middle of their logo stands for "God." One obvious truth is that it stands for "GOLD.")

Joint Resources

Then the Bible came to print. The market for this tome was not the wealthy. They already had a handwritten copy. Nor was it the tenants. They were far too poor to make this purchase. The market was the tradesmen—and the book was still so costly that it took the combined life savings of siblings to buy a family Bible. The other reason the tradesmen were in the market was they had also been taught how to read as part of their apprenticeship. As contractors they had to know how to do that! Other than the families of the Super-Rich (and the priests) nobody else knew how to read.

Swear No Oaths

These men were blown away when they read Jesus' command against swearing oaths (Matt. 5: 33-37). This was news to them. For well over a millennium they had been trusting the Church—originally just the Church of Rome, but now also the Church of England—that had been telling them everything they needed to know in that book. Then they found out that Jesus said, "Swear no oaths." Talk about an eye-opener!

Imagine seeing a conspiracy revealed that went back over 1000 years. Without oaths there would have been no tenants laboring for the nobility and receiving mere subsistence in return. The whole society was premised on oaths; the whole society CLAIMED it was Christian, yet it violated a very simple command of Christ! And the tradesmen had done it, too, by demanding sworn contracts of indenture for apprentices and giving their own oaths to the guilds. They had no way of knowing that was prohibited by Jesus! They were angry. "Livid" might be a better term. The governments had seen this coming. What could they do? Ban the book? The printing would have simply moved underground, and the millennium-long conspiracy would be further evidenced in that banning. They came up with a better scheme. We now call it the "Reformation."

In an unprecedented display of unanimity, the governments of Europe adopted a treaty. This treaty would allow anyone the State-right of founding a church! The church would be granted a charter. It only had to do one very simple thing to obtain that charter. It had to agree to the terms of the treaty.

Buried in those provisions, most of which were totally innocuous, was a statement the Church would never oppose the swearing of lawful oaths. Jesus said, "None." The churches all said (and still say), "None, except . . ." Whom do you think was (is) right?

> To show their absolute displeasure with those who had kept this secret for so long, they refused to give anyone in Church or State any respect.

Black Hats and the Quaker Rebellion

The tradesmen got even angrier! They had already left the Church of England. But with every new "reformed" church still opposing the clear words of Christ, there was no church for them to join—or found.

They exercised the right of assembly to discuss the Bible. Some of them preached it on the street corners, using their right of freedom of speech. But they could not establish a church, which followed Jesus' words, for that would have required assent to that treaty which opposed what Jesus had commanded. To show their absolute displeasure with those who had kept this secret for so long, they refused to give anyone in Church or State any respect. It was the custom to doff one's hat when he encountered a priest or official. They started wearing big, ugly black hats, just so the most myopic of these claimed "superiors" would not miss the fact the hats stayed atop their heads. Back then the term "you" was formal English, reserved for use when speaking to a superior. "Thee" was the familiar pronoun, used among family and friends. So they called these officials only by the familiar pronoun "thee" or by their Christian names, "George, Peter, Robert," etc. We call these folk "Quakers." That was a nickname given to them by a judge. One of them had told the judge that he would better, "Quake before the Lord, God almighty." The judge, in a display of irreverent disrespect replied, "Thee are the Quaker here." They found that pretty funny, being such a total misnomer (as you shall soon see), and the nickname stuck. With the huge membership losses from the Anglican Church—especially from men who had been the more charitable to it in the past—the Church was technically bankrupt. It was not just the losses from the Quakers. Other people were leaving to join the new "Reformed Churches." Elsewhere in Europe, the Roman Church had amassed sufficient assets to weather this storm. The far newer Anglican Church had not.

Tax Without Jurisdiction

But the Anglican Church, as an agency of the State, cannot go bankrupt. It becomes the duty of the State to support it in hard times. Parliament did so. It enacted a tax to that end. A nice religious tax, and by current standards a very

> ## Absent their oaths establishing this servitude, there was "no jurisdiction." And they were right.

low tax, a tithe (10%). But it made a deadly mistake in that. The Quakers, primarily as tradesmen, recognized this income tax as a tax "without jurisdiction," at least so far as they went. As free men, they pointed out that they did not have to pay it, nor provide a return. Absent their oaths establishing this servitude, there was "no jurisdiction." And they were right. Despite laws making it a crime to willfully refuse to make a return and pay this tax, NONE were charged or arrested.

That caused the rest of the society to take notice. Other folk who had thought the Quakers were "extremists" suddenly began to listen to them. As always, money talks. These guys were keeping all they earned, while the rest of the uninformed, thinking this tax applied to them, forked over the prescribed 10%. Membership in the Anglican Church fell even further, as did charity to it. The taxes were not enough to offset these further losses. The tithe (income) tax was actually counterproductive to the goal of supporting the Church. The members of the government and the churchmen were scared silly. If this movement continued to expand at the current rate, no one in the next generation would swear an oath. Who would then farm the lands of the nobility? Oh, surely some-one would, but not as a servant working for subsistence. The land would need to be leased under a contract, with the payment for that use established in the market, not on the unilateral whim of the nobleman. The wealth of the nobility, their fat purses, was about to be greatly diminished. And the Church of Eng-land, what assets it possessed, would need to be sold off, with what remained of that Church greatly reduced in power and wealth. But far worse was the dimin-ishment of the respect demanded by the priests and officials. They had always held a position of superiority in the society. What would they do when all of society treated them only as equals?

Anarchy

The Quakers began to use the term "anarchy." But England was a monarchy, not an anarchy. And that was the ultimate solution to the problem, or so those in government thought. There is an aspect of a monarchy that Americans find somewhat incomprehensible, or at least we did two centuries ago. The Crown has divine right, or at least it so claims. An expression of the divine right of a Crown is the power to rule by demand. The Crown can issue commands. The King says, "Jump!" Everyone jumps.

Why do they jump? Simple. It is a crime NOT to jump. To "willfully fail (a familiar term) to obey a Crown command" is considered to be a treason, high treason. The British Crown issued a Crown command to end the tax objection movement.

Did the Crown order that everyone shall pay the income tax? No, that was not possible. There really was "no jurisdiction." And that would have done nothing to cure the lack of respect. The Crown went one better. It ordered that every man shall swear an oath of allegiance to the Crown! Damned Christian thing to do, eh? Literally!

> . . .the prisons of England filled with adolescent females, serving the life sentences for their dads. Those lives would be short.

High Treason

A small handful of the tax objectors obeyed. Most refused. It was a simple matter of black and white. Jesus said "swear not at all." They opted to obey Him over the Crown.

That quickly brought them into court, facing the charge of high treason. An official would take the witness stand, swearing he had no record of the defendant's oath of allegiance. Then the defendant was called to testify, there being no right to refuse to witness against oneself. He refused to accept the administered oath. That refusal on the record, the court instantly judged him guilty. It took all of ten minutes. That expedience was essential, for there were another couple hundred defendants waiting to be tried that day for their own treasons against the Crown.

Children Starved

In short order the jails reached their capacity, plus. But they were not filled as you would envision them. The men who had ten minutes were not there. Their children were. There was a "Stand-in" law allowing for that. There was no social welfare system. The wife and children of a married man in prison existed on the charity of Church and neighbors, or they ceased to exist, starving to death. It was typical for a man convicted of a petty crime to have one of his kids stand in for him for 30 or 90 days. That way he could continue to earn a living, keeping bread on the table, without the family's having to rely on charity. A man convicted, though, of more heinous crimes would usually find it impossible to convince his wife to allow his children to serve his time. The family would prefer to exist on charity rather than see him back in society. But in this case, the family had no option. The family was churchless. The neighbors were all in the same situation. Charity was nonexistent for them. The family was destined for quick starvation, unless one of the children stood in for the breadwinner. Unfortunately, the rational choice of which child should serve the time was predicated on which child was the least productive to the family earnings.

That meant nearly the youngest, usually a daughter. Thus, the prisons of England filled with adolescent females, serving the life sentences for their dads. Those lives would be short. There was no heat in the jails. They were rife with tuberculosis and other deadly diseases. A strong man might last several years. A small girl measured her remaining time on earth in months. It was a Christian holocaust, a true sacrifice of the unblemished lambs. (And, we must note, completely ignored in virtually every history text covering this era, lest the Crown, government and Church be duly embarrassed.) Despite the high mortality rate the jails still overflowed. There was little concern that the daughters would be raped or die at the brutality of other prisoners.

Criminals Set Free

The other prisoners, the real felons, had all been released to make room. Early release was premised only on severity of the crime. High treason was the highest crime. The murderers, thieves, arsonists, rapists, etc., had all been set free. That had a very profound effect on commerce. It stopped. There were highwaymen afoot on every road. Thugs and muggers ruled the city streets. The sworn subjects of the Crown sat behind bolted doors, in cold, dark homes, wondering how they would exist when the food and water ran out. They finally dared to venture out to attend meetings to address the situation. At those meetings they discussed methods to overthrow the Crown to which they were sworn! Call that perjury! Call that sedition! Call it by any name, they were going to put their words into actions, and soon, or die from starvation or the blade of a thug. Here we should note that chaos (and nearly anarchy: "no Crown") came to be, not as the result of the refusal to swear oaths, but as the direct result of the governmental demand that people swear them! The followers of Jesus' words did not bring that chaos; those who ignored that command of Christ brought it.

Children Released

The Crown soon saw the revolutionary handwriting on the wall and ordered the release of the children and the recapture of the real felons, before the government was removed from office under force of arms. The courts came up with the odd concept of an "affirmation in lieu of oath." The Quakers accepted that as a victory. Given what they had been through, that was understandable. However, Jesus also prohibited affirmations, calling the practice an oath "by thy head." Funny that He could foresee the legal concept of an affirmation 1600 years before it came to be. Quite a prophecy!

American Colonies Founded

When the colonies opened to migration, the Quakers fled Europe in droves, trying to put as much distance as they could between themselves and the Crown. They had a very rational fear of a repeat of the situation. That put a lot of them here, enough that they had a very strong influence on politics. They could have blocked the ratification of the Constitution had they opposed it. Some of their demands were incorporated into it, as were some of their concessions, in balance to those demands. Their most obvious influence found in the Constitution is the definition of treason, the only crime defined in that document . . .

The remainder of this article deals with federal income taxes which are beyond the scope of this book.

We found the complete article at:
http://www.chrononhotonthologos.com/lawnotes/index.html

NOTE: Editing of the original article has been done to provide clarity.

Appendix B

Statutory Trusts

This is not a complete list of Statutory Trusts, and we recommend discussing the particulars with Trust trained professionals. Much of the information from this list has been taken from *Irrevocable Trusts, Third Edition* by George M. Turner, published by West Group.

Trust Name	Description
Accumulation Trust	Describes the application of throwback rules to a Trust that accumulates undistributed funds from one year to the next.
Charitable Remainder Uni-trust	Income Beneficiaries get a fixed percentage of the fair market value (F.M.V.) of the corpus, with F.V. recomputed annually. Be sure to review Private Letter Ruling 9120016.
Charitable Annuity Trust	Income Beneficiaries get annual payment equal to at least 5% of original value of the corpus.
Children's Trust	Gifts can be given to children.
Crummey Trusts, (a life insurance Trust with a Crummey provision)	Applicable to gifts of a future interest as a gift of the present interest and hence have it qualify for the annual gift tax exclusion.

Trust Name	Description
Dynasty Trust, also known as Legacy Trusts, Mega Trusts, Super Trusts	To provide for Beneficiaries who extend to multiple generations. This is the Trust most closely designed to the Irrevocable Common-Law Trust.[146]
Educational Trusts with Use of Gift and Lease Arrangement	How education of family members can be accomplished through a series of transactions to shift income from parent-taxpayer . . . to children . . . in a lower tax bracket
Generation Skipping Trusts	Using a series of Trusts for the benefit of the children. This takes into consideration the various capabilities, weaknesses, and strengths of each child and allows each to keep his or her financial affairs segregated as much as possible.
Life Insurance Trusts	Purchase life insurance products through a technique to minimize both income taxation and estate taxation at death. Not applicable to term insurance.
Medicaid Trust	Established for the benefit of a senior citizen accepting Social Security Benefits who is entitled, generally on the basis of medical and financial need, to the benefits of a government program. It allows additional funds to go into a Trust to allow for a small supplemental income to the recipient, and the Beneficiary is the State or the federal government, unless the Beneficiary is also disabled.
Public Charitable Trust	A nonprofit Trust organization formed per Internal Revenue Code Section 501(c)(3).
Rabbi Trust	Members of a synagogue provide a retirement benefit for the Rabbi.

---

[146]   Clifton Beale, *The Trust Bible*, p. 118; George M. Turner, Irrevocable Trust, Third Edition, 23 Dynasty Trusts.

Trust Name	Description
Special Needs Trust	Primarily for disabled or dysfunctional children. Basically, the same principles apply as for the Medicaid Trust.
Sprinkling or Spray Trusts	Combined with other Trusts where the Trustee is given authority to make distribution of income and/or principal among Beneficiaries using discretion considering the particular needs of the individual.
Term Trusts	Transfer the income taxation on earnings to a Beneficiary in a lower tax bracket for a term of no less than ten years
Testamentary Trust	The assets of a Will are turned over to court-appointed Trustees through an act of Probate per the terms of the Will.

Appendix C

Conspiracy, Fraud . . . and Treason

On May 23, 1933, Congressman Louis T. McFadden brought formal charges against the Board of Governors of the Federal Reserve Bank system, the Comptroller of the Currency and the Secretary of United States Treasury for numerous criminal acts, including but not limited to, conspiracy, fraud, unlawful conversion and treason.

The petition for Articles of Impeachment was thereafter referred to the Judiciary Committee and has *yet to be acted on.*

Remarks in Congress, 1934

The quotations are from several speeches made on the Floor of the House of Representatives by the Honorable Louis T. McFadden of Pennsylvania. Mr. McFadden, due to his having served as Chairman of the Banking and Currency Committee for more than 10 years, was the best posted man on these matters in America and was in a position to speak with authority of the vast ramifications of this gigantic private credit monopoly. As Representative of a State which was among the first to declare its freedom from foreign money tyrants it is fitting that Pennsylvania, the cradle of liberty, be again given the credit for producing a son that was not afraid to hurl defiance in the face of the money-fund. Whereas Mr. McFadden was elected to the high office on both the Democratic and Republican tickets, there can be no accusation of partisanship lodged against him. Because these speeches by Congressman McFadden are set out in full in the Congressional Record, they carry weight that no amount of condemnation on the part of private individuals could hope to carry.

The Federal Reserve-A Corrupt Institution

"Mr. Chairman, we have in this Country one of the most corrupt institutions the world has ever known. I refer to the Federal Reserve Board and the Federal Reserve Banks, hereinafter called the Fed. The Fed has cheated the Government of these United States and the people of the United States out of enough money to pay the Nation's debt. The depredations and iniquities of the Fed have cost enough money to pay the National debt several times over.

"This evil institution has impoverished and ruined the people of these United States, has bankrupted itself, and has practically bankrupted our Government. It has done this through the defects of the law under which it operates, through the maladministration of that law by the Fed and through the corrupt practices of the moneyed vultures who control it.

> "This is an era of misery, and for the conditions that caused that misery, the Fed are fully liable."

"Some people think the Federal Reserve Banks are [part of the] United States Government institutions. They are private monopolies which prey upon the people of these United States for the benefit of themselves and their foreign customers; foreign and domestic speculators and swindlers; and rich and predatory money lenders. In that dark crew of financial pirates there are those who would cut a man's throat to get a dollar out of his pocket; there are those who send money into states to buy votes to control our legislatures; there are those who maintain international propaganda for the purpose of deceiving us into granting of new concessions which will permit them to cover up their past misdeeds and set again in motion their gigantic train of crime.

"These twelve private credit monopolies were deceitfully and disloyally and foisted upon this Country by the bankers who came here from Europe and repaid us our hospitality by undermining our American institutions. Those bankers took money out of this Country to finance Japan in a war against Russia. They created a reign of terror in Russia with our money in order to help that war along. They instigated the separate peace between Germany and Russia, and thus drove a wedge between the allies in World War. They financed Trotsky's passage from New York to Russia so that he might assist in the destruction of the Russian Empire. They fomented and instigated the Russian Revolution, and placed a large fund of American dollars at Trotsky's disposal in one of their branch banks in Sweden so that through him Russian homes might be thoroughly broken up and Russian children flung far and wide from their natural protectors. They have since begun breaking up of American homes and the dispersal of American children. Mr. Chairman, there should be no partisanship in matters concerning banking and currency affairs in this Country, and I do not speak with any [hesitation].

National Reserve Association Bill

"In 1912 the National Monetary Association, under the chairmanship of the late Senator Nelson W. Aldrich, made a report and presented a vicious bill called the National Reserve Association bill. This bill is usually spoken of as the Aldrich bill. Senator Aldrich did not write the Aldrich bill. He was the tool, if not the accomplice, of the European bankers who for nearly twenty years had been scheming to set up a central bank in this Country and who in 1912 had spent and were continuing to spend vast sums of money to accomplish their purpose.

"We were opposed to the Aldrich plan for a central bank. The men who rule the Democratic Party then promised the people that if they were returned to power there would be no central bank established here while they held the reins of government. Thirteen months later that promise was broken, and the Wilson administration, under the tutelage of those sinister Wall Street figures who stood behind Colonel House, established here in our free Country the worm-eaten monarchical institution of the "King's Bank" to control us from the top downward, and from the cradle to the grave.

"The Federal Reserve Bank destroyed our old and characteristic way of doing business. It discriminated against our 1-name commercial paper, the finest in the world, and it set up the antiquated 2-name paper, which is the present curse of this Country and which wrecked every country which has ever given it scope; it fastened down upon the Country the very tyranny from which the framers of the Constitution sought to save us.

President Jackson's Time

"One of the greatest battles for the preservation of this Republic was fought out here in Jackson's time; when the second Bank of the United States, founded on the same false principles of those which are here exemplified in the Fed, was hurled out of existence. After that, in 1837, the Country was warned against the dangers that might ensue if the predator interests after being cast out should come back in disguise and unite themselves to the Executive and through him acquire control of the Government. That is what the predator interests did when the came back in the livery of hypocrisy and under false pretenses obtained passage of the Fed.

"The danger the Country was warned against came upon us and is shown in the long train of horrors attendant upon the affairs of the traitorous and dishonest Fed. Look around you when you leave this Chamber and you will see evidences of it in all sides. This is an era of misery, and for the conditions that caused that misery, the Fed are fully liable. This is an era of financed crime and in the financing of crime the Fed does not play the part of a disinterested spectator.

Misleading Public Opinion

" . . .The Aldrich bill . . .was a copy, in general a translation of the statues of the Reichsbank and other European central banks. One-half million dollars was spent on the part of the propaganda organized by these bankers for the purpose of misleading public opinion and giving Congress the impression there was an overwhelming popular demand for it and the kind of currency that goes with it, namely, an asset currency based on human debts and obligations. Dr. H. Parker Willis had been employed by Wall Street and propagandists, and when the Aldrich measure failed—he obtained employment with Carter Glass, to assist in drawing the banking bill for the Wilson administration. He appropriated the text of the Aldrich bill. There is no secret about it. The text of the Federal Reserve Act was tainted from the first.

"The Fed Note is essentially unsound. It is the worst currency and the most dangerous that this Country has ever known."

"A few days before the bill came to a vote, Senator Henry Cabot Lodge, of Massachusetts, wrote to Senator John W. Weeks as follows:

'New York City,

December 17, 1913

'*My Dear Senator Weeks: Throughout my public life I have supported all measures designed to take the Government out of the banking business. This bill puts the Government into the banking business as never before in our history.*

`The powers vested in the Federal Reserve Board seem to me highly dangerous especially where there is political control of the Board. I should be sorry to hold stock in a bank subject to such dominations. The bill as it stands seems to me to open the way to a vast inflation of the currency. I had hoped to support this bill, but I cannot vote for it because it seems to me to contain features and to rest upon principles in the highest degree menacing to our prosperity, to stability in business, and to the general welfare of the people of the United States.'
Very Truly Yours, Henry Cabot Lodge.

"In eighteen years that have passed since Senator Lodge wrote that letter of warning all of his predictions have come true. The Government is in the banking business as never before. Against its will it has been made the backer of horse thieves and card sharps, bootleggers smugglers, speculators, and swindlers in all parts of the world. Through the Fed, the riffraff of every country is operating on the public credit of the United States Government.

Machinery

"Meanwhile and on account of it, we ourselves are in the midst of the greatest depression we have ever known. From the Atlantic to the Pacific, our Country has been ravaged and laid waste by the evil practices of the Fed and the interests which control them. At no time in our history, has the general welfare of the people been at a lower level or the minds of the people so full of despair.

> "The people who have thus been driven out are the wastage of the Fed. They are the victims of the Fed. Their children are the new slaves on the auction blocks in the revival of the institution of human slavery."

"Recently in one of our States, 60,000 dwelling houses and farms were brought under the hammer in a single day. 71,000 houses and farms in Oakland Count, Michigan, were sold and their erstwhile owners dispossessed. The people who have thus been driven out are the wastage of the Fed. They are the victims of the Fed. Their children are the new slaves on the auction blocks in the revival of the institution of human slavery.

The Scheme of the Fed.

"In 1913, before the Senate Banking and Currency Committee, Mr. Alexander Lassen made the following statement: "The whole scheme of the Fed with its commercial paper is an impractical, cumbersome machinery–is simply a cover to secure the privilege of issuing money, and to evade payment of as much tax upon circulation as possible and then control the issue and maintain, instead of reducing interest rates. It will prove to the advantage of the few and the detriment of the people. It will mean continued shortage of actual money and further extension of credits, for when there is a shortage of money people have to borrow to their cost.

"A few days before the Fed passed, Senator Root denounced the Fed as an outrage on our liberties. He predicted: `Long before we wake up from our dream of prosperity through an inflated currency, our gold—which alone could have kept us from catastrophe—will have vanished and no rate of interest will tempt it to return.'

"If ever a prophecy came true, that one did."

"The Fed became law the day before Christmas Eve, in the year 1913, and shortly afterwards, the German International Bankers, Kuhn, Loeb and Co., sent one of their partners here to run it.

"The Fed Note is essentially unsound. It is the worst currency and the most dangerous that this Country has ever known. When the proponents of the act saw the Democratic doctrine would not permit them to let the proposed banks issue the new currency as bank notes, they should have stopped at that. They should not have foisted that kind of promises to pay namely, an asset currency, on the United States Government. They should not have made the Government [liable on the private] debts of individuals and corporations, and, least of all, on the private debts of foreigners. "As Kemerer says: 'The Fed Notes, therefore, in form, have some of the qualities of Government paper money, but in substance, are almost a pure asset currency possessing a Government guarantee against which contingency the Government has made no provision whatever.'

"Hon. L.J. Hill, a former member of the House, said, and truly: 'The are obligations of the Government for which the United States received nothing and for the payment of which at an time, it assumes the responsibility: looking to the Fed to recoup itself.'

"If this United States is to redeem the Fed Notes, when the General Public finds it costs to deliver this paper to the Fed, and if the Government has made no provisions for redeeming them, the first element of unsoundness is not far to seek.

"Before the Banking and Currency Committee, when the bill was under discussion Mr. Crozier of Cincinnati said: 'The imperial power of elasticity of the public currency is wielded exclusively by the central corporations owned by the banks. This is a life and death power over all local banks and all business. It can be used to create or destroy prosperity, to ward off or cause stringencies and panics. By making money artificially scarce, interest rates throughout the Country can be arbi-

> "This is a life and death power over all local banks and all business. It can be used to create or destroy prosperity, to ward off or cause stringencies and panics."

trarily raised and the bank tax on all business and cost of living increased for the profit of the banks owning these regional central banks, and without the slightest benefit to the people. The 12 Corporations together cover and monopolize and use for private gain—every dollar of the public currency and all public revenue of the United States. Not a dollar can be put into circulation among the people by their Government, without the consent of and on terms fixed by these 12 private money trusts.'

Private Credit Corporation

"In defiance of this and all other warnings, the proponents of the Fed created the 12 private credit corporations and gave them an absolute monopoly of the currency of these United States—not of the Fed Notes alone—but of all other currency! The Fed Act provided ways and means by which the gold and general currency in the hands of the American people could be obtained by the Fed in exchange for Fed Notes—which are not money—but mere promises to pay.

"Since the evil day when this was done, the initial monopoly has been extended by vicious amendments to the Fed and by the unlawful and treasonable practices of the Fed.

Money for the Scottish Distillers

"Mr. Chairman, if a Scottish distiller wishes to send a cargo of Scotch whiskey to these United States, he can draw his bill against the purchasing bootlegger[147] in dollars and after the bootlegger has accepted it by writing his name across the face of it, the Scotch distiller can send that bill to the nefarious open discount market in New York City where the Fed will buy it and use it as collateral for a new issue of Fed Notes. Thus the Government of these United States pay the Scotch distiller for the whiskey before it is shipped, and if it is lost on

---

[147]   Bootlegged whiskey.

the way, or if the Coast Guard seizes it and destroys it, the Fed simply write off the loss and the government never recovers the money that was paid to the Scotch distiller.

Bootlegging

"While we are attempting to enforce prohibition here, the Fed are in the distiller business in Europe and paying bootlegger bills with public credit of these United States.

"Mr. Chairman, by the same process, they compel our Government to pay the German brewer for his beer. Why should the Fed be permitted to finance the brewing industry in Germany either in this way or as they do by compelling small and fearful United States Banks to take stock in the Isenbeck Brewer and in the German Bank for brewing industries?

"Mr. Chairman, if Dynamit Nobel of Germany, wishes to sell dynamite in Japan to use in Manchuria or elsewhere, it can draw its bill against the Japanese customers in dollars and send that bill to the nefarious open discount market in New York City where the Fed will buy it and use it as collateral for a new issue of Fed Notes while at the same time the Fed will be helping Dynamit Nobel by stuffing its stock into the United States banking system.

"Why should we send our representatives to the disarmament conference at Geneva while the Fed is making our Government pay Japanese debts to German munitions makers?

"Mr. Chairman, if a German wishes to raise a crop of beans and sell them to a Japanese customer, he can draw a bill against his prospective Japanese customer in dollars and have it purchased by the Fed and get the money out of this Country at the expense of the American people before he has even planted the beans in the ground.

"Mr. Chairman, if a German in Germany wishes to export goods to South America, or any other Country, he can draw his bill against his customers and send it to these United States and get the money out of this Country before he ships, or even manufactures the goods.

"Mr. Chairman, why should the currency of these United States be issued on the strength of German beer? Why should it be issued on the crop of unplanted beans to be grown in Chile for Japanese consumption? Why should these United States be compelled to issue many billions of dollars every year to pay the debts of one foreigner to another foreigner?

"Was it for this that our National Bank depositors had their money taken out of our banks and shipped abroad? Was it for this that they had to lose it? Why should the public credit of these United States and likewise money belonging to our National Bank depositors be used to support foreign brewers, narcotic drug vendors, whiskey distillers, wig makes, human hair merchants, Chilean bean growers, to finance the munition factories of Germany and Soviet Russia?

For the remainder of this article go on line at:
http://www.freedomdomain.com/redemption/mcfadden1.html

The Art of Passing the Buck - Volume I

Appendix D

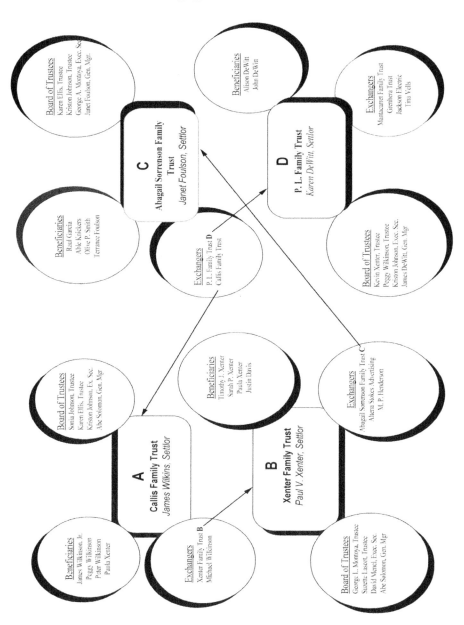

C
Abagail Sorrenson Family Trust
Janet Foulson, Settlor

Board of Trustees
Karen Ellis, Trustee
Kriston Johnson, Trustee
George A. Montoya, Exec. Sec.
Janet Foulson, Gen. Mgr.

Beneficiaries
Raul Garcia
Able Knickers
Olive P. Smith
Terrance Foulson

Exchangers
P. L. Family Trust **D**
Callis Family Trust

D
P. L. Family Trust
Karen DeWitt, Settlor

Beneficiaries
Alison DeWitt
John DeWitt

Exchangers
Mantacarrel Family Trust
Grethera Trust
Jackson Electric
Tina Vells

Board of Trustees
Kevin Xenter, Trustee
Peggy Wilkinson, Trustee
Kriston Johnson, Exec. Sec.
James DeWitt, Gen. Mgr.

A
Callis Family Trust
James Wilkins, Settlor

Board of Trustees
Sonia Johnson, Trustee
Karen Ellis, Trustee
Kriston Johnson, Ex. Sec.
Abe Solomon, Gen. Mgr.

Beneficiaries
James Wilkinson, Jr.
Peggy Wilkinson
Peter Wilkinson
Paula Xenter

Exchangers
Xenter Family Trust **B**
Michael Wilkinson

B
Xenter Family Trust
Paul V. Xenter, Settlor

Beneficiaries
Timothy J. Xenter
Sarah P. Xenter
Paula Xenter
Justin Davis

Exchangers
Abagail Sorrenson Family Trust **C**
Altera Stokes Advertising
M. P. Henderson

Board of Trustees
George L. Montoya, Trustee
Suzette Lascot, Trustee
David Menel, Exec. Sec.
Abe Solomon, Gen. Mgr.

Wheels Within Wheels Collective Overview

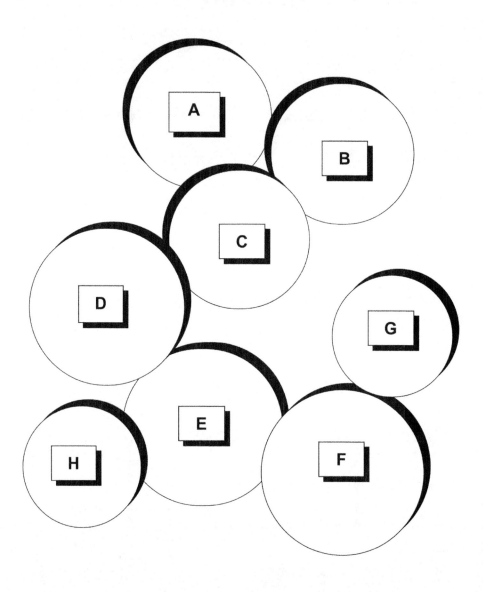

Appendix E

Trust Choices

Services	Type of Instrument					
	Will	Living Trust	Statutory Revocable	Statutory Irrevocable	Common-Law	Corporation
Avoids probate			✔	✔	✔	✔
Protects assets			✔	✔	✔	✔
Gift distribution	✔	✔	✔	✔	✔	
Pass-through			✔	✔	✔	✔
Privacy					✔	
Requires administration			✔	✔	✔	
Distributes during life of Settlor	✔++	✔	✔	✔	✔	
Probate before distribution	✔	✔				
Heirs must have direct relationship to grantor		✔	✔(?)			
Trustees Court Appointed**	✔		✔	✔		

++ Both a Will and a Living Trust can give gift distributions to reduce the taxable income, but distributions on profits are paid by the Trust Grantor before the Beneficiaries receive funds.

** If a Will sets up a Testamentary Trust, the Trustees are appointed by the Judge, even if the people are specified in the Will. If a Living Trust is contested, a stranger could be appointed by the court as a Trustee. Only if a Common-Law Trust cannot get another Trustee and funds are significant can the Beneficiaries petition a court to get a Trustee.

Appendix F

Reasonable Skill

Reasonable skill: "Such skill as is ordinarily possessed and exercised by persons of common capacity engaged in the same business or employment. *Mechanics' Bank v. Merchants' Bank,* 6 Metc. (Mass.) 13, 26." The legal system makes liberal use of an indefinite but assumed standard of reasonableness. *(Black's Law Dictionary)* effort at defining the slippery concept "reasonable" is "(f)air, proper, just, moderate, suitable under the circumstances. . . . Thinking, speaking, or acting according to the dictates of reason. Not immoderate or excessive, being synonymous with rational, honest, equitable, fair, suitable, moderate, tolerable."

The same source sees "reason" as "a faculty of the mind by which it distinguishes truth from falsehood, good from evil, and which enables the possessor to deduce inferences from facts or from propositions." The reverse of negligence is "reasonable care," defined in *Black's Law Dictionary* as "that degree of care which a person of ordinary prudence would exercise in the same or similar circumstances." Words like "average," "ordinary," "competent," "prudent" and "diligent" show up again and again in the definitions of such terms as "reasonable and probable cause," "reasonable belief," "reasonable diligence," "reasonable doubt," "reasonable skill," etc.

Appendix G

Definition of United States

There are three meanings of the United States

- The federal corporation located in the District of Columbia, identified as the United States of America and often referred to as United States.[148]

- The collection of 50 states.

- Territories governed by the federal government.

At one time, before the 14th Amendment, citizenship was established in each particular state. There was no such classification as federal citizen, or U.S. Citizen. The term Federal Citizen came into existence with the 14th Amendment. It originally referred to black slaves, who did not have a citizenship in reference to the state. These people became a rich source of taxation, for they had to pay for the privileges of becoming citizens and having access to the courts.

To get Social Security, you must claim to be a U.S. Citizen, which is a fictitious status. By voluntarily agreeing to become a U.S. Citizen, though, you become taxable.

The issue of citizenship has been so lost in the legal quagmire, and deliberately obscured by the over-eager tax authorities who get a large chunk of your paycheck, that to oppose that thinking, no matter how legally correct you may be,

---

[148]   *Diversified Metals Products, Inc. v. T-Bow Company Trust, et al*, 93-405-E-EJL United States' Answer and Claim, point 4. District of Idaho.

is a battle. Absent the battle, though, states and citizens alike become ever more enmeshed in federal regulations.

The following references found in the Internal Revenue Code define the term State:

1.   The term "State" means the District of Columbia, the Commonwealth of Puerto Rico, Guam, and American Samoa.[149]

2.   The United States is located in the District of Columbia.[150]

3.   The term "United States" when used in a geographic sense includes the District of Columbia, the Commonwealth of Puerto Rico, Guam, and American Samoa.[151]

4.   This statement does not include, nor mean the 50 States.[152]

Further issues of definition and a discussion of the Article II Courts and territories start on the next page.

---

[149]   IRC §3121, (e), (1)

[150]   California Commercial Code §9307(h)

[151]   IRC §3121, (e), (2)

[152]   IRC §4612 (a) (4)

SUMMERS v. U S, 231 U.S. 92 (1913): It is established that the courts of the territories may have such jurisdiction of cases arising under the Constitution and laws of the United States as is vested in the cir- [231 U.S. 92, 102] cuit and district courts, but this does not make them circuit and district courts of the United States.

UNITED STATES v. BURROUGHS, 289 U.S. 159 (1933): Where a statute uses this or similar language to define the jurisdiction of a court such a court is authorized to try statutory actions declared to be cognizable by district courts, as if the tribunal were in fact a district court of the United States. And the same rule is applicable to appellate proceedings. Compare In re Cooper, 143 U.S. 472, 494 , 12 S.Ct. 453; Hine v. Morse, 218 U.S. 493 , 31 S.Ct. 37, 21 Ann. Cas. 782; Federal Trade Commission v. Klesner, 274 U.S. 145, 154 , 47 S.Ct. 557; United States v. California Coo perative Canneries, 279 U.S. 553, 558 , 49 S.Ct. 423. But vesting a court with 'the same jurisdiction as is vested in district courts' does not make it a district court of the United States. This has been repeatedly said with reference to territorial courts. Reynolds v. United States, 98 U.S. 145 , 154; Stephens v. Cherokee Nation, supra, page 476 of 174 U.S ., 19 S.Ct. 722; Summers v. United States, 231 U.S. 92, 101 , 34 S.Ct. 38.

REYNOLDS v. U.S., 98 U.S. 145 (1878): As to the constitutionality of the Poland Bill. Rev. Stat., sect. 5352. Undoubtedly Congress, under art. 4, sect. 3, of the Constitution, which gives 'power to dispose of and make all needful rules and regulations respecting the territory or other property belonging to the United States,' and under the decisions of this court upon it, may legislate over such territory, and regulate the form of its local government. But its legislation can be neither exclusive nor arbitrary. The power of this government to obtain and hold territory over which it might legislate, without restriction, would be inconsistent with its own existence in its present form. There is always an excess of power exercised when the Federal government attempts to provide for more than the assertion and preservation of its rights over such territory, and interferes by positive enactment with the social and domestic life of its inhabitants and their internal police...By sect. 1910 of the Revised Statutes the district courts of the Territory have the same jurisdiction in all cases arising under the Constitution and laws of the United States as is vested in the circuit and district courts of the United States; but this does not make them circuit and district courts of the United States. We have often so decided. American Insurance Co. v. Canter, 1 Pet. 511; Benner et al. v. Porter, 9 How. 235; Clinton v. Englebrecht, 13 Wall. 434. They are courts of the Territories, invested for some purposes with the powers of the courts of the United States. Writs of error and appeals lie from them to the Supreme Court of the Territory, and from that court as a territorial court to this in some cases.

Mandel v. The Boston Phoenix, Inc., No. 05-1230 (1st Cir. August 03, 2006) Summary judgment on the issue of status in a defamation case is vacated and remanded where there was insufficient evidence in the record with which to determine plaintiff's status. Denial of defendants' motion for judgment as a matter of law is affirmed.
http://laws.lp.findlaw.com/1st/051230.html

HOOVEN & ALLISON CO. v. EVATT, 324 U.S. 652 (1945) The term 'United States' may be used in any one of several senses. It may be merely the name of a sovereign occupying the position analogous to that of other sovereigns in the family of nations. It may designate the territory over which the sovereignty of the United States ex- [324 U.S. 652, 672] tends, or it may be the collective name of the states which are united by and under the Constitution. 6

United States v. Lexington Mill & E. Co., 232 US 399, pp. 409. (1914) "We are not at liberty to construe any statute so as to deny effect to any part of its language. It is a cardinal rule of statutory construction that significance and effect shall, if possible, be accorded to every word. As early as in Bacon's Abridgment, 2, it was said that 'a statute ought, upon the whole, to be so construed that, if it can be prevented, no clause, sentence, or word, shall be superfluous, void, or insignificant.' This rule has been repeated innumerable times." Justice Strong,

Mookini v. United States, 303 U.S. 201 (1938) The term 'District Courts of the United States,' as used in the rules, without an addition expressing a wider connotation, has its historic significance. It describes the constitutional courts created under article 3 of the Constitution. Courts of the Territories are legislative courts, properly speaking, and are not District Courts of the United States. We have often held that vesting a territorial court with jurisdiction similar to that vested in the District Courts of the United States does not make it a 'District Court of the United States.' Reynolds v. United States, 98 U.S. 145, 154; The City of Panama, 101 U.S. 453, 460; In re Mills, 135 U.S. 263, 268, 10 S.Ct. 762; McAllister v. United States, 141 U.S. 174, 182, 183 S., 11 S.Ct. 949; Stephens v. Cherokee Nation, 174 U.S. 445, 476, 477 S., 19 S.Ct. 722; Summers v. United States, 231 U.S. 92, 101, 102 S., 34 S.Ct. 38; United States v. Burroughs, 289 U.S. 159, 163, 53 S.Ct. 574. Not only did the promulgating order use the term District Courts of the United States in its historic and proper sense, but the omission of provision for the application of the rules to the territorial courts and other courts mentioned in the authorizing act clearly shows the limitation that was intended. (See also Longshoremen v. Juneau Spruce Corp., 324 U.S. 237; Reynolds v. U.S., 98 U.S. 145, 154; McAlister v. U.S., 141 U.S. 174; U.S. v. Burroughs, 289 U.S. 159, 163.)

This is where two elements must be considered: First, the "United States District Court" is a territorial court (Balzac v. Puerto Rico (1922)), where the "District Court of the United States" is the first-level Article III court of the United States (Mookini v. United States (1938)). Second, the "United States" is the proper principal of interest in courts of the United States other than territorial courts, where the "United States of America, ss, President of the United States" is the principal of interest in insular possession territorial courts (see judicial provisions for Puerto Rico & the Virgin Islands in Title 48 of the United States Code). (Other cases using this case: GLIDDEN COMPANY v. ZDANOK, 370 U.S. 530 (1962); LONGSHOREMEN v. JUNEAU SPRUCE CORP., 342 U.S. 237 (1952); STAINBACK V. MO HOCK KE LOK PO , 336 U.S. 368 (1949); ROY SYLVESTER PARROTT v. GOVERNMENT OF THE VIRGIN ISLANDS UNITED STATES COURT OF APPEALS FOR THE THIRD CIRCUIT No. 99-3688

ROY SYLVESTER PARROTT v. GOVERNMENT OF THE VIRGIN ISLANDS UNITED STATES COURT OF APPEALS FOR THE THIRD CIRCUIT No. 99-3688 The District Court's power originates under Article IV, S 3, which authorizes Congress to regulate the various U.S. territories. See Binns v. United States, 194 U.S. 486, 491 (1904) (recognizing Congress's plenary power to define institutional relationships in territories). Congress exercises this authority through the Revised Organic Act, which serves as the Virgin Islands constitution. See 48 U.S.C. SS 1541-1645 (West 1987 & Supp. 2000); Brow, 994 F.2d at 1032. As such, the Revised Organic Act is also the source of authority for the Virgin Islands Legislature. See 48 U.S.C. S 1574(a). It is through the Revised Organic Act that Congress authorizes the local legislature to grant the Territorial Court its jurisdiction. See 48 U.S.C. S1611(b). Consequently, both the Territorial Court and the District Court derive their respective jurisdictional grants from the same sovereign -- namely, Congress, exercising its authority under Article IV, S 3.

As a result, the District Court does not derive its jurisdiction, as do other federal courts, from Article III. See United States v. George, 625 F.2d 1081, 1088-89 (3d Cir. 1980).11 Nor has the District Court previously been treated...

[I]n a federal Territory and the Nation, as in a city and a State, "[t]here is but one system of government, or of laws operating within [its] limits." City and State, or Territory and Nation, are not two separate sovereigns to whom the citizen owes separate allegiance in any meaningful sense, but one alone.

United States v. Wheeler, 435 U.S. 313, 321 (1978) (internal citations omitted). Moreover, "vesting a territorial court with jurisdiction similar to that vested in the District Courts of the United States does not make it a `District Court of the United States.' " Mookini v. United States , 303 U.S. 201, 205 (1938). See also Barnard v. Thorstenn, 489 U.S. 546, 551-52 (1989) (holding that Supreme Court lacked supervisory power over District Court of the Virgin Islands because that court was not an Article III federal district court). Before the created by act of Congress, under the power to make rules and regulations respecting the territory belonging to the United States given by Article IV, section 3 of the Constitution, but is not a court of the United States created under Article III, section 1. 625 F.2d at 1088-89.

MCALLISTER v. U S, 141 U.S. 174 (1891); These cases close all discussion here as to whether territorial courts are of the class defined in the third article of the constitution. It must be regarded as settled that courts in the territories, created under the plenary municipal authority that congress possesses over the territories of the United States, are not courts of the United States created under the authority conferred by that article...For the reasons we have stated it must be assumed that the [141 U.S. 174, 185] words 'judges of the courts of the United States,' in section 1768, were used with reference to the recognized distinction between courts of the United States and merely territorial or legislative courts.

Bonds v. Tandy, No. 05-60478 (5th Cir. July 19, 2006) 21 U.S.C. section 877 limits petitions for judicial review to those litigants with Article III standing and who are also arguably within the zone of interests of the Controlled Substances Act (CSA). A petition for review of the Drug Enforcement Administration's denial of a waiver application that would have allowed a pharmacy to hire petitioner is dismissed for lack of jurisdiction. http://caselaw.lp.findlaw.com/data2/circs/5th/0560478cv0p.pdf

Appendix H

Metaphysics and Wealth

We believe the following article explains, in a way that nothing else does, the **real** reasons not only why a belief in reincarnation to this day remains largely suppressed in the West, but why the Irrevocable Common-Law Trust, despite its myriad advantages, financial clout, tax benefits, and proven track record in asset protection and growth, remains untaught and all but unknown. You see, and we know this will seem outrageous and bizarre, the Super-Rich do not want the people at large to know about their financial super weapon and key means for ensuring not merely their dominance and dominion in the here and now, but in lifetimes to come!

Many members of what the ordinary people may term the Super-Rich, despite all their denials and carefully cultivated appearance of worldliness, are deeply involved with and schooled in the esoteric and the occult. Through magickal (as distinguished from stage "magic") means, many members of the Super-Rich believe that they can "manipulate the system" such that lifetime after lifetime, they will reincarnate into the same powerful families where, thanks to the power of Trusts, they will find themselves equipped with every conceivable advantage as they ceaselessly pursue their self-aggrandizement and relentless accumulation of power. The Bohemian Club,[153] and Skull and Bones,[154] are but

---

[153]   *Fairness and Accuracy in Reporting*, Inside Bohemian Grove: "The Story People Magazine Won't Let You Read," December 1991: http://www.fair.org/index.php?page=1489

[154]   Alexandra Robbins, *Secrets of the Tomb: Skull and Bones, the Ivy League and the Hidden Paths of Power*, Bay Back Books (2002); Kris Millegan (editor), *Fleshing Out Skull & Bones: Investigations into America's Most Powerful Secret Society*, Trine Day; New Edition, October 1, 2004; Antony C. Sutton,

two organizations that thrive on hidden mysteries. The esoteric point of view provides a belief in the continuation of the soul, thus through their initiations they believe they can control nothing less than the placement of it from one incarnation to the next.

Perhaps what we should be doing is setting up our next game plan. That is the true purpose of the Irrevocable Common-Law Trust. Not to leave the assets for the Beneficiaries, but to leave them for yourself. When you come back, you want to be well positioned.

This fascination with the occult is reported and demonstrated by documentary film maker Alex Jones. He infiltrated the Bohemian Grove, videotaped and wrote of his shocking discoveries there. This included robed world leaders and their worship of an enormous owl representing Moloch.[155]

At the bottom of the web page are still photos of Bohemian Grove, a free video trailer includes links to order the full video. Here you will also find other links regarding this and similar subjects.

You may think we are not exactly "right in the head," about all of this, so we refer you to our next startling moment in the following article titled, "The Origins of Reincarnation." We think it will become perfectly clear to you, why the rich are so eager to renew the perpetual contract to hold the Trust money in a safe place.

Please note the spiritual slant in the following article is not part of our point of view. We feel the vivid overview of religious history and a belief in the system of rebirth, though, offers a deep insight into why the rich may look to the Trust system as a way to preserve wealth through the ages. Oddly, though, this perpetual birth cycle is precisely why the Empress Theodora instigated the destruc-

---

America's Secret Establishment: An Introduction to the Order of Skull & Bones, Liberty House Press, Billings, Montana, 1986

[155] Http://www.prisonplanet.com/alex_jones_tell_his_ story.html

tion of this belief. Only through the tangled web of evolution has the subject been so twisted. Her desire to avoid judgment resulted in suppressing the belief in reincarnation and this has proved much to the advantage of those who hold power.

The article is only in part. Footnotes explaining the people ,or other side information have been omitted.

Origins of Reincarnation [156]

A Political and Religious History

by Chris Populi

Despite efforts by traditional Western religions for 1,200 years to deny its existence, reincarnation has not gone away. Instead, it provokes increased interest among all religions.

Why such persistent denial? Incredible as it may seem, reincarnation's rejection was ordered by a pagan empress.

> Soul is older than body. Souls are continuously born over again into this life. Plato (427-347) B.C.

Reincarnation is not a new subject. It dates back to time immemorial. The *Vedas,* Krishna, Buddha, the *Zendavesta*, the *Cabala,* the *Book of the Dead*, etc., all spoke of man's many rebirths. Socrates and Plato mention it (rebirth) in their teachings.

Shakespeare, Emerson, Thoreau, Thomas Huxley, William James, Benjamin Franklin, and many others believed in it.

---

[156]   Reprinted, with minor editing, from *Perceptions* magazine (out of print), Spring 1994

Often, those interested in reincarnation have read case studies in the books of Dr. Ian Stevenson, in which children vividly recollect their previous lifetimes.

In the highly publicized book, *The Search for Bridey Murphy*, Morey Bernstein reports the case of a Pueblo, Colorado housewife who, when placed under hypnotic regression, vividly described the town, shops, and many townspeople from her previous life in Ireland as a lass named Bridey Murphy–facts the Colorado housewife could not have known.

Unfortunately, the idea of reincarnation met with such disbelief in 1956, that after a few years the book fell into oblivion. People were not prepared for such *avant-garde* ideas.

Author and teacher Origen (185-254 AD), a Roman Catholic Church father, spoke about reincarnation. He explained that man needs successive lives to correct the apparent inequities of human condition. Early Church leaders respected and endorsed his teachings, which were based on Plato's teachings.

According to the Greek Orthodox Church, which branched out of the Roman Church:

> When man is dead, he always lives; when our terrestrial existence ends, we must wait, because we will return to it again.

Edgar Cayce, one of America's best known psychics, says that reincarnation is not a theory; it is a practical collection of ethical laws affecting men's morality. His readings unquestionably accept it.

The Gospels According to Spiritism by Allan Kardec, who founded Spiritism in 1860 states:

The entry of spirits into the physical life is necessary so as to carry out God's purposes. The activities they are compelled to perform help them develop their intelligence. God, being sovereignly just, treats all His children equally.

Many distinguished modern scientists and universities now study reincarnation and are scientifically proving its existence. Among them are Ian Stevenson and Dr. Raymond Moody.

The "New Age" has presented much interesting research in this area. In Brazil, countless bestsellers, allegedly based on real life stories, cover two and three lives of the characters.

Why the Roman Catholic Church Rejects Reincarnation

Despite its acceptance by many respectable religious and illustrious masters, including Jesus, many westerners and traditional religions stubbornly deny reincarnation.

According to *Edgar Cayce on Reincarnation*, by Noel Langley, *Pageant of the Gods*, by John Forrow, *Secret History*, by Procopius and Leon Denis, and to Brazilian Spiritists in general, Byzantium's Emperor Justinian (483-565 A.D.) was pressured by his wife, the powerful and wicked Empress Theodora, to banish reincarnation from the Scriptures.

> . . .Byzantium's Emperor Justinian (483-565 A.D.) was pressured by his wife, the powerful and wicked Empress Theodora, to banish reincarnation from the Scriptures.

The ruthless Theodora, who wielded immense power, ordered anyone who opposed her insatiable ambitions to be eliminated. She also exerted great control over her emperor husband.

Theodora did not like the idea of reincarnation. Through its mechanical laws of cause and effect, the imperial titles and prestige of her and her husband would have to be expunged after death. She wanted instant deification.

Furthermore, the humiliation of being judged like a common, delinquent spirit, and then to take later incarnation based on rectifying the consequences of her many thousands of crimes, were too much for Theodora to accept.

Though Justinian at first endorsed reincarnation, Theodora convinced him otherwise. Fearful of his own crimes, he surrendered to Theodora's pressure. Anyone who dared to oppose her nefarious plans against reincarnation found sudden death.

Through Theodora's constant instigation, Justinian pressured the Church of Rome for years to approve the so-called Anathemas. These Anathemas would banish belief in the pre-existence of the soul and of reincarnation from the Scriptures, as well as from all the teachings of Origen's that confirmed reincarnation.

Pope Agapetus and then his successor Pope Silverius, tried to convince Justinian not to impose such Anathemas. Both found an early and sudden death–apparently executed through Theodora's henchmen.

As a successor to Pope Silverius, who was sent into exile where he expediently died, Theodora appointed his assistant, Bishop Virgilius, as Pope, in hopes that he would agree with her anti reincarnation ideas. He did not.

When Theodora died in 548, Justinian continued pressing Pope Virgilius. To force his consent to the Anathemas, he held him prisoner for eight years. In 553 A.D., Justinian summoned an Ecumenical Council at Constantinople, ostensibly to approve an old, harmless law, called the "Two Edict" (see *Catholic Encyclopedia*), but actually it was to approve the Anathemas. Justinian controlled all 159 Greek bishops, Pope Virgilius refused to attend the council because he was denied an equal number of Roman bishops; only six were allowed to attend.

By order of the irreverent pagans, Justinian and Theodora, the Anathemas against reincarnation and against Origenism were approved by the Constantinople Ecumenical Council. A short time later, under suspicious circumstances a greatly embittered Pope Virgilius died.

One of the Anathemas reads:

> Whosoever shall teach the pre-existence of the soul and the strange opinion of its return to earth, to him be anathema.

Apparently the Anathemas were never approved by the Roman bishops, nor signed by the Pope, who only approved the "Two Edict.

Erasing references to reincarnation from the Scriptures, along with all of Origen's teachings, became the infamous task fo Emperor Justinian.

Increased Control of the Roman Catholic Church

After Justinian's death in 565 A.D. the teachings of Origen could have been reinstated safely into the Scriptures. Why weren't they? The Church of Rome and its bishops had never approved of the Anathemas.

In Reincarnation, *The Phoenix Fire Mystery*, Joseph Head and S.L. Cranston explain why reincarnation was so offensive to "defenders of the faith." The implicit psychology of reincarnation may be the best explanation:

The believer in this teaching tends to be responsible for his own progress and salvation. Such a person has no need of priests, and little regard for external dead-letter observance, rite or conformity.

The devices (such as the confessional) of a redemption conferred by institutional authority were, to believers of evolution through rebirth: transparent, fraudulent or false. Hence, the persecution over the many centuries while dogmatic religion remained in power.

According to Emmanuel channeled through Chico Xavier in *Emmanuel,* and to *Emmanuel* and to *Denis in Death*, the following transpired:

> At first it was convenient for the Roman Church not to do anything regarding reinstating reincarnation into the Scriptures because to ignore it [reincarnation] facilitated its [the Church's] temporal control.

After Emperor Focas consolidated the power of the papacy in 607 A.D., the Church gained considerable political and spiritual power, exerting increased influence not only over the masses, but also over the emperors.

Temporal power gained acceptance, and the pagans who converted into Christianity began to gradually adapt the rituals and pomp of the emperors for their papal ceremonies, and from pagan rituals for their liturgy. Slowly they abandoned the simplicity and humility of the early Christians. Jesus, who did not possess even a rock upon which to rest his head, never used temples, but chose nature to convey his teachings.

> The Vatican lavishness, its sumptuous churches, and its ostentatious ceremonies are a reminder of the polytheistic dissipation of the Roman society . . . "Emmanuel"

The Church's control over the masses was maintained through the fear of hell and eternal damnation. Such beliefs provided a tremendous source of income for the Church and the states. Through payments of penitence, tithes, celebration of masses, and fees for absolution and the deliverance of "sinner," the Church maintained its increased control over the state and the people for 1,200 years, starting in 607 A.D., until declaring the Pope infallible in 1870.

The Inquisition Persecutes Believers in Reincarnation

According to Dr. Bezerra de Menezes in *Dramas of Obsession*, to *Emmanuel and Denis in After Death*, and to *Emmanuel,* after the Crusades ended, which were wars of conquest to take the Holy Land from the Muslims in the XI, XII and XIII centuries, the feared and ignoble Inquisition (1231-1820) began.

Also called the "Holy Calling," the Inquisition was established by the papacy to punish "heretics,"–people who believed in an afterlife, in reincarnation and in the occult, threatened the universal control of the Church.

The papacy proclaimed such beliefs to be the work of the devil, witchery and heresy. Those accused of heresy were sent to gloomy dungeons to be tortured into recanting or killed if unwilling to do so. Unfortunately, fears of prosecution and damnation became inculcated in the minds of most westerners. Throughout the centuries their deep subconscious mind became conditioned.

If everyone could be saved by being reborn in another body, the Church would lose its main excuse to save sinners from eternal Hell and damnation. Priests would lose their prestige and the Church its source of income.

According to Hand and Cranston:

> After the Renaissance, the iron hand of the "holy" Inquisition descended over most of Europe, and for several centuries heretic hunting on the part of the masses and clergy alike raged with an unparalleled fury. It sent to the stakes as sons of Satan hundreds of thousands of brave, freethinking Christians.

Gradually the night of enslavement over the human mind came to an end. But as to reincarnation, the supposed curse against preexistence of A.D. 553, followed later by the indefatigable work of the Inquisitors, proved exceedingly effective. Reincarnation was now dead to the masses of people in the West. Henceforth, and until the latter half of the nineteenth century, only among philosophers, writers and a few daring theologians was the doctrine to be quietly welcomed.

Despite being a religious court, the Inquisition was based on civil powers. The clergy and the state, in collusion, also found a great source of wealth by confiscating the properties and assets of those condemned of heresy.

Reincarnation was part of the Jewish dogmas, being taught under the name of resurrection. They believed that man could live again.

Referring again to *The Gospels According to Spiritism*:

The most vicious persecutions of the Inquisition occurred in Italy, Portugal and Spain. According to Dr. Menezes, it was a good excuse to get rid of enemies. The most persecuted heretics were the Jews because they possessed most of the wealth. Their financial power was even greater than that of the nobility.

Many Jews were given the chance to convert to Catholicism. To save their families, most did. But through the extraction of tithes, gratuities, permits and fees to "save" their souls, they were relentlessly persecuted and exploited.

Inquisitors did not bother with the mystic beliefs of the independent gypsies or the Moors because they were of a lower class and had no money. However, lest we be self-righteous about the Catholic Church, through the laws of reincarnation, many of us may have condemned others through the Inquisition, only to suffer its persecutions in later reincarnations.

Reincarnation Is One of the Many Laws of the Universe

Man is reborn into the physical world hundreds of times. Such a sequence of existences is called reincarnation. Jesus to Nicodemus, a ruler of the Jews, said, "Truly, truly, I say to you, unless one is born again, he cannot see the Kingdom of God," John 3:3.

Spiritism, *Emmanuel* and in Denis in *After Death* and Emmanuel in *Emmanuel* teach that God is not careless, nor unjust, nor irresponsible nor biased; He does not dispense blessings and punishments at random or indiscriminately. The Universe and its beings are ruled by perfect and just laws.

Reincarnation can explain the reasons for all injustices, birth defects, mental retardation, deformities and handicaps, unavoidable accidents and life reverses, etc. These are most likely the result of past existence misdeeds— and chance may play a part, too.

God's Perfect Laws—Causes of Afflictions

St. Augustine said, "According to the divine justice, in this world cannot exist an unfortunate individual that has not deserved his misfortune."

Denis feels the theory of reincarnation is far more preferable than the idea that God created some of us poor, others rich, some with physical or mental handicaps, or with incurable diseases, while others are born healthy, intelligent and wholesome. And none of them performed any good deeds or misdeeds to deserve their good or bad fate.

Spiritism teaches that on each reincarnation man gradually acquires knowledge, wisdom and responsibility. His bodily shape is also perfected. He confronts his errors on the extra-physical world and attempts to rectify them in the school of hard knocks of the physical world. He also consolidates his intellectual, moral and spiritual achievements, as well as his good inclinations to the physical body–unfortunately, sometimes his bad tendencies as well.

God's Laws are Just and Infallible

As the days of my terrestrial life end, I shall wait, because I shall return to it again.[157]

Again, Denis and *The Gospels According to Spiritism* by Kardec explain that man never escapes the consequences of his faults, because he is controlled by perfect and never-failing laws. Such laws are known for millennia by Eastern religious schools as the Laws of Cause and Effect and of Karma.

Jesus warned us, "That which we sow we shall reap."

———————————

The above article continues, exploring more of the spiritual side of reincarnation. Should you want to read the entire article, please write the publisher.

———————————

[157]   The writer attributed this quote to Job. We were unable to verify it.

Index

Under no circumstances should you rely on the content of either volume of *The Art of Passing the Buck* in determining a trust's federal income tax liability, whether that trust presently exists or is to be created in the future. For all such matters, you should seek appropriate professional assistance (e.g., from an attorney, certified public accountant, or otherwise properly licensed and reputable tax return preparer).

Printed in Great Britain
by Amazon

14195610R00210